PUBLIC EDITOR #1

ALSO BY DANIEL OKRENT

Great Fortune: The Epic of Rockefeller Center

The Way We Were:
New England Then, New England Now

Nine Innings

PUBLIC EDITOR #1

. . .

The Collected Columns
(with Reflections, Reconsiderations, and Even a
Few Retractions) of the First Ombudsman of
The New York Times

DANIEL OKRENT

PublicAffairs
New York

Book design and composition by Mark McGarry, Texas Type & Book Works
Set in Electra

Library of Congress Cataloging-in-Publication Data is available
ISBN-13: 978-1-58648-400-2
ISBN-10: 1-58648-400-1

FIRST EDITION
10 9 8 7 6 5 4 3 2 1

*For Mimi, Arika, Joel, Sarah,
and Karen, and in memory of David*

If they hang you, I'll always remember you.

—Humphrey Bogart to Mary Astor,
in *The Maltese Falcon*, quoted in an e-mail
message from a *New York Times* reader

Contents

Notes on an Unendearing Profession

The creation of the public editor position at The New York Times was announced by the paper's executive editor, Bill Keller, on his first day on the job, in July 2003. Keller had been named to succeed Howell Raines, who had been asked to resign not two years into his tenure. The apparent cause of Raines's firing was the long series of journalistic crimes committed under him by the rogue reporter Jayson Blair; additional reasons had surfaced in a fateful meeting convened in a Manhattan theater that May by publisher Arthur O. Sulzberger Jr. At the meeting, an angry staff aired a catalog of grievances about Raines's managerial style, his journalistic practices and much else. I was not alone at the time in thinking that Raines couldn't possibly hold on to his job once so many demons had come out into the open. But of course I didn't imagine that one of the consequences would be the creation of the position I would come to occupy later that year.

American journalism's first ombudsmen—the most common term for reader representatives at United States newspapers—had shown up in the 1960s, notably at the Louisville Courier-Journal and the Washington Post. The Times, however, had for more than three decades steadfastly refused to hire one, citing the presumed obligation of the paper's own editors to represent the readers. Because so much of the newspaper industry looked to The Times to set standards, one of the consequences of the paper's resistance was a slowdown in the growth of the ombudsman business. Another consequence, conceivably, was Jayson Blair.

I'm not suggesting that an ombudsman—or public editor, as The Times would eventually have it—would definitely have caught Blair in the act of plagiarizing other papers, fabricating interviews and events and otherwise amassing a staggering rap sheet of journalistic felonies. Nor zwas Jayson Blair the only person in the early years of the 21st century responsible for despoiling the reputation of The Times specifically and American journalists generally. But there certainly was the possibility that complaints from readers, from people Blair wrote about and from other members of the paper's staff would have been heeded by someone specifically charged to listen to them. All those editors who presumably were representing the readers had other things to do—chiefly, they had to put out a newspaper every day.

Before managing editor John Geddes called me that September to ask if I'd be interested in interviewing for the public editor job, he and I had never met—in fact, I don't think he'd ever heard my name. But we knew several people in common, among them his former Wall Street Journal boss Norman Pearlstine, for whom I had worked at Time, Inc. Pearlstine recommended me for the job.

Geddes's call was hardly one I was expecting, or even imagining. Though I knew many people at The Times, I just wasn't a newspaper guy, nor was I a particularly devoted reader of press criticism and commentary. I had taken early retirement two years previously from Time, Inc., where I had served as an editorial executive for the previous decade, and had embarked on what I thought would be the last phase of my working life, writing books. My entire career had been in books and magazines; I had last worked for a newspaper as a college student in the 1960s. A book I had written about New York in the 1920s and 1930s was about to be published when Geddes called, and I was about to begin another, about the United States during Prohibition.

But The Times was The Times, and I was a journalist, and it was impossible to ignore Geddes's invitation. A live conversation followed, as did a series of meetings with various members of newsroom management. Bill Keller and I spoke twice in person, and then once on the phone, before he offered me the job.

Only then did I meet Arthur Sulzberger. (Given that I'd already accepted Keller's offer, this was powerful evidence of the independence of the news operation from the publisher's procedural interference.) Sulzberger, whose manner at times might be described as a sort of aggressive informality, opened our meeting with a characteristic comment: "Why on earth would you want to do this?" I had no answer other than "Because it's The Times." It turned out to be a pleasant enough conversation, in which the publisher made it clear that although I was Keller's hire, he supported the idea of a public editorship. The only question he asked that seemed to approach a sensitive matter was whether I would ever recommend, in my column or in conversation, that he fire somebody. Absolutely not, I replied; I was willing to be a one-man jury, but he'd have to be the judge.

. . .

Keller didn't hand me a job description, nor did I prepare one for him. This was a process of invention, and Keller effectively handed me the keys to the laboratory and walked away. We agreed that I would have a regular, semiweekly space in the Sunday Week in Review section; that my copy would be seen by no one but my copy editor until the paper was on press; that if I wanted space without waiting two Sundays, I could have it on demand; and that I would be free to write what I wanted to write, using my own voice (no Timesian "Mr. Bush" or "Ms. Clinton" for me). We also agreed that I would serve for 18 months, and at my request we further agreed that there would be no possibility of renewal, and that I would state this publicly at the outset. I had a life I knew I would want to get back to, but beyond that I also didn't want any reader to think I was pulling my punches in order to win favor with those who would decide whether to renew my contract.

Keller's decision to distance himself from both the definition of the job and the policing of its occupant was extremely savvy: it would enable him to hold me at all times at arm's length. Whenever I criticized a Times journalist Keller could give the bruised (or enraged) staff member a figurative hug, noting that Okrent spoke only for himself, and that management judged staff performance entirely independently of what I had to say.

At times, Keller's support of his people could be combative—a style he demonstrated most forcefully in his intense response to my criticism of two editors in the culture department (see the notes following "Arts Editors and Arts Consumers: Not on the Same Page," on page 183). Neither did he have any difficulty defending his people, and criticizing me, in interviews or public appearances. But when it was appropriate he backed me as well, at times citing my columns in speeches to the staff; with Sulzberger, inviting me to speak to the New York Times Co.'s board of directors; and, though this may not have been directly attributable to my work, authorizing a "credibility committee," under the leadership of assistant managing editor Allan M. Siegal, that beginning in the spring of 2004 took up a formal study of several issues I had raised in my columns, and several of whose members met with me to discuss them further. Keller twice got fairly bumptious about the way I wrote about (or even reported) certain subjects (see notes to "When the Right to Know Confronts the Need to Know," on page 130, in addition to those on the "Arts Editors . . ." column), and he never shied from letting me know when he disagreed with me. But he never came after my space, and he never was anything but cooperative in his responses to my queries. As I recall, the only time he declined to answer my questions was when I was probing territory that involved unnamed sources—a subject that would bring him much woe after my tenure had ended, in the person of reporter Judith Miller.

My introduction to the staff came in three forms: once, before I formally started, when I sat in on the daily Page 1 meeting, so I'd have at least some idea of the decision-making process; next, on the first of what would be scores of trips through the third-floor newsroom to meet with Al Siegal, a maiden voyage most memorable to me for all the pairs of regarding eyes peeping up from behind their computer monitors; and then, most revealingly, on a trip to Washington to meet with the staff of the paper's most important bureau.

There, over sandwiches and sodas, I attempted to field about 90 minutes of questions from the bureau's reporters and editors, no more than four or five of whom I had ever met before. Among those was bureau chief Philip Taubman, who introduced me to the group; our sons had gone to high school together. Taubman and I were only nodding acquaintances, really, but it was reassuring to have someone I knew, even slightly, sitting next to me. If you ever have the opportunity to submit to a grilling by several dozen members of the New York Times Washington staff, you will learn why that reassurance seemed necessary. It was the middle of the winter, but as I left I was soaked in sweat.

The editors and reporters weren't unfriendly. They just wanted to know how I had come to take this job; what my qualifications were; how I proposed to go about my work; whether I was fully aware of the agendas of pressure groups who had it in for The Times; whether I knew how sensitive—and competitive—was the practice of journalism, particularly within the Beltway; and whether I had anything in my experience or training that could possibly qualify me to look into Times reporting on matters involving the CIA and other intelligence agencies.

There was one other question that stuck in my mind that day, and for the nearly 18 months to follow. A reporter I would later come to admire enormously for her skills, her ethics and her ungrudging willingness to discuss criticism of her work, asked, "Are you going to mention *names* in your column?"

I don't remember if I said what I thought: "What do you do for a living?"

. . .

One of the regular tropes in the charges tossed at me by outside critics was about my evident laziness. (I've included directions to a particularly vivid assault of this nature, in the context of my post-vacation column in September 2004, on page 147.) My failure to dwell repeatedly on their particular issues was bad enough, these critics said, but really inexcusable given how I only troubled myself to write a column every other week. Not only had The Times marginalized me by allowing me to appear so infrequently, they seemed to think, but I blithely went along with it because 1,500 words every 14 days was not exactly heavy lifting.

In fact, the column was not even the largest part of my job. The typical column was a two-to-three-day enterprise for me — a day or two of reporting, a day or so of writing (following, in most instances, several late nights and early mornings staring at the bedroom ceiling and thinking about the subject at hand). Most of each two-week cycle was spent handling the e-mail, which abated somewhat after a first, explosive spurt of pent-up complaint (see the note following my first column, on page 33), but which nonetheless continued at a healthy pace of roughly 500-to-1,000 messages a week for as long as I was there.

Every one of these messages was read by my assistant, Arthur Bovino, who had spent three years as a Times news clerk before he signed up with me. Arthur, I am sure, came to know The Times's readership better than anyone else in the building, consumed as he was in a 24/7 conversation with the readers over an 18-month period. Once we had a system in place, every e-mail message got an automated response containing answers to standard questions (how to find the address of a particular reporter; how to locate articles I'd mentioned in my column; how to submit articles to the Op-Ed page) and letting the inquirers know that if a response was called for, they would be hearing back from us.*

That reduced the in-basket by half. Another quarter of the incoming mail emanated from mass campaigns provoked by particular interest groups, and could be answered by a single response either posted on my Web journal or sent back via e-mail. Others that went unanswered were those containing abusive language (some of which was truly shocking), irrelevant and often prurient nonsense (in the early months, one man wrote nearly daily to ask, "Is Maureen Dowd really as hot as she looks in her pictures?") or complaints that the ink in the paper came off on the reader's fingers.

The remainder—maybe 75 to 100 messages a week—got personal attention. Often this would mean a quick reply explaining a particular conventional newsroom procedure. Sometimes Arthur or I would forward a complaint to an editor, and ask the reader who had made the complaint to come back to us if the response was either unsatisfactory or dilatory. Another frequent reply reported the results of corrections editor Bill Borders's examination of a claim of error.

Those who received the most personalized (and, when our systems were working, the most timely) replies were people who had been written about in the paper and felt they had been misquoted, mischaracterized or otherwise treated unfairly. If the complaints contained the words "sue," "libel" or "lawyer," copies

---

* I'll confess that those who came to us through the easily managed medium of e-mail got much faster service than those who left messages on voice mail, sent their complaints via the post office, or, like those corporate communications functionaries bearing elaborate binders detailing their companies' mistreatment at the hands of The Times, arranged to have them delivered by hand directly to my office—or, in one unpleasant instance, to my home.

went immediately to The Times's legal department. These were joined in the most urgent category by any message that alleged unethical behavior by a Times reporter.

In those cases, and in several dozen others every week, I would attempt to discern the merit of a complaint by some form of investigation. This would usually take the form of e-mail queries to editors responsible for the article in question, further inquiries with the reporter who wrote the piece and conversations with top newsroom management (usually Al Siegal). Almost always, I learned enough to respond—with an explanation of either why I believed The Times to be blameless, or why I felt the complainant was correct. If the latter, our correspondence would usually conclude with a correction, an editors' note, a note of direct apology from an editor or writer—or, at the very least, an acknowledgment from me, to be used however the complainant wished, that The Times had erred, but that the editors disagreed with me.

At most, the same complaint would become a column—particularly when something in the complaint touched on an issue at the center of The Times's way of doing business. For instance, the complaint of a few parents about the way a controversy at a high school basketball game was reported (see "Setting the Record Straight—But Who Can Find the Record?," on page 75) became material for a column because I felt it illustrated a continuing problem characteristic of contemporary journalism. How that particular basketball game was covered was crucially important to a small group of parents; that the mistakes made in The Times's coverage of the game were part of an ongoing problem was, I believed, important to all the paper's readers.

· · ·

Arthur Sulzberger had wondered why I'd want the job for fairly
obvious reasons. Early on, a reader sent me a note with a quotation from I.F. Stone: "persuading others to virtue," he said, "is
not an endearing profession." Neither is serving in the internal
affairs division, wearing the badge of an inspector general or setting oneself up as thumbs up/thumbs down executioner—three
of the unpleasant roles that various people at The Times
likened to my position. Joann Byrd, a member of the committee that had recommended to Keller the creation of the public
editor's position, had been the ombudsman at the Washington
Post; she'd said that after concluding her tenure in the job, her
only remaining friends in the Post building were two loyal souls
who worked well out of the line of fire, in the paper's library.

I'm sure people at the Post can be pretty rough, but at The
Times—arrogantly convinced of its primacy, historically dismissive of both critics and competitors—an outsider given space to
knock the work of its staff was not likely to receive the warmest
of welcomes, nor be extended the most willing cooperation. As
someone without a newspaper background, I couldn't possibly
understand the nature of the work. As someone who'd never
worked at The Times, I couldn't possibly be accepted as a peer.

But I'd known people at The Times for decades, and what
had always struck me was how unhappy the place seemed to be.
I do not recall a time when a culture of complaint was not the
prevailing weather on West 43rd Street.* In my time at the
paper, I came to realize that this was not because of anything
the management did or did not do, but because of The Times's
singular place in American journalism, and what that meant to

---

* The possible exception: the early stages of Max Frankel's tenure as executive editor, in the mid–1980s, when the conclusion of A.M. Rosenthal's long
reign gave way to several years of relative glasnost.

those who aspired to work there. For most print journalists, The Times has long been Everest, and most people got there after a long climb. If you were the best reporter at a small paper in, say, central Kentucky, you'd soon be plucked away by the Louisville Courier-Journal. There, your work might be noticed by editors at the Chicago Tribune. After a few years in Chicago, or maybe at a Tribune bureau in Washington or overseas, The Times would come calling.

At each of your stops along the way, you were a star. Then, having finally pulled yourself up to this exalted summit, you look around and see that there are a thousand other people already there. Another metaphor: after several years of being Best in Show, you're now just another dog running on a treadmill.

For me, the generalized discontent inside the kennel made my job in at least one way easier than I had expected. Although there were maybe a dozen really nasty cases who made my life difficult whenever they could, most of the people I dealt with, at least after the first few months, saw me as just another irritant to grumble about. Or, as another pair of ears to grumble *to*, for many of them were more than willing to turn their discontent into useful material for me. With surprising frequency, staff members would come to me to discuss a perceived act of questionable journalism committed by someone else. Sub-editors would rat out desk heads, Washington bureau reporters whispered sourly about national editors and the hard news types threw roundhouse punches at articles featured on the cover of the Sunday magazine.

Fielding these complaints wasn't exactly pleasant—if not an internal affairs cop, I often did feel like the assistant principal of an unruly high school. But from these self-interested sources I often got useful insight into the paper's operations, and over time it made reporting about the insides of the institution relatively easy: alienated laborers, once one has discounted their motivations, make good sources.

Except, of course, when what they were alienated from was *me*. No one on the staff was compelled to answer my questions, respond to my e-mail messages, return my phone calls or give me the time of day. All I could do in response was to press my reporting elsewhere—that, and mention the name of the uncooperative writer or editor in my column, indicating what questions he or she had chosen not to answer. A few people occasionally engaged in some mildly unpleasant forms of obstruction. Only once, though, did I find someone pursuing a grossly unfair form of sabotage. It occurred about three months into my tenure, and it made for my single worst day on the job, followed by a weekend over which I seriously considered resigning.

David Cay Johnston, a reporter in the business section, learned that I had just been elected to the board of a very small public company called TESSCO Technologies (its entire market capitalization was roughly $60 million; by way of comparison, the New York Times Co. market cap around the same time exceeded $6.5 billion). He immediately announced my apparent perfidy to many colleagues and sent me a blistering message accusing me of causing widespread "outrage in the newsroom" because of my undisclosed conflict of interest. "The last thing we need is another scandal," Johnston wrote. "But now we have one."*

---

* I should point out that I had already had one nasty tangle with Johnston, who had opened a meeting with the business news staff by accusing me of sabotaging the career of a young reporter (who sat next to him, visibly uncomfortable, while he pounded the table); putting the paper's reputation at risk (by sending out to a reader an extremely mild acknowledgment that an article the young reporter had written "was not The Times at its best"); and otherwise abusing my position as public editor.

What Johnston didn't know, and hadn't bothered to inquire about, was that before Keller and I formally agreed on my hiring, I had given him a complete accounting of all my outside activities and engagements, including the then-pending election to the TESSCO board. Hired as I was for a fixed 18-month tenure, I could not afford to give up all my non-Times activities; I'd still need to earn a living when my term concluded in May 2005. Keller, as he later told Johnston, had considered the potential conflicts; we had agreed that I would disclose or recuse myself if any of them arose in my work. This included my membership on the board of the National Portrait Gallery, a division of the Smithsonian Institution. ("And the Smithsonian is part of the federal government," Johnston had written ominously. "Are trustees paid?" Ah, if only!)

After Keller informed Johnston of my disclosures and our discussions ("Obviously [Okrent] would not be in the job if I thought he was going to embarrass us through unethical behavior, but if he did the embarrassment would be chiefly to himself"), and after John Geddes and Al Siegal talked me down from my contemplated resignation (I had invoked to them an essential life principle, "Who needs this shit?")—after all that, Johnston sent me another e-mail. I'll quote the whole thing: "Keller says he is cool and it is his call. :)"

Johnston was one of a kind. So was deputy Metro editor Joe Sexton, who managed to be entirely cordial, yet determinedly uncooperative. Sexton, who had been one of the most outspoken people at the staff meeting in May 2003 that precipitated Raines's departure from the paper, wrote to me in March 2004, after I had asked him about a complaint from the office of the New York City corporation counsel.

"I think I have come to conclude that I am going to invoke my right not to respond directly to you or your inquiries," he wrote.

> It's a decision I like to think is based on something approaching principle for me, and not one of convenience or insecurity. I think the creation of the public editor's job was a profound mistake for the paper. But I will not in any way be an obstructionist. I will do my best to facilitate having reporters and editors who want to respond to you to go ahead and do so, and to provide them with what information I have to assist them. I am a passionate loyalist for Metro and would not want my silence to harm its reputation and credibility. It's possible that even that decision is somehow contradictory. But that's where I am at the moment.

If Sexton wanted to be a conscientious objector, I had two choices: live with it, or complain to Keller. The former option simply meant I'd have to do my Metro reporting elsewhere. The latter would have required me to become more dependent on Keller than I cared to. Working around Sexton turned out to be fairly easy.

If I became dependent on anyone at all (other than Arthur Bovino, of course), my rock was Al Siegal. I think we disagreed on half the positions I took, but Siegal never—well, almost never—told me what he thought of anything I'd written. It was Siegal, the paper's assistant managing editor for standards, who had chaired the committee that had recommended the creation of the public editor position. He had known that, once hired, the public editor would be out of management's control, and he would have to live with whomever Keller selected. Siegal chose to live civilly.* He was the man I went to when I wanted to understand Times policies and procedures, or when I wanted to know why certain rules were in place, why some rules in place were not necessarily followed and, generally, the processes that enabled a group of 1,200 people scattered around the world to get out a coherent, lively and largely accurate paper every day. Over his four decades at The Times, Siegal had developed a reputation among some members of the staff for rudeness, even nastiness—so on those very rare occasions when I encountered that side of him, I knew not to take it personally.

But Siegal also had a reputation for generous mentoring and an incorruptible devotion to the highest standards, two traits I admired greatly and exploited fully. Over the months my trips down to the third-floor newsroom to meet with him became so commonplace that all those pairs of eyes that had earlier peeked over the rows of computer monitors whenever I entered the enormous room ceased to note my presence. Reporters who had seemed nothing but suspicious when I had called or written them generally began to treat me with polite indifference. Some editors occasionally sought me out to discuss a pending issue, and if it didn't pertain to something not yet published, I was happy to be a sounding board.† In general, people at the

---

* Not that he was without reason to do so: I think Siegal derived a certain joy from having someone else take the blows from unhappy readers that had previously fallen on his shoulders. As he once wrote me when I sent him an e-mail noting how a dismayed reader had turned to me after getting the brush-off from one of the paper's senior editors, "Why do you think I invented you?"

† These conversations often had to do with complaints they had received about specific reporters, or about whether I'd heard from anyone outside the paper about a story that had just run. However, after one early mistake, at no

paper began at least to tolerate my presence—largely, I believe, because they had learned that no matter what I said in my column, when they came to work on Monday morning, the paper was still theirs.

That was good news for them, obviously. For me, the most gratifying news, which filtered back to me from a number of people in the newsroom, was that on those same Monday mornings, in many departments the day would begin with people arguing about what my column had said the day before. They might not have liked what I had written, they might not even think it merited saying—but they were necessarily engaged in a discussion of the issues my column had raised. Getting people at The Times to think about how readers perceived various aspects of their work wasn't the whole battle, but it was a very large part of it.

With one exception, every column I wrote grew out of inquiries or objections I received from readers or from people who had been written about in the paper. For that exception (see "There's No Business Like Tony Awards Business," on page 98), I gave myself a free pass: it was a column motivated by displeasure I had experienced as a Times reader.

The Tony Awards piece provoked a strong response from

[*continued*]

time would I ever discuss anything about a story before it appeared in print, lest I be asked to comment on it later, just as I attended no story meetings and took no part in policy discussions. The early mistake occurred when I heard from an acquaintance about a matter that seemed ripe for coverage in The Times. An editor agreed, assigned the story, and shepherded it onto the front page, where it landed heavily burdened with anonymous quotations. The next day, a party to the story called to urge me to investigate. Obviously, I could not.

people in the New York theater community. But in some quarters very far removed from Broadway, the white hot response enabled me to gain crucial insight into the way The Times is perceived by certain of its most critical readers. For months after the piece was published, those who disapproved of my take on aspects of The Times's political coverage cited the Tonys column as damning evidence of my failure at my job. Anyone concerned with such trivia, they argued, was unfit for the position of public editor. Similarly, many ideologically driven readers expressed their anger (or their dismissiveness) at various places around the Web whenever I failed to address in print what they had written to me about, or if I failed to send them a personal response to their complaints.

I understood their frustration, but they seemed not to grasp what the newspaper meant in the lives of readers other than themselves (nor, apparently, were they aware of the volume of mail I received). If the focus of your life is the war in Iraq, or the state of abortion law in the United States, or the way your book is reviewed or your company is described, it can be difficult to understand that hundreds of thousands of others are picking up the paper each day with no agenda other than wishing to be informed, enlightened and perhaps entertained. Of course the Tony Awards were not as important as United States foreign policy—but the Tony Awards, the pennant races, the movie grosses, the restaurant scene and a thousand other comparably inessential subjects were covered in The Times and meant something to substantial portions of the readership.

Apart from handling the e-mail and writing the column, the last large chunk of my time was taken up in meetings—not with

Times staff (although I did make a round of lunches and coffee dates with most editorial departments in my first several months on the job), but with outside parties. The line of people waiting at my door the day I started in the job convinced me that getting out into the world, or inviting the world into The Times, would enable me not only to explain my responsibilities but also, in a way, to determine what my responsibilities were.

I spoke to school groups, community groups, religious groups. I met with angry emissaries from the largest New York City municipal employees union, from the firefighters' union and from the Statue of Liberty Foundation. A group of scholars and Armenian activists came to me to try to persuade The Times to use the word "genocide" to describe what the Turks had done to the Armenians 75 years ago; after Keller changed the policy, I received a delegation of dismayed Turks. The provost, athletic director and two other officers of Ohio State University came bearing a bill of complaint about the sports section in my first month on the job, a Tufts University professor of cellular biology dismayed by science coverage visited during my last, and in the very last week of my tenure I addressed the membership of The Ombudsman Association of New York.* And throughout, I would meet or have extended conversations with lawyers, public relations specialists and crisis managers representing Wal-Mart, Newmont Mining Corp., Purdue

---

* These were largely from universities, public agencies and corporations. The trade association for people like me was an international group called the Organization of Newspaper Ombudsmen (or, aptly, ONO), the fellowship of whose members I valued, but whose annual conventions in such places as London, Paris and Istanbul seemed rather junket-like for a group of professional moralists. Then again, I may feel that way because the one convention that I could get to was in the decidedly unexotic St. Petersburg, Florida.

Pharma and a wide variety of other large companies who felt bruised by The Times.

These especially well-financed, well-lawyered and well-connected parties posed one of the thorniest problems I had to confront. Much as we might deny it, I believe most journalists get most defensive when their accusers come from the ranks of the overprivileged: large corporations; government agencies; political figures. With a few exceptions (notably reporter Walt Bogdanich's temperate, measured responses to the complaints from CSX Corp. about his series on safety at railroad crossings), reporters and editors alike seem to enter these disputes in a defensive crouch. They dismiss the complaints as self-interested, the elaborate supporting documents presented with them as attempts to obfuscate or intimidate. They do not begin by asking, "Is it possible that they have a point? Did we maybe get something wrong?"

Of course, when things are working, that second question is asked before publication. Time and again, I would see how first-rank investigative reporters like Bogdanich, David Barstow or Scott Shane would have already presented their findings to the individuals or entities under examination, giving them the opportunity to disprove or mitigate those findings before publication. But that wasn't always the case, and the three-way conversations that ensued—The Times, the story subject, me—were among my most difficult: it's hard to look at Halliburton or Wal-Mart as the disadvantaged party in a conflict. However, when they're up against The Times, they might well be.

Back when my appointment was announced in the fall of 2003, the one reaction that resonated most with me, and that proved most prophetic, appeared in an article by Mark Jurkowitz in the Boston Globe. Alex Jones, a former Times reporter (and co-author with Susan Tifft of *The Trust*, a superb family biography of the Sulzbergers), said that whatever I wrote "will be amplified tremendously by the enemies of The Times." (See the notes to "Is the New York Times a Liberal Newspaper?," on page 141, and to "13 Things I Meant to Write About But Never Did," on page 266.)

Leaders of some interest groups, and the bloggers who run with them, would praise me when I wrote something they agreed with, then dismiss me as incompetent, dishonest or a fig leaf for the paper when I disagreed with them.* E-mail messages I sent out taking issue with something in The Times's Middle East coverage would be reproduced and scattered by whichever side saw its viewpoint advanced by my comment—and then, the next month, they'd find me saying something they didn't like, and, as often as not, ascribe it to my buckling to pressure from Arthur Sulzberger, Bill Keller, Exxon Mobil or the Elders of Zion.

I was glad my mother, who was still living then, didn't surf the Web, or she would have had to suffer some pretty ugly stuff. Some critics, however, maintained an evenness of tone and an openness of communication no matter how much they disagreed with what I wrote, and I was all the more grateful to them for their courtesy. Notable among these were the leaders of the Gay and Lesbian Alliance Against Defamation, Partners

---

* Advice to aspiring public editors: try not to serve during a presidential election campaign.

for Peace and the Committee for Accuracy in Middle East Reporting in America.

Still, I tried not to close my ears to the impolite, the intemperate or the just plain offensive, recognizing that whatever provoked their rage should still be judged evenly and fairly. The complaint from the left that seemed to have the most merit arose from my admission that I felt it necessary to listen especially closely to critics who did not share my views. I had chosen to engage myself with a number of people on the right, running the risk—as I acknowledged in my first column—that "the effort at impartiality . . . can sometimes make you lean over so far backward that you lose your balance."

I'm sure I toppled at one time or another. I tried to compensate for that and for other failings of perspective or wisdom by making it a policy to publish in a monthly letters column only those reader messages that criticized my position or took a different one. But looking back, I have to say bending over backwards was worth it, if only for the chance of opening my ears and my mind to people whose views I might not encounter in a year of social and intellectual interaction in Manhattan.

I especially valued a dialogue I engaged in with David Mastio, a former USA Today editor and Detroit News reporter, and later a Bush administration speechwriter. Mastio argued that if The Times suffered from a lack of ideological diversity on its news staff it was not entirely its own fault, given the nature and coloration of the newspaper business in the United States. By the time reporters had become sufficiently accomplished to be hired by The Times, he explained, those with nonnormative views had already been flushed out of the system. Mastio says that he was more closely questioned and often directly challenged when he wrote things—particularly about environmental issues—

"that didn't fit the standard narrative" tacitly accepted in so many American newsrooms.

Two newsroom conservatives who did survive (and thrive) at The Times told me they were constantly made aware of their differences, much as black and Hispanic journalists I've known have experienced a persistent feeling of separateness from many of their white colleagues—not because of arrant racism, but simply because of dissimilarities in their backgrounds, and in the specific perspective they bring to their work *because* of that background.

In fact, there was more than ideological diversity at issue. There weren't enough political conservatives on the staff of The Times, but neither were there enough gun owners, or military veterans, or political liberals who happened to be evangelical Christians—just as there had long been a shortage of African-Americans or acknowledged gay men and lesbians, or (back in the day when writers named Abraham reduced their first names to initials in their bylines) even enough observant Jews.

Now, though, staff diversity was more important than it had ever been, for now The Times was a decidedly national newspaper, seeking both to understand the nation and to speak to it as it never had before. In 2003, Sunday circulation inside New York City and 26 surrounding suburban counties was, for the first time, exceeded by circulation in the rest of the country; two years later, national circulation of the daily edition also surpassed local circulation. At the same time, the rapid nationwide growth of nytimes.com threw the New York/Not New York division even more out of balance. The Times could choose to speak to its nationwide—even worldwide—audience by addressing only those who shared its general angle of vision, or it could try to widen that angle by being more inclusive intellectually. And, consequently, more effective journalistically.

If I erred in listening too closely to those who saw The Times as the voice of a New York–centric urban liberalism, I guess it was because I felt it reasonable to represent those people who weren't reading The Times, but ought to have been. Certainly I believe the country (much less the paper) would be better off if more people did read it.

For I remain convinced that The Times is our one truly essential newspaper. The sheer ambition of its daily task is unmatched anywhere else in journalism. It competes every day with the Washington Post and the Los Angeles Times on national news with the Wall Street Journal on business and economic news, and on international news with the combined foreign forces of all three of those. It competes with everyone on sports and style, and expends large sums on the resources that enable it to stand far above the rest of the American press in the space and effort it gives to cultural coverage. In New York City, it's engaged in a daily battle with the tabloids and the local broadcast stations.

For all its distinctiveness, The Times, as its former columnist Sydney Schanberg pointed out to me, is hardly the only paper that suffers from what Schanberg aptly calls "journalism's diseases." It is, he says, "just the most important one and the standard-maker."

That's why I heard from other journalists constantly, beginning with Brooke Unger, an Economist reporter based in Brazil who disagreed with the position I took in my second column ("You Can Stand on Principle and Still Stub a Toe," page 35), fearing that my argument might hamper the work of reporters everywhere, simply because The Times's prestige within the profession automatically accrued to its ombudsman. When I published the name of a reader who had sent an especially vile message to a staff reporter, some reporters at other papers (as well as one old friend at The Times) chastised me for abusing the power that came with a byline in The Times (see "How Would Jackson Pollock Cover This Campaign?," on page 155, and the notes following "A Correction," on page 169). Others took issue with specific columns that, they feared, might persuade their own readers that there was something pervasively unhealthy in American journalism generally.

Mostly, though, I received support from other journalists— and, especially and most movingly, from former journalists. A few Times retirees clearly saw me as their cat's paw, hoping I would take a paddle to editors they didn't like, or point out that the paper wasn't nearly as good (or as noble or important or ethical or valuable) as it had been in their day. But it was striking how many retired journalists—from The Times and elsewhere—were supportive of my work. It was as if their distance from newsroom culture had enabled them to see what those who are immersed in it may not notice: the distortions caused by a perpetually antagonistic stance; the dissimulating overreliance on anonymous sources; the mindless pursuit of empty scoops; the sometimes cruel incursions into private lives; the entire complex of taken-for-granted practices that have led to the diminished faith in journalism that so many Americans now express.

Not only the diminished faith that they express—but the general suspicion that leads them to begin their discourse with their daily paper in a posture of suspicion and mistrust. Take, for instance, the woman who was "deeply offended" by part of a Times headline that was, she felt, "insensitive, offensive and probably racist." The story, about pedestrian workers on Long Island, most of them immigrants who were endangered by speeding traffic, bore the main headline, "Peril Afoot in the Land of Four Wheels." My correspondent said she objected to the subhead, "Careless Immigrants Find Risk on Long Island Roadways," and asked why the subhead didn't attribute the carelessness to "the people who, speeding in the safety of their cars, run over innocent pedestrians or cyclists? Who is likely to be more careless, he who has nothing to lose or the walker who knows he is risking his life by crossing the highway, and has no other transportation, or safer option?"

I was about to forward the e-mail message to Metro editor Susan Edgerley when I thought to look at the article — always a good idea — to see if there was anything in Patrick D. Healy's reporting that might possibly have justified this patently offensive adjective, likely inserted in the headline by an editor so arrogant that he could not perceive the wounds the description could inflict. This close reading of the text determined my response to the woman:

"I'm happy to be able to tell you that what you perceived was not the case," I wrote. "The subhead on the article was '**Carless** Immigrants Find Risk on Long Island Roadways,' not 'Careless Immigrants' . . . "

Just another day in the life of Public Editor Number One.

A Note to the Reader

Except for some slight changes in punctuation and the deletion of one name (explained, in context, on page 169), all of the columns reprinted here—my complete published output as public editor—appear as they did in The Times. In both the columns and in the notes that follow each of them, I refer to individual editors by the titles they held at the time the column was written.

In a few of the columns and in several of my notes on the columns, I mention newspaper articles, blog postings and other texts, including criticisms of what I wrote in The Times. When the context does not provide enough information (headline, date of publication, place of publication) for the reader to locate a Web version of the reference easily, I have inserted [@], indicating that the mentioned item can be linked to from www.publicaffairsbooks.com/publiceditor#1. In some instances, of course, these links will lead you to a site that insists on either membership or a fee.

All of my Public Editor columns, as well as letters about them from readers, are available free of charge through a link at the same address. You can pursue references to items in my Web journal from this page as well.

· · ·

An Advocate for Times Readers Introduces Himself

. . .

December 7, 2003

WHEN The New York Times invites you to be the first person charged with publicly evaluating, criticizing and otherwise commenting on the paper's integrity, it's hard to say no: this is a pretty invigorating challenge. It's also hard to say yes: there are easier ways to make friends.

Reporters and editors (the thickness of their skin measurable in microns, the length of their memories in elephant years) will resent the public second-guessing. The people who run the newspaper may find themselves wondering how they might get away with firing me before my 18-month term is up. Too many combatants in the culture wars, loath to tolerate interpretations other than their own, will dismiss what I say except when it serves their ideological interests.

But those are their problems, not mine. My only concern in this adventure is dispassionate evaluation; my only colleagues are readers who turn to The Times for their news, expect it to be fair, honest and complete, and are willing to trust another such reader—me—as their surrogate.

So who am I?

By training and experience, I'm a journalist: for 25 years a magazine writer and editor, for the last couple of years (and during various other between-gigs intervals) a writer of books; earlier in my career, I spent nearly a decade as a book editor. When I was in school in the 1960s, I was a not-very-good campus correspondent for The Times, a little on the lazy side, rarely willing to make the third or fourth phone call to confirm the accuracy of what I'd been told on the first one. Instead I expended my energies in that hyperventilated era as a shamelessly partisan and embarrassingly inaccurate reporter for my college newspaper. Early in my magazine career, I at times participated in a form of attack journalism that today fills me with remorse — picking a target and sending out a reporter to bring back the scalp. I got fairer, and better, as I got older.

By upbringing and habit, I'm a registered Democrat, but notably to the right of my fellow Democrats on Manhattan's Upper West Side. When you turn to the paper's designated opinion pages tomorrow, draw a line from The Times's editorials on the left side to William Safire's column over on the right: you could place me just about at the halfway point. But on some issues I veer from the noncommittal middle. I'm an absolutist on free trade and free speech, and a supporter of gay rights and abortion rights who thinks that the late Cardinal John O'Connor was a great man. I believe it's unbecoming for the well-off to whine about high taxes, and inconsistent for those who advocate human rights to oppose all American military action. I'd rather spend my weekends exterminating rats in the tunnels below Penn Station than read a book by either Bill O'Reilly or Michael Moore. I go to a lot of concerts. I hardly ever go to the movies. I've hated the Yankees since I was 6.

To the degree that I've been the subject of Times reporting or commentary, I've generally been treated fairly. In 1985, though, a book of mine was clobbered in the Book Review (" . . . [it] has difficulties with detail, pace and even words. . . . When Mr. Okrent is not forcing phrases, he collapses into cliché.. . . ") by someone whose own book I had reviewed negatively—for The Times!—not three years earlier. My wife tells me I should get over it, but a grudge like this is much too nourishing to give up after only 18 years. It's also a reminder that real people can get hurt by a newspaper's missteps, and maybe I was made to suffer that review so I could empathize with similarly aggrieved parties two decades later.

Since my appointment was announced, I've heard complaints about the paper so intense they could peel paint. A former colleague told me she canceled her subscription because of The Times's "virulent anti-Catholicism." An acquaintance's parents consider the paper "prima facie anti-Semitic." One of my oldest friends is boycotting The Times because of what he considers its conscious hostility to conservatives and its "institutional inaccuracy." Another friend, inflamed by what he deems the absence of coverage of post-Taliban Afghanistan, asks, "Isn't The N.Y. Times as complicit as the Bush administration in ignoring this poor country?"

Let me acknowledge a theological principle of my own: I believe The Times is a great newspaper, but a profoundly fallible one. Deadline pressure, the competition for scoops, the effort at impartiality that can sometimes make you lean over so far backward that you lose your balance altogether—these are inescapably part of the journalism business. So is the boiling resentment toward men and women in power that can arise in a trade that requires, as Russell Baker once wrote, "sitting in marble corridors waiting for important people to lie" to you.

Journalistic misfeasance that results from what one might broadly consider working conditions may be explainable, but it isn't excusable. And misfeasance becomes felony when the presentation of news is corrupted by bias, willful manipulation of evidence, unacknowledged conflict of interest—or by a self-protective unwillingness to admit error. That's where you and I come in. As public editor, I plan on doing what I've done for 37 years, reading the paper every day as if I, like you, were asking it to be my primary source of news and commentary (and ruefully expecting it to enrage me every so often as only a loved one can). But to enable me to represent you effectively when you have a complaint about The Times's integrity, the top editors are granting me open access to the entire staff, and space right here, every other week (more often if I think it's necessary), to comment on its work.

My copy will not be edited, except for grammar, spelling and the like. Staff members are not required to answer my questions about coverage, presentation or other aspects of journalistic practice, but if they choose not to, I'll say so. In the interest of open communication with my fellow readers, I will try very hard not to speak to anyone at The Times off the record, on background, not for attribution or under the cover of any of the other obfuscating cloud formations that befog modern journalism. I want to be able to let you know what I know—to remain a reader, even if a reader with an all-access backstage pass. I never want to be in the position of saying, "I know they did this right, but I'm not allowed to tell you why." The paper's operations may not always be transparent, but I hope my own arguments, assertions and, as necessary, indictments will be.

If I were running for re-election, you'd have every reason to doubt my independence; consequently, on May 29, 2005, by mutual agreement with executive editor Bill Keller, my name will disappear from the head of this column and from The Times's payroll ledger. Until then, I'll let my fellow readers decide if I'm doing my job honestly. Here's wishing good luck, and good will, to us all. See you in two weeks.

· · ·

This first piece was a revision of a tryout column I had written during the period in which Bill Keller and I were discussing the possibility of my taking the public editor job. I had thought it wise to let Keller know the tone of voice I intended to use—my goal was to be conversational, to provoke at least the illusion of intimacy with the readers, to level with them on my politics and prejudices. Keller apparently bought into it, but Al Siegal sagely suggested that I delete a line summarizing my position on the Israeli-Palestinian conflict. In essence, he said, "Why do you want to lose a chunk of your readership in your very first column?" From what I would come to learn about the way that every word dispatched from the paper's Jerusalem bureau could provoke uncontained rage, I'm certain Siegal was right.

I was stunned by the response that the column provoked. Within 24 hours of its appearance—unheralded, except for a plug at the bottom of the front page of the Week in Review section—my published e-mail address had been overwhelmed with more than a thousand messages from readers. Many were dismissive: a typical e-mail message read, "I would not be interested in what you have to say. Your bias is already evident (and wrong)." Responses like that shouldn't have dismayed me as much they did; naïveté had led me to expect even the paper's most vehement enemies to give the public editor experiment at least a chance. I had to give credit to those critics who had a sense of humor: "You pretend to be middle-of-the-road, but it sounds like the road is Broadway in front of Zabar's, which tells me all I need to know."

But by the time I had finished reading a broad selection of the incoming artillery, I had come to understand that the intensity of response was not simply the result of the political passion that would later dominate so much of the reader mail. For much of the first week, Arthur Bovino and I faced a flood of grievance that previously had had no effective outlet. People who had been written about years before told their tales of woe, which usually began with perceived acts of unfairness or inaccuracy committed by the paper, then segued directly into complaints about letters unanswered, voice mail messages unreturned or messages that could never have been returned because the complaint numbers printed in the newspaper were attached to voice mailboxes that were perpetually full. The Times had long had systems to handle reader complaints; they just didn't use them terribly often.

Press response was mixed, but the most memorable comment made me flinch (in itself no surprise: my skin's as thin as anyone else's). The Los Angeles Times's excellent media columnist, Tim Rutten, blasted me for a variety of reasons, but especially for (a) narcissism, and (b) undue attention to alleged media bias, when the only issue that mattered was accuracy.[@] Rutten may still not like what I ended up doing in my 18 months, and it would be awfully narcissistic of me to argue the narcissism charge—but I hope he came to recognize during and after the 2004 presidential campaign that perceived bias is a matter of great concern for many readers.

The only thing I wish I could take back from the column is the suggestion that I wouldn't let Times editors and writers explain themselves off the record. Within weeks, off-the-record conversations became a necessary part of my reporting.

You Can Stand on Principle and Still Stub a Toe

· · ·

December 21, 2003

MOST people who are subjects of newspaper articles they believe to be unfair or inaccurate have few avenues of recourse.

You can write a letter to the editor, and if you're extraordinarily lucky, it will leap out of the enormous haystack (The Times gets more than 300,000 letters and e-mail messages every year) and into print. You can ask for a correction, which even if granted isn't likely to be seen by nearly as many people as the original story. If you've got a lot of money and a lot of time, you could even hire a lawyer.

Some complainants have both the will and the resources to carry on a sustained war. In my experience, the most determined are corporations that abide by the dictum expressed by one Washington-based consultancy: "A culture of attack permeates today's business world." They fight fire with fire, rolling out the lawyers, the public relations specialists, the "crisis management" commandos. Sometimes they fight cinders with fire. In 1997, I.B.M. stopped advertising in Fortune after the magazine published what any disinterested reader would have considered an unexceptionable profile of the company's chief executive, Louis Gerstner. It didn't return its millions of dollars of business to the magazine until after Gerstner's retirement in 2002.

I'll leave it to I.B.M. stockholders to determine how this action might remotely have served their interests. But while I.B.M.'s tactic may not have been pretty, it was perfectly fair. The company didn't own a major business magazine in which to make its case. Nor does Purdue Pharma, the drug company that makes OxyContin and has long felt put upon by The Times.

Back on Feb. 9, 2001, The Times published an article headlined "Cancer Painkillers Pose New Abuse Threat." In the next 13 months, co-author Barry Meier's byline appeared above an additional 13 stories detailing the painkiller's horrifying abuse as a recreational drug, its salutary medical uses, the dispute between federal agencies about its impact, and the marketing strategies used by Purdue Pharma. The company objected to what it still considers Meier's "sensationalized and skewed account" of its actions. In December 2001, company officials visited The Times to make their case to newsroom managers, who, a Purdue Pharma lawyer told me, "blew us off." Times editors believe they gave their visitors full consideration, and Meier continued to write about both the drug and the company until shortly after he began work on a book about OxyContin in the spring of 2002.

I'm not in a position to pass definitive judgment on the fairness of Purdue Pharma's charges. But after reading through Meier's work and the company's detailed rebuttals, and after talking to authorities both parties directed me to, I believe Meier's reporting was generally accurate and fair, even if the way some of the pieces were played—placement, headline, frequency, etc. — sometimes seemed the work of an especially ferocious terrier that had gotten its teeth into someone's ankle. In the 18 months after Meier moved off the story to write his book, The Times published two more articles and one brief item about Purdue Pharma and its controversial drug. Then Rush Limbaugh showed up.

Limbaugh's announcement this fall that he was taking a leave of absence to treat his addiction to painkillers presented The Times with the occasion for a story. It presented Meier, whose book had been published just weeks before, a reason to return to a subject on which he was the paper's acknowledged expert. Aware of the sensitivities involved, on Oct. 16 he asked assistant managing editor Allan Siegal for permission, as he wrote in a follow-up e-mail message, "to proceed with occasionally writing about issues related to narcotic painkillers in light of the recent publication of my book."

"My concern," he continued, "was that critics of The Times, including the manufacturer of the drug that is at the center of my book, might contend publicly that I was using The Times as a platform to promote my book." Siegal gave Meier permission to proceed with a story for the Tuesday Science Times section that was not a news account but a Limbaugh-connected consideration of painkillers and addiction. "He promised me that the piece he had in mind was only peripherally about OxyContin," Siegal told me.

Meier kept to his word; the article that eventually appeared on Nov. 25 didn't mention OxyContin or Purdue Pharma until the 11th paragraph. Howard Udell, Purdue Pharma's chief legal officer, acknowledged that although he had some minor problems with it, he thought it was "the fairest piece Barry has written."

But back when Meier first approached Purdue Pharma for comment for the article, Udell demanded that The Times take the reporter off the story, asserting that the recent publication of Meier's book posed a conflict of interest. Because Meier was out on the talk show circuit promoting the book, Udell argued, he had a financial interest in seeing stories about his subject in the pages of the paper. Siegal defended the paper's position in a letter to Udell: "Mr. Meier's current assignments are not centrally or principally concerned with your company or its products." Udell was not appeased. In his response, he argued that if there is the appearance of a conflict (The Times's written policy, he noted, says that "staff members must never give an impression that they might benefit financially from the outcome of news events"), there is a conflict.

When a news subject tries to get a reporter removed from a story, a challenge has been issued to the core of a newspaper's self-image: its integrity. Unless editors see a clear case of bias or conflict, they tend to respond the way you or I would respond to, say, an insult to a family member. They stiffen with indignation. They try at the same time to support the wounded loved one. Were they to concede, the humiliation could hurt more than the charge itself.

The classic instance of this sort of immune-system response occurred in 1963, when President Kennedy asked Arthur Ochs Sulzberger, who had just been named the paper's publisher, to recall reporter David Halberstam from Vietnam. (Interestingly, as historian Robert Dallek writes in his recent biography of Kennedy, Halberstam's "irrefutable accounts of U.S.-South Vietnamese failings in the war" had implied that "greater

American involvement was necessary.") Times editors had been planning to reassign Halberstam, as part of the normal rotation of reporters serving difficult assignments. But Kennedy's intervention led both Sulzberger and Washington bureau chief James Reston to resist: if you want him off so badly, they effectively said to the White House, we are compelled to keep him on.

That was the proper defense of a central principle in a clearcut case of enormous importance. In the OxyContin case, Times editors found themselves instinctively defending the principle, but perhaps at the cost of credibility. Even if Meier's Limbaugh article mentioned his book (it did not); even if it had appeared at the moment that Limbaugh was in the news (it took more than five weeks to get into the paper); even if the piece had sensationalized or magnified the issue at hand (not even close), it is almost certain that Meier would not have benefited financially: the functional connection between his article and his book was thinner than the page you're holding. (The positive review of Meier's book in the paper last Wednesday was infinitely more valuable, but the complicated matter of Times reviews of books by Times staff members will have to be the subject of another column.)

And here's another string of even-ifs: Even if Barry Meier was not going to see dollars pouring in from writing about OxyContin, and even if he was the Times reporter who knew the most about oxycodone-based painkilling medication, and even if Udell's demand was perceived as a disingenuous effort to intimidate the paper into altering its coverage—despite all this, there did exist the appearance of a conflict.

A newspaper shouldn't take a reporter off a running story because of complaints from subjects if it doesn't find the complaints valid. But neither should a newspaper automatically defend this principle when it is neither material nor mission-critical. Meier had not been covering Purdue Pharma or OxyContin for 18 months, and the paper and its readers could have been well served on the Limbaugh piece by one of the reporters currently on the beat. Certainly the paper's reputation could have been served by removing even the slightest hint of conflict. Assistant managing editor Siegal acknowledges that giving Meier the go-ahead—which Meier properly sought under The Times's own rules and procedures—was "probably a mistake."

This wasn't a matter of a president leaning on a newspaper to back off a story of critical importance, but The Times's T cells didn't make the distinction. As I asked people at the paper about this episode, some felt that whatever complaints Purdue Pharma might have, its concern about the Limbaugh-pegged story was, as one said, "making a mountain out of a molehill."

Problem is, when you put out a paper the size of The Times, with scores of individual articles, day after day, many will seem like molehills. But when you're at the other end of the telescope, when you're the subject of a story—even if you're a big pharmaceutical company—each one looks like Everest. Reporters and editors need to place the paper's readers someplace in between, and give them an unobstructed, and unconflicted, view of both.

. . .

The reaction to this piece included the first affirmation (of scores to come) of the point Alex Jones had made in the Boston Globe article about my appointment: how anything I wrote critical of The Times "will be amplified tremendously by the enemies of the Times." On Slate.com, a writer who had objected strongly to much of Barry Meier's coverage said that my column had "dealt with [anti-] Oxycontin bias," and suggested I believed Meier guilty of it. Slate immediately ran a lengthy correction when this and other errors were brought to their attention.

In at least one fashion, I did Meier a disservice with this column. Within a couple of weeks I would come to determine that my world had to have begun on December 1, 2003: I decided I could not address—in print, online, or in e-mail—anything that had appeared in the paper before my first day on the job. To do otherwise would have had me disappear into those endless tunnels of past grievance that had been revealed in the reader reaction to my first piece. Meier's Limbaugh-launched piece had beaten my starting date by six days—not much, but fine points are still points.

My favorite example of the complaint that predated my arrival at The Times would soon come in a letter from a woman in Chicago, who nearly three years before had made futile objections to a "Vows" column about her ex-husband's remarriage. The original article had said that the newlyweds had met after the husband and my pen pal had separated; in fact, she said, they had conducted a lengthy, adulterous affair. She had a genuine grievance, but for the paper to publish a correction on such a matter more than two years after the event would have been kind of weird. The woman was eventually mollified by an appropriate, and official, apology from Al Siegal.

Speaking of Siegal: this column brought out one of his very rare comments about my work—I had failed to include his middle initial. A modest crime, perhaps, but none of us owns anything as valuable as our names. As for Louis Gerstner and the long ago Fortune piece that had inflamed him: what had apparently gotten him so angry was the suggestion that he had bad manners on the golf course.

The Quote, the Whole Quote and Nothing but the Quote

. . .

January 4, 2004

THE first true blizzard of the first public editor's first season began Sunday, Dec. 21. The lead headline on the front page of The Times declared, "Strong Support Is Found for Ban on Gay Marriage." Reading the article over my morning coffee, I wondered why a single poll—The Times's own, co-sponsored by CBS—was itself considered news (at least one other released around the same time showed substantially different results). But for the next two weeks, rising drifts of e-mail provoked by the piece made me realize my attention belonged elsewhere.

Most correspondents felt that the 55 percent of those polled favoring a constitutional amendment against same-sex marriage did not constitute "strong support." Many others, called to arms by the Gay and Lesbian Alliance Against Defamation, objected to the phrasing of the poll questions, and to the unequal number of pro- and anti-amendment respondents quoted in the article (three to one). Additionally, read the complaint posted on GLAAD's Web site, "the story sensationalized and misrepresented poll results, failing to ask basic poll questions that would have allowed respondents to consider the full range of issues at play."

These are substantive objections, but each seems arguable: a 55–40 split (the rest had no opinion) would constitute a landslide in any election this side of Beijing. I'm not convinced that any poll questions on so volatile an issue can be truly nonprejudicial. And as for the imbalance of interview subjects, when man bites dog, you talk to the dog: the news here was the increased support for the proposed amendment relative to previous polls.

I'm still puzzled by the notion that a poll conducted by The Times is front page material. Without a detailed explanation of methodology, how can a reader figure out why this poll is more reliable than those conducted by competing news organizations? And wouldn't a thorough piece of journalism at least report on other polls that have different results? The Times isn't alone in this habit, of course, but when any news organization touts its own polls while failing to note reputable polls conducted by others, I pat my pocket to make sure my wallet is still there. This isn't news; this is awfully close to promotion.

But my gravest concern about the piece, shared by scores of my correspondents (both supporters and opponents of the amendment), has to do with a dicier journalism issue: the fair representation of quotations. In this case, the problem was not the alteration of words, but their absence. Seven paragraphs into the article, reporter Katharine Q. Scelye, who shared the byline with Janet Elder (one of the editors who supervise The Times's polling operation), quoted a comment President Bush had made a few days earlier: "I will support a constitutional amendment which would honor marriage between a man and a woman, codify that."

But the president had actually teed up his statement, made to Diane Sawyer in an ABC News interview, with a potent qualifier: "If necessary," he said, "I will support...." I cannot believe that these were words the president uttered lightly. I imagine they were arrived at with a great deal of forethought, analysis and even calculation. The rumbling they evoked from pro-amendment as well as anti-amendment partisans indicates how fragile a hedge the president was cultivating. "If necessary" could suggest that the president wouldn't support a constitutional amendment if the recent Massachusetts court decision were reversed by the Legislature; or if the Supreme Court got involved; or who knows, maybe not if "Queer Eye for the Straight Guy" dropped out of next season's Bravo lineup. Politically, you could reasonably assume that the truly necessary part of the president's statement was "if necessary."

The elision in the Seelye-Elder article was not, as several of my correspondents insist, "politically motivated," or "unethical" or a "blatant manipulation of the facts." It was a simple mistake. When first reported in The Times by White House correspondent Elisabeth Bumiller on Dec. 17, the president's comments appeared in two separate sentences: the news ("I will support") followed immediately by the qualification ("But Mr. Bush said he would support an amendment only 'if necessary' to preserve traditional marriage"). Washington editor Rick Berke asked Seelye to freshen the poll data (it was more than a week old) by referencing the president's recent comment. After searching the Times database, Seelye told me via e-mail, "I took the quote directly from Elisabeth Bumiller's story, which, unbeknownst to me, was foreshortened." No one caught it during the editing process, and foreshortened it remained.

In the months before I started in this job, two instances of Times columnists' truncating or eliding quotations made some readers apoplectic. I'm trying to stay away from issues that arose before I started here, except insofar as they relate to running stories, so I'll leave further discussion of those incidents to critics, polemicists and the columnists' loved ones. But deciding when a quote begins and when it ends is something that nearly every writer faces in nearly every story, and there are no firm rules to follow. Even The Times's detailed policy on quotations doesn't address this. "Readers should be able to assume that every word between quotation marks is what the speaker or writer said," according to the paper's "Guidelines on Our Integrity." [@] "The Times does not 'clean up' quotations." (I'd better play by strict rules here: The policy continues for another eight sentences, but none concerns the beginning or ending of quotations. Trust me.)

Whether plucked from a press conference or a barroom conversation, quotes are not just reported—they're selected. Subject goes on at length; reporter picks a few especially revealing, juicy or simply interesting sentences; presses roll; and, later, the subject cries, "Taken out of context!" But except when a newspaper prints verbatim transcripts, all quotations are taken out of context. The context is the actual conversation or press conference in which words get uttered; the printed pages of a newspaper can only rudely duplicate it.

The business of quoting is inherently artificial. Selection is editing. Ask any film critic who sees his words misappropriated for an advertisement. Newspaper reporters and editors may be more conscientious than movie studio promotion departments (and they don't slap an exclamation point on the tail of every sentence), but the hunt for words to put between quotation marks may be a relic no more vital than the hardened city editor of long ago, green eyeshade on his brow and Lucky Strike hanging from his lip, barking to the trembling cub reporter, "Go back and get me a quote!" A worthy quote? A revealing quote? A quote for its own sake? Doesn't matter—just get me one. When Joe DiMaggio was a young ballplayer and a reporter asked him for a quote, he didn't know what the man was talking about. "I thought it was some kind of soft drink," DiMaggio remembered.

Defenders of quote-chasing say it's necessary for verisimilitude (even if the selection process is arbitrary), for color (if so, that's an unhappy comment on a writer's ability to render a scene vividly) and, crucially, for balance. But even this last motivation often leaves us listening in on banter that wouldn't dignify an elementary school playground, especially during a political season. Just last week, a Howard Dean spokeswoman told a Times reporter asking about a John Kerry criticism, "What you're seeing is a career politician desperate to save his political career." This is not to knock the spokeswoman, whose rebuttal was no less dignified than those made by her counterparts in the other candidates' camps, but for all the enlightenment this provided Times readers she might as well have said, "And so's your mother." Wouldn't it be sufficient—and maybe even raise the level of the public conversation an inch or two—for the reporter simply to write, "A Dean spokeswoman dismissed Senator Kerry's charge as political"?

But I'm afraid we'll see reporters stop chasing quotes around the same time dogs stop chasing cars. Until then, we just have to hope that quotations are rendered accurately and fairly. (Is this a shot across the bows of columnists, editorial writers and the public editor? You bet it is.) The Times seems to be pretty good about rectifying misquotations; in early December, when Mississippi State football coach Sylvester Croom's spoken "ain't" was prettified into standard English [@], a correction appeared swiftly. So too with the missing "if necessary," restored to the president's lips three days after its unfortunate disappearance.

But the two instances are different. In addition to being rendered inaccurately, Coach Croom's words may have lost a little of their flavor in the process; President Bush's were stripped of a crucial part of their meaning. Deputy national editor Alison Mitchell told me that "as soon as we became aware" of the shortened Bush quote, "we made a correction, and we believe the correction was sufficient." But maybe there's a new category of correction needed for errors that distort meaning, as distinct from errors that fumble facts. There's a difference between misspelling St. Catharines, Ontario (not "St. Catherine's," readers of the Corrections column learned on Christmas morning) and misreporting the president's words. Judging by the reader mail that snowed me under in the days after Dec. 21, it's partly the paper's grudging unwillingness to acknowledge the relative importance of an error that makes some readers think that innocent missteps, like the dropped "if necessary," are willful misdeeds. All quotations may be created equal, but all misquotations are not.

. . .

I don't think Katharine Seelye was terribly happy with this piece, and if she felt vindicated when the president's definition of "necessary" proved to be extremely accommodating, she had every right to be. Two months later, he declared that a constitutional amendment was necessary, and the elided words had lost whatever meaning they'd once had. I'll stick by the central point, though: all quotation is selective, and as most journalism tries to be interesting as well as accurate, most reporters will lean on the pithiest comment a source provides them while making infrequent use of the temporizing, qualification and reconsideration that afflicts most civilized people.

The strongest reaction I got came from Janet Elder. What did I know about polling that qualified me to criticize The Times's polling operation? Why hadn't she been given a chance to respond? Throwing off a side comment in the course of a column about another subject was nothing like the columns that most other ombudsmen did, and why had I done it? Elder later got strong support from Bill Keller, who said in an interview that my comments on the poll issue were "ill-informed." (Keller did, however, institute a policy change, asking that a box explaining a poll's methodology be printed not just on the first day a poll's data is reported, but in all subsequent articles that, like Seelye and Elder's, drew on a previously published poll.)

If I was in fact ill-informed, it was Rich Meislin, who headed the paper's polling operation at the time, who would later do a good job of informing me. Meislin pointed out that a Times poll was like a Times article—prepared and interpreted by Times staff, to Times standards. The Times would cover a political news event without acknowledging how other papers covered it, and public attitudes, as measured and weighed by The Times, are certainly news.

It's a good point. Still, the authority of numbers is powerful. Numbers may not be unimpeachable (see "Numbed by the Numbers, When They Just Don't Add Up," on page 209), but they do tend to take on an authoritative halo. If The Times wants to lead with its own take—its own numbers—that's perfectly fine, but acknowledging different (or similar!) numbers gathered by other reputable news organizations would give readers a deeper understanding. Around the same time that The Times poll was in the field, an Annenberg Public Policy Center poll on the subject, with the question phrased somewhat differently, came up with a nearly mirror-opposite response (40 percent for the amendment, 51 against).

Finally, should a poll ever lead the newspaper? Well, when there's no real news to report—an all too common circumstance in Sunday and Monday papers—you're kind of stuck. But if you're willing to go with news you actually make, editors on that Sunday could have led with the first, riveting part of David Barstow and Lowell Bergman's unassailable series on workplace safety, which ran in a less prominent spot on Page One. That was news that really mattered.

Dr. Dean Assumes His Place on the Examining Table

. . .

January 18, 2004

JODI WILGOREN has been the lead Times correspondent on Howard Dean's campaign plane since last summer. She was among the first national reporters to recognize the propulsive force of the Dean movement, in July, when she wrote a front-page article studded with phrases describing how the candidate "burst from his obscurity to rank among the top contenders" and his "stunning surge" in the fund-raising race; a subhead read, "Standing Up for His Beliefs." People in the Dean campaign believe she's an excellent reporter. I've never met her, but as a faithful reader I think so, too.

But judging by my e-mail and my Web surfing (which

included a stop at a blog called "The Wilgoren Watch"), she has a lot of detractors. Not Gephardtians angry about what they perceive as The Times's obsession with their candidate's fund-raising difficulties. Not Kucinichers who believe that The Times "has for many months and from very early on been a heavy promoter of Dr. Dean; I don't think too many people would dispute that," as the congressman's press secretary, David Swanson, told my associate Arthur Bovino. No, Wilgoren seems to have become the face on the dartboard for Dean supporters.

Nearly every time there's a story about Dean in the paper, my in-box fills with complaints from his fans. (Every time there isn't a story providing a précis of a new policy statement from the Dean camp, it's almost the same.) They attack the editors of The Times, Wilgoren, national political correspondent Adam Nagourney and other staff reporters for misrepresenting, ridiculing or attempting to sabotage Howard Dean. They especially object to The Times's microscopic inspection of their candidate while, many say, the depredations of George W. Bush go unexamined.

One reader asks, "Is The Times reprising its relentless attacks on Clinton by now using the Democratic front-runner" as its target? Another calls one senior reporter a "Republican operative." A third has canceled her subscription to the paper because of an analysis she considered an "effort to topple Howard Dean." Some complain that The Times is improperly obsessed with Dean's personality, or unfairly digging into his past or—a complaint common, it seems, to all the campaigns— too interested in handicapping the electoral horse race while ignoring substantive policy positions.

I took a few days off from scanning the incoming artillery before calling Dean headquarters last week. Campaign spokesman Jay Carson understandably didn't want to comment on the quality of The Times's coverage, but he did have something to say about what the e-mail barrage represents: The Dean crusade (my term, not his, and meant as a compliment) is "the greatest grass-roots campaign in modern history," he said, and he continued: "These people write letters, they make phone calls, they give money. It's just a very high level of commitment."

I'll say. The complaints from Dean's adherents have struck me with such force that they've triggered Bennet's Corollary, a formulation of The Times's Jerusalem bureau chief, James Bennet: "Just because everyone is mad at you doesn't necessarily mean you're doing the right thing." (It's a phrase that most journalists, who play defense even more aggressively than they play offense, should etch into their computer screens.) This past week, it led me to reread The Times's Democratic campaign coverage since Dec. 1.

The paper has made mistakes. Wilgoren's description of Dean listening to Al Gore announce his endorsement (Dec. 10) was inappropriate in a news article: "Dr. Dean smirked his trademark smirk"; that's columnist language. The visual used to illustrate an article on Dean's temper (Jan. 3) was more problematic; it was the cover of a recent issue of National Review, with the face of an inflamed Dean above the headline, "Please Nominate This Man." The caption noted that National Review is a "conservative journal," but there's no escaping the fact that this wasn't an example of Dean's temper, but of what an avowedly partisan publication thinks of Dean's temper.

Some headlines understandably aroused the troops. David Halbfinger's fine Jan. 4 piece detailing the potential mechanics of a Dean collapse (if you're an electoral horse-race fan, it was irresistible; if you're a Dean fan, it was probably alarming) appeared under the words "Yes, Howard Dean Can Be Toppled and How." Halbfinger, uttering a line that is a version of every reporter's mantra, says, "I've long since stopped worrying about headlines, as I have no control of them." Week in Review editor Katy Roberts, who does, admits that "the headline, in trying too hard to be cute (with the double meaning of 'and how'), may have misrepresented the story."

In the news pages on Jan. 9, the head over a piece chiefly about Dean voters in Iowa read, "Tide of Second Thoughts Rises Among Democrats." Judging by what appeared in the article, the "tide" consisted of the four Iowans quoted in the story and some unknown portion of the "dozens" of others with whom the writers spoke.

I found the front-page play given one story peculiar and inappropriate. Managing editor Jill Abramson stoutly defends the placement of "Vermont Auditors Faulted Dean Aide on Contract in '92" (Jan. 6), by Rick Lyman, because "this was a revealing example of how Dean handled the award of a lucrative state contract to a company connected to a close political ally." I think it was a revealing example of how newspapers tend to inflate their own scoops.

Abramson says the story was additionally relevant because of the way "Dean and the Democrats are also assailing the Bush administration for secrecy." But a story so old, and so tenuously connected to Dean's own actions, didn't need to shout. Page 1 is a megaphone, and the same piece, run inside the paper and at less imposing length, could have been delivered at a more appropriate volume. Executive editor Bill Keller believed that the story was important, but he told me, "I concede we might have overplayed it."

That's what I found in seven weeks of intense coverage: one sentence; one picture; two headlines; and an overplayed story. I'm sure I missed some other questionable phrasings, but certainly not enough that could signify a pattern of behavior or betray a partisan agenda. It's true that many thoughtful Dean supporters have carefully dissected a variety of other pieces to reveal a tilt against Dean. But the tilt they identify is invariably a part of the story under examination. An article detailing what Dean's opponents perceive to be his weaknesses is legitimate news. All the "on the one hands" and "on the other hands" you could stuff into such a piece wouldn't dissipate the negative aura it necessarily emits. Individual articles may be rough on the candidate, but individual articles do not constitute coverage. What the paper does over time, through the long slog of a campaign, is what matters.

I have a suggestion for angry Deaniacs (including those who objected to reporter Todd Purdum's use of the term "Deaniacs" on Jan. 11, even though many of Dean's own supporters use the term themselves—see www.deaniacs.org). Think of a politician you dislike—maybe one of the Democrats Dean is battling— and substitute his name for Dean's in any piece about your man. If it still sounds unfair, there's the possibility it is. But without passing such a test, you're left not with "an insult to our democracy," as one of my correspondents calls the paper's campaign coverage, but with journalism.

I think Jay Carson is right—the grass-roots activists Dr. Dean has inspired should absolutely make phone calls, write letters, hound public editors. But they have to recognize that the full-body physical their candidate has to endure is a sign of good fortune, the direct consequence of being in front. By my count (I did it quickly, so don't arrest me if I'm off by two or three), from

Dec. 1 through this past Friday, The Times published 59 major stories or editorials about Dean. Wesley Clark has been up for view 30 times. No other candidate has enjoyed (or suffered) more than 20 appearances in the paper. Carol Moseley Braun got only three shots—and two of those were about her decision to leave the race.

Memo to Dean supporters: If you think it's rough when The Times has you under observation, be prepared to strap on your seat belts if he wins the nomination.

The following item ran under the heading "Editors' Note," but over my byline, the next Sunday, January 25:

Readers of the Public Editor column will remember that on Jan. 4, I made a lot of clucking noises about quotations that are truncated in such a way as to be misleading. Journalists, I said, are obligated to be extremely careful with the words of those they write about.

But in rendering a quote for my column last Sunday I committed a blunder that could qualify for the headline "Caesar's Wife Slips on Freudian Banana." Sloppiness led me to leave the false impression that reporter David Halbfinger disapproved of an editor's headline on an article he had written for the Week in Review ("Yes, Howard Dean Can Be Toppled and How," Jan. 4).

"I've long since stopped worrying about headlines, as I have no control of them," I quoted him as saying. But I failed to mention that he went on in the same sentence to add that "the headline, to me, was aptly tongue in cheek." To make matters worse, Halbfinger actually used the words "control over them," not "of them."

I suppose I could try to explain how I managed to mistranscribe a quotation in an e-mail message sitting right in front of me, or go through the reasoning that had me cut Halbfinger's comment short. But explanation is not justification.

The mistake was entirely my own, and a pretty embarrassing one it is. My apologies to David Halbfinger, and to the readers.

See you next week.

. . .

Shortly after I began working on the Howard Dean column, I started to hear rumblings from various people in the Washington bureau about the questions I had been asking. As I would throughout my tenure, I had sent out a number of e-mail queries to writers and editors about various aspects of campaign coverage. One of these went to R.W. Apple Jr., the celebrated Times correspondent (Apple was celebrated for his decades of political coverage long before he became celebrated, as a food writer, for the apparent size of his expense account).

Apple had gone to one of the bureau editors to express his view that I was asking questions that were, if not inappropriate, then certainly—by his standards—"ill-informed" (a phrase that was threatening to sound like a chorus). Apple never gave me any trouble directly, and at various times during my tenure he was quite helpful. But isn't asking questions a way of becoming *well*-informed?

More troubling was a question raised by deputy national editor Alison Mitchell, who was running the New York end of the campaign coverage. Mitchell was disturbed by my having called Jay Carson of the Dean campaign to get his reaction to Wilgoren's coverage. By doing so, she argued, I had inappropriately, and possibly influentially, introduced myself into the relationship between reporter and subject without being asked to by either. She was absolutely right; judges should take evidence, not go out hunting for it. I never did it again.

Maureen Dowd had her own take on this piece: writing on The Times's Op-Ed page later the same week, and picking up on what I had characterized as "columnist language," she twitted George W. Bush for "smirking his trademark smirk." Touché.

All the News That's Fit to Print? Or Just Our News?

. . .

February 1, 2004

THIS week, it's time for some journalism heresy. I'd like to suggest that newspapers with aspirations to greatness—like the one you're holding in your hands—learn to be generous to their rivals, and in the process provide value for their readers.

It has long been Times policy to credit other news organizations for their scoops: "Such and so was first reported Monday in 'The Daily Bugle.'" It has even longer been part of the paper's genetic code never to let someone else's scoop lie unmassaged by Timesian hands. "What can we add?" goes the editors' refrain. Sometimes—often—that works. Sometimes, though, the effort at addition becomes, for the reader, an act of subtraction.

In the last several weeks, three stories launched elsewhere have been either diminished or disregarded by The Times. (Of course, among major news organizations, this not-invented-here attitude is no more exclusive to The Times than are commas.) In each case, the effort to maintain a high level of what people around here call "competitive metabolism" has not served the readers well.

Last October, The Blade in Toledo, Ohio, published a series of articles revealing that "members of a platoon of American soldiers known as Tiger Force slaughtered an untold number of Vietnamese civilians over a seven-month period in 1967." The series was the product of 10 months of research conducted on two continents and in seven states.

When The Blade series broke, The Associated Press sent out a story summarizing its findings. Many newspapers picked up the A.P. report; some, including the Times-owned International Herald Tribune, put it on the front page. In the Times newsroom, Roger Cohen, who was foreign editor at the time, thought it an important story, but, he recalls, he was "focused on Iraq" and "did not give it the attention it deserved." National editor Jim Roberts tried to get something rolling that the paper could call its own, but reporters who knew their way around the Pentagon were otherwise engaged. Editors felt that running 10 inches of A.P. copy would not represent the story fairly.

In The New Yorker of Nov. 10, Seymour Hersh, who as a young reporter broke the story about the massacre at My Lai, praised The Blade series, noting along the way that the four major networks and most major newspapers had all but ignored it. Hersh's article provoked The Times's executive editor, Bill Keller, to order up a lengthy piece on The Blade's discoveries. John Kifner's "Report on Brutal Vietnam Campaign Stirs Memories," which sought to place The Blade series in historical perspective, finally ran on Dec. 28 — a report on a two-month-old story about events that took place 37 years ago. The Blade's publisher and editor in chief, John Robinson Block, felt that The Times's late weigh-in, which included a sizable help-ing of the skepticism that re-examination will almost inevitably provoke, was an insult to his paper and its reporters.

Keller told me that if his own staff had developed The Blade series, he would have put it on the front page. Yet at least partly because it was someone else's, it ended up diminished, delayed and, in some eyes, devalued.

Scores of readers wrote me earlier this month about The Times's failure to put former Treasury Secretary Paul O'Neill's bombshells about the early days of the Bush administration on the front page. Most suggested (and many insisted) that the story was played down for political reasons.

There are several more practical explanations that could be invoked by Times defenders. They might note that the careful-ly leaked morsels of news that fed the story were intended to propel the book containing O'Neill's revelations onto the best-seller list. They could point out that O'Neill himself wasn't available to The Times; his first broadcast interview had been locked up exclusively by "60 Minutes," and his first print inter-view had been promised to Time magazine. Most persuasively, Times editors had very little to go on as they tried to fashion their first story for Saturday, Jan. 10, and what they had was frus-tratingly manipulative: promoting its exclusive Sunday evening interview with O'Neill, CBS spooned out a few juicy nuggets to newspapers on Friday and Saturday—enough to entice readers to watch "60 Minutes," yet not enough to make them feel they'd already seen it.

The 10-paragraph Associated Press story The Times ran on Jan. 10 may not have been a prizewinner, but it did have a for-mer cabinet member comparing the president who appointed him to a "blind man in a roomful of deaf people," which certainly sounds like Page 1 news to me. But if it didn't make the front page because CBS had locked down the story, once The Times did have access both to the book and to O'Neill himself, it didn't make the front page because—well, because by then the news was no longer new. For the historical record provided by the newspaper of record, explosive revelations about a sitting president by one of his appointees were consigned to Pages A11, A22 and A13.

The most important not-invented-here in recent weeks, and the one that crystallized the issue for me, was a story that ran in The Washington Post on Jan. 7. "Iraq's Arsenal Was Only on Paper," by Barton Gellman, was so stunning a piece of reporting that it led Bill Keller to tell The New York Observer that it "caused everyone who competes with [Gellman] a serious case of indigestion followed by admiration." In a conversation in his office last week, Keller elaborated: Gellman's piece, he said, was "rich and subtle and deeply reported." I asked him why, if it was so good, it didn't merit a story in The Times recounting its main points, especially since The Times's own reporting on Iraqi weapons programs last winter has continued to suffer a hurricane of criticism. Keller said that trying to do a summary of Gellman's work for Times readers ran the risk of oversimplification—that the nuances that made the piece so strong would not survive reduction to summary form. Gellman's piece, he said, was "easy to admire, hard to represent."

Or, as former Times managing editor Gene Roberts once said by way of explaining the difficulty of handling other papers' big stories, "You can't steal an elephant." The necessary checking and re-reporting The Times had to go through to run its own version of The Blade's Vietnam story required several weeks. Tracking down Gellman's Iraqi sources might have taken years. Breaking through the fortress of exclusivity erected around Paul O'Neill by CBS and Simon & Schuster would have taken a safecracker.

But it's not as if The Times, and every other newspaper on the planet, doesn't consistently publish material it hasn't gathered on its own. When a district attorney announces an indictment, The Times doesn't assume it needs weeks to interview witnesses, check allegations or otherwise vet the prosecutor's charges. When a politician makes a speech, there's often so much taken at face value a critic could argue (and in my e-mail, many, many do) that the paper is shilling for the politician. Having read Barton Gellman's words for many years, why can't Times editors have as much faith in them as in John Kerry's, or Dick Cheney's, or the Santa Barbara County prosecutor's? They—the editors—may read The Washington Post. But how many of their readers do?

There's no question that the competitive electricity powering a news organization produces a great deal of benefit, just as it would in a soap company fighting for market share or in a research team trying to beat the other guys to a medical breakthrough. I understand why competition is necessary to inspire the troops. I also understand that Macy's never carried anything with a Gimbel's label sewn into it. But maybe The Times's insistence on stamping its own brand on everything it touches ends up diminishing what it delivers. If the goal of newspapering is to inform the readers and create a historical record, shouldn't the editors be telling us about everything they think is important, no matter where they find it?

I've been trying to stick to one theme in each of my biweekly columns, but as that may be more a product of vanity than necessity, I'm going to break the pattern here. Last Sunday's Times Magazine cover story on sex slavery, "The Girls Next Door," by contributing writer Peter Landesman, has provoked a great deal of controversy, and the article's detractors and its defenders have made their cases forcefully. Go to www.slate.com/Landesman [@] for a wide-ranging assault on the piece by Slate editor at large Jack Shafer and for a comprehensive defense by Times Magazine editor Gerald Marzorati. For those who missed it, a link to the original story may be found at nytimes.com/weekinreview [@].

.   .   .

Richard Pérez-Peña, a Metro reporter who soon became one of my most intellectually stimulating sparring partners, thought my point about how newspapers unquestioningly repeat the declarations of prosecuting attorneys was "sophistry."

If it diminished my argument, I'll take it back. The point is a simple one, and it's one that is at the core of what I believe are the most foolish aspects of the news business: the fanatical belief in scoops, and the associated disregard for the scoops of others. Neither trait has anything to do with informing the public.

The Blade's Tiger Force piece, by the way, won the 2004 Pulitzer Prize for investigative reporting.

It's Been 11 Weeks.
Do You Know Where Your Ombudsman Is?

. . .

February 15, 2004

IN the two-and-a-half months since I stepped into this job, my mother isn't the only person who has asked how it's going. Many, many readers have written or called to express their pleasure, their disappointment, their conviction that I'm a fig leaf for Times management, their concern that management isn't backing me up. Some want to know why I haven't answered their messages, and others ask when I'm going to fire one or another of the paper's columnists.

These and many other questions made me think I ought to sit for an interview about how this new adventure — for both The Times and me — is playing out. I could hardly have a Times reporter ask the questions, so I turned to the nearest available journalist: me.

Q. So tell me, Dan. How are they treating you at The Times?

A. I'm glad you asked. It has been both better and worse than I expected — better because a lot of people here believe that The Times should be as open to examination as those The Times itself examines each day; their welcome has been generous and heartening. What's worse than I expected is the overt hostility from some of those who don't want me here.

Q. Is it aimed at you, or at the job?

A. Both. One reporter ripped me up and down about how offensive it was that the staff had to endure public second-guessing, how it makes reporters vulnerable to further attack, how the hovering presence of an ombudsman can hinder aggressive reporting. When I objected—"I don't think your complaint's with me; I didn't invent this job"—the reporter hissed, "You accepted it!"

Others have complained that as a former magazine writer and editor, I don't know anything about newspapers; as a non-Timesman, I don't appreciate how The Times is different from all other media institutions; or as an idiot, I don't know anything about anything. They may well be right. But all those deficiencies may enable me to ask the stupid questions no insider ever would.

Then there are the people in between, who say that I'm doing a good job and taking the right positions—except on those subjects in which they're involved. Fair enough; in this regard, they're just like a lot of the people The Times writes about.

Q. What about the bosses?

A. So far, everyone in the paper's management has behaved well. Some have criticized me for specific acts (executive editor Bill Keller told The Washington Post that one of my columns was "ill informed"), but that's their prerogative. As long as I have unhindered access to this space and to The New York Times on the Web (nytimes.com), as well as the right to say what I wish in e-mail correspondence and interviews, I have no complaints.

Q. How are you dealing with readers?

A. I've received more than 11,000 e-mail messages from readers. A majority have complaints about The Times, many of them substantive. Another source consists of people who don't read The Times but write to me because they've been rallied by a Web-based organization.

For instance, the director of national letter-writing (a real title!) at the Committee for Accuracy in Middle East Reporting in America (CAMERA) sends out alerts about objectionable articles to the "CAMERA E-Mail Team," with my address attached; other groups, like the Gay and Lesbian Alliance Against Defamation, paste my name and address to the text of a complaint—all that its constituents need to do is hit "send."

When I answer the mail that pours in as a result, I do it only in the Web journal that I recently set up at nytimes.com/danielokrent.

All messages overheated by abusive language or intemperate accusations go into the bin otherwise reserved for solicitations from Nigerian billionaires. And I've found that answering someone who is writing from a position of unshakable ideological conviction is generally a futile endeavor for both of us.

Q. Why aren't you addressing complaints about The Times's reporting last year on Iraqi weapons of mass destruction?

A. I determined early on that looking into articles published before I started in the job on Dec. 1 would make me disappear into an endless tunnel. Each day's mail brings something new to address. If I were obliged to look backward, I'd never complete, say, my current examination of The Times Magazine's Jan. 25 piece on sex slavery.

Q. Any advice for readers?

A. E-mail is better than the telephone. Keep your messages short. Check to see if I address your concern in my Web journal. Do not try to get me to prove my independence by daring me to investigate the secret pact the Sulzberger family has made with the Trilateral Commission and Pete Rose to take over the Grammy Awards.

Also, be wary of telephone calls that purport to be from this office. In December, the subject of a Times investigation hired a private detective to pose as my representative. She telephoned several people a Times reporter had interviewed, indicated there was a problem with the reporter's work and told the sources I wanted to review the questions the reporter had asked. If anything like this should happen to you, ask to return the call. If the number you're given doesn't begin with (212) 556-, don't do it. Instead, send me an e-mail message immediately.

Last bit of advice: don't call me "you," as in "Why did you [or "your people"] put such-and-such on the front page?" I'm not The Times; I'm an independent contractor. I don't attend editorial meetings, engage in personnel discussions or review anything before it gets into print—nor should I be able to. That's why newspapers have editors.

Q. Speaking of editors, when are you going to write about the editors' evident pro-Bush, anti-Republican, Likud-sponsored, Israel-hating bias?

A. Not soon. I'm reading carefully; I'm taking notes; a few readers have kindly offered to keep track of what they perceive to be bias. I'm going to wait until I've bird-dogged this one over time before I come to any conclusions.

Q. What about the editorial page and the columnists? You never write about them.

A. As it largely should be. Most correspondents who complain to me about opinions expressed in editorials or in the space allotted regular columnists are likely to receive this reply: "Editorial writers and columnists are free to express whatever opinions they wish, and readers are free to disagree with them."

However, some related issues that have come up have attracted my attention. One is whether (or how) The Times's editorial positions determine its news coverage. Another is whether columnists should be free, as they are now, to decide whether and when to publish corrections of their own mistakes. One especially determined critic keeps asking "whether there is such a thing as an unfair opinion." (An e-mail note I received this week charged that one columnist "has crossed the line from acceptable or at least standard partisan nonsense to actual irresponsible journalism.") These are all provocative questions, and I hope to be addressing each of them at some point—the corrections policy first, certainly within the next couple of months.

Q. One critic said you write like "a pensioned insider," while many of your readers would prefer you to attack wrongdoers with cracking whips and howling dogs. Why are you so, well, polite?

A. Because I'm interested in a conversation, not an argument. The purpose of my column, my Web journal, my e-mail messages to readers and my very presence here is to open a window. Screaming won't help; discussion may; transparency definitely will.

Q. Any last words?

A. Yes—but they shouldn't be mine. That's why, starting next Sunday, this space will periodically be given over to readers' letters about subjects I address in my columns. Letters most likely to be published are those that are brief, temperate and take a position different from or critical of my own. Somebody's got to ombud the ombudsman.

. . .

Sure, I know that the self-interview is a cheap trick, but tricks become cheap precisely because they're easy, and the first few months had been so intense I needed a break. Tricks also make some people very mad, as evidenced by the later fulminations of Bob Somerby of DailyHowler.com, a liberal blogger who couldn't bear my politics (even though I don't really think he knew what my politics were), nor very little else about me and my public editor gig—I'll give you a link later on, when I provoke one of his angriest responses.

At times, I inadvertently handed over a few stout sticks to my detractors, and let them take whacks at me. It was in this column, when I posited the virtue of stupid questions, that I gave a bunch of people at The Times a tool some would use over and over. "Well, I certainly agree he asks stupid questions," or "Why doesn't he say how stupid his questions are?"—quotations like these usually came back to me from reporters from other papers who were writing about The Times's experiment with a public editor. Maybe they kept calling the same source (I know that Jonathan Landman—a masthead editor who deserves credit for always speaking his mind on the record—was one).

So let me put it differently: you learn nothing if you take anything for granted, or if you presume you know something before you've explored it.

On the matter of some readers' belief that I was being undercut by management when Bill Keller criticized me in public (notably the "ill-informed" statement about my comments on The Times's reporting on its own reporting): I appreciated their concern, but it was misplaced. There was no better way to establish my independence than by accepting Keller's (or Landman's or anyone else's) right to criticize whenever he wished—so long as I continued to control a visible chunk of the Week in Review section every other Sunday morning.

The private investigator who represented herself as my representative was working for the imprisoned Russian oil billionaire Mikhail Khodorkovsky. I didn't mention his name in the published version of the piece because reporter Timothy L. O'Brien was still working on his article. I tried never to comment on unpublished articles because I didn't think it appropriate for me to influence works in progress. I made an exception in this case because I genuinely feared that others would attempt to do what Khodorkovsky's agent was doing. I made a later exception (see "There's No Business Like Tony Awards Business," on page 98) because what The Times was about to do was what it had been doing for years. And because I wanted to write about the Tony Awards.

Lee Green of CAMERA wrote to say that her title was "national letter-writing group director," not "director of national letter-writing."

What Do You Know, and How Do You Know It?

. . .

February 29, 2004

AT the beginning of the most controversial article published in The Times in the last few months, writer Peter Landesman described a house in Plainfield, N.J., that had once harbored a sex slavery ring.

"When I stood in front of it on a breezy day in October," he wrote in The Times Magazine on Jan. 25, "I could hear the cries of children from the playground of an elementary school around the corner. American flags fluttered from porches and windows. The neighborhood is a leafy, middle-class Anytown."

I visited Plainfield last week, and I can assure readers that every detail in Landesman's description is accurate. I can also assure you that every detail in my own description is accurate:

"When I stopped my car in front of the house on a wintry day in February, the loudest noise came from the traffic roaring past. Across the street stood a pair of body shops; virtually next door, Friendly Check-Cashing conducted its desultory business. Yards away sat the single-story home of the Faith Tabernacle Church, and just beyond that the rotting hulk of an enormous 90-year-old Mack Truck factory, a dark satanic mill that would have been at home in any dying industrial city."

Not every journalist sees every fact from the same angle.

The assault on "The Girls Next Door" and its assertions of widespread sex slavery in the United States began within hours of its publication, mostly on the Web: alarmist, unconvincing, undersourced. Soon after, I received the first of several messages from Times reporters expressing similar views, their tone ranging from studied skepticism to barely contained outrage.

From Times staffers? Don't be so surprised. The antipathy directed toward The Times Magazine by many of the daily paper's writers and editors is decades old. Standards at the magazine are deficient, many say; at a meeting I attended recently with several dozen members of The Times's Metro staff, one reporter said, "No one in this room would have written that story."

The magazine's defenders make the case that their standards are in fact tougher than those in force at the daily paper. Newspaper reporters aspire to corroboration of disputed facts by relying on more than one source; magazines, say those on the other side, do the same but may not provide the evidence in print. They also subject their stories to examination by checkers who review every fact. Magazine people say most newspaper stories aren't written well enough, or dramatically enough, to engage the reader; newspaper people say magazine writers excel not at storytelling but at embroidery.

Both sides are better at offense than defense. It's impossible to read a typical day's Times without corroboration being attributed to . . . well, to people who asked not to have their words attributed to them. "Sources say," "analysts say" and all the similarly empty variants suggest corroboration but don't confirm it. The Times's new policy on anonymous sources, announced last week and available at www.nytco.com/sources, may mitigate this practice, but imagining a modern newspaper without unattributed quotes is like imagining the Arctic without ice.

At magazines, fact-checking can help you get details right, but can't pin down the un-pindownable: sometimes, a source will make an assertion—for instance, that he saw women walking through Cottonwood Canyon, Calif., in high heels. (An Editors' Note addressing this and some other matters relating to Landesman's article appeared in The Times on Feb. 15. [@]) Virtually all the fact-checker can do is call the source and ask, "Did you see women walking through Cottonwood Canyon in high heels?" The firmest "yes" doesn't even approach proof. It's often not the fact that gets checked, but the fact that someone said it was a fact.

Newspaper reporters engage in a daily dialectic, and try to follow a controversial declaration with a balancing statement from someone on the other side. Magazine writers, believing in the primacy of narrative, will withhold contrary views until the end of the piece—or, often, withhold them altogether. Magazine writing, says Gerald Marzorati, editor of the Sunday magazine, "encourages point of view and authorial opinion." Newspaper writing does not. (Except, of course, when it does.)

For Landesman, the dialectical approach would have been pretty difficult—it's not easy to find people who'll make the case for sexual slavery. But there are always doubters, and I know Landesman talked to several. In a newspaper story, they would have been quoted or paraphrased, even if left unidentified; in a magazine story, practitioners argue, it's often enough for the author to assimilate contrary views and then make a judgment. Persuaded by his own reporting, and able to convince his editors of its accuracy, Landesman marshaled all the evidence he could find to support what became a piece of advocacy journalism.

But Landesman and the editors carried the advocacy to a fault. In possession of a horrifying story, they didn't allow it to speak for itself. I won't use the word "hype," which connotes a mendacity that was in no way present here. The verb I prefer is "shout," which the magazine did in two different voices, one presentational and one rhetorical.

The presentational excess began with the cover line, "Sex Slaves on Main Street," with the Anytown implication it carries. The cover photograph depicted a partly obscured young woman who we later learn is 19 years old, but whose clothing (knee socks, kilt, sweater vest) suggested someone much younger. Inside, the display type above the headline declared that "perhaps tens of thousands" of young women "are captive and pimped out for forced sex" in the United States. Always beware "perhaps," the most dangerous word in journalism. As often as not, it's a synonym for "Who knows?"

The barely more refined number—30,000–50,000—in the piece itself, put forward by the president of America's largest anti-slavery organization, is an example of the article's rhetorical problems. If your material is strong enough—and I believe Landesman's was—you don't need to underscore, capitalize or quantify, especially when there is really no way of coming up with a number accurate enough to be meaningful.

If your material is strong enough, you don't need to cite prosecutions that may have involved smuggling women for voluntary or temporary prostitution, but not for what you'd call slavery. You don't need to bring in tangential references to other forms of sexual horror that have nothing to do with slavery. You don't need to rely on the testimony of a pseudonymous young woman, "Andrea," for the most dramatic, detailed and harrowing description in the entire piece. I've read the transcript of Landesman's interview with Andrea, and despite some internal contradictions, it is impossible not to believe it in its outlines and in much of its detail. But excerpting it without qualification, or without a convincing explanation of why Andrea's detailed memories of events that happened many years ago are believable, only undercuts its credibility. The question is not whether Landesman believes Andrea—what matters is whether he can persuade the rest of the world to believe her.

When I first read Landesman's piece, I found him credulous. Having examined the article more closely, and having done some reporting of my own, I'm convinced that the proper adjective would be "inflamed." As he went deeper into his reporting, the degradation and the horror he encountered rendered him passionate—hardly an insult, but in the newspaper business often a disqualifier. He brought into the story figures, facts and circumstances that he felt added to his argument. Instead they turned some readers into skeptics, some skeptics into critics.

In the weeks after Landesman's article went to press, authorities in both Mexico and the United States brought charges against what The Associated Press described as "a family-based ring that lured girls and women into sex slavery in Mexico and in New York"—an operation based in the town of Tenancingo and described in detail in Landesman's article. In late January federal officials busted a suspected sex slavery ring in Queens. A few days later, Los Angeles authorities broke up another operating out of a motel across the street from Disneyland.

The road from West Front Street to Anaheim is a long one, and every mile along the way provides a battlefield for the ongoing war between newspaper reporters and magazine writers. One journalist presents one set of facts; the other presents another. Both make choices that shape the terrain of an article. Each relies on a different descriptive technique, and on different claims of proof. Based on my examination of Landesman's materials, on conversations with law-enforcement authorities and on the internal evidence itself, his choices were fairly arrived at. But they weren't justified terribly well.

So do you tear Landesman apart because you don't believe his sources, or because you can't locate an audit trail to some of his assertions? Or do you accept the hideous realities he describes and emerge convinced that sex slavery is a genuine problem? I do the latter—I just wish he and his editors had been more circumspect in making the case.

(**March 7, 2004**) Correction: The Public Editor column last Sunday, about a recent Times Magazine article on sex slavery, misidentified the police officers who broke up a suspected slavery ring operating from a motel near Disneyland. They were from Anaheim, not Los Angeles.

. . .

As someone who has spent most of his career in the magazine business, I've long debated with various colleagues the virtues of fact-checking. Much as I love a good fact-checker, and as often as the good ones have saved my neck, I do think an undue faith in fact-checking can lead to laziness on the part of reporters and credulousness on the part of editors. "There are TK trees in Russia," goes the old journalism joke (first uttered, I believe, by Otto Friedrich of Time)—"TK" being journalese for "to come," itself another way of saying, "Could the fact-checker look this up?" The very notion that the number of trees could possibly matter suggests that some editor believes precise numbers can lend a piece the aura (hardly the reality) of scientific authority.

And any breach in fact-checking procedures can leave a newspaper or magazine open to damaging accusations. After Newsweek in May 2005 published in its "Periscope" section an item asserting that American troops in Guantanamo had flushed a copy of the Koran down the toilet, the magazine's editors acknowledged that "Periscope" items were not checked as thoroughly as the rest of the magazine. Yet nowhere on the "Periscope" page do readers see a warning such as, "Items on this page are not checked as thoroughly as the rest of the magazine," or "Items on this page may not be as accurate as the rest of the magazine."

This column did contain one gratuitous aside I'd like to take back: the parenthetical "Except, of course, when it does," following the assertion that newspaper writing does not encourage "point of view and authorial opinion." I had intended this to carve out an exception for editorials, signed columns, and arts criticism. But by resorting to a snappy comeback instead of a sober explanation, I cheapened my description of the differences between newspaper and magazine writing.

Setting the Record Straight —
But Who Can Find the Record?

. . .

March 14, 2004

LATE in January, Colonel Pete Mansoor, an Army brigade commander in Baghdad, sent an e-mail message to some 50 friends and relatives. One of those forwarded it to me, with some disturbing words inserted into the subject line: "N.Y. Times Falsely Reports Americans Killed Iraqis — that's my take."

The offending story had been published in The Times on Jan. 13, under the headline "G.I.'s Fire on Family in Car, Killing 2, Witnesses Say." Colonel Mansoor's message, sent several days later, established that those witnesses were wrong; the victims had been killed by shrapnel from a terrorist bomb. He concluded with this admonition to his friends and relatives: "Although you can read both sides of the story in this e-mail, the American people only know the original story as printed in The Times, which never issued a retraction or clarification. Let the reader beware."

In fact, The Times not only published a clarification the day after the first story appeared, but did it under a robust five-column headline. Yet, just like Colonel Mansoor, you'd never know it unless you were looking for it, because of a squirrelly journalistic dance step known to old-timers as a "rowback."

As a prominent editor told his readers last week, "It is inevitable that in producing an entirely new newspaper containing more than 100,000 words on deadline, every day of the year, we will make mistakes."

Leonard Downie Jr., executive editor of The Washington Post, wrote those words, but he could have been speaking for the competition as well. Reporter Edward Wong, who wrote the Times story that inflamed Colonel Mansoor, did everything he could to get the story right. He asked questions of every available witness and all available authorities; he tried to interview survivors at a nearby hospital; he attributed assertions of American responsibility to named individuals.

Not 24 hours later, though, American authorities informed Wong that an investigation indicated that the two civilians had been killed by bomb shrapnel. Wong immediately sent in an update to The Times's online edition and reported the clarifying details in the next day's paper, under that five-column headline. Problem was, the headline read "Army Copter Downed West of Baghdad in Hotbed of Anti-U.S. Sentiment," and the clarification appeared almost as an aside, in the 17th paragraph of a story otherwise far removed from the deadly explosion on Palestine Street.

The editors who decided to handle the clarification this way may not know the term, but this was a classic example of the rowback. The one definition I could find for this ancient technique, from journalism educator Melvin Mencher, describes a rowback as "a story that attempts to correct a previous story without indicating that the prior story had been in error or without taking responsibility for the error." A less charitable definition might read, "a way that a newspaper can cover its butt without admitting it was ever exposed."

It happened again on Feb. 7, on the front page of the Metro Section, in a story about an incident at a private-school basketball game. (Actually, it happens fairly frequently, but these two stories make especially vivid examples.) For those not attuned to the folkways of Manhattan elites, this one may have escaped your attention; for those more plugged in to local rites, there was no way of avoiding it. An enraged parent attending a contest between the Trinity and Dalton Schools charged that Trinity students had hurled anti-Semitic imprecations at a Dalton player.

The resulting coverage wasn't The Times at its best. Reporter Jane Gross and deputy education editor Jack Kadden took as corroboration a Trinity official's allusions to an ongoing disciplinary investigation. It was the sort of story, editors told me, that might not have made the paper on a newsier day. But on a Friday afternoon, with word going around that a local television station was preparing to break the story, even the unavailability of corroborating witnesses couldn't slow the train down. The article and its headline—"Anti-Semitic Slurs Mar Game at Top Private School"—didn't even suggest that there was a difference of opinion over what had happened. When I asked education editor Suzanne Daley why the story hadn't been postponed for a day or so while Gross sought corroboration more palpable than the Trinity official's ambiguous reticence, she replied, "Because we're a newspaper."

And, you might say, because The Times is a newspaper, the default corrective turned out to be a rowback. A week after Gross's article appeared, the paper published a story by Tamar Lewin that provided the textured detail that had been either unavailable or unexplored in the first piece: the fact that one of the accused Trinity students was himself Jewish; that the "slurs" resembled the sort of harmless, if juvenile, byplay you expect to

find in an Adam Sandler film; and that some Trinity parents had
charged that the Dalton parent who triggered the first story had
gotten into "a physical altercation" with Trinity students. But
nowhere in the second piece was there acknowledgment that
anything had been missing from the first one — nor, in fact, that
there had even been a first one.

Last month, when I was able to inform Colonel Mansoor
how Edward Wong's efforts had led to a clarification that
appeared in the paper, however obscurely, he was grateful.
Similarly, I know that some of the Trinity parents felt somewhat
mollified by Lewin's follow-up. But if you find either Wong's
first piece or Gross's article in an electronic archive, neither is
linked to the rowback. "Correction Appended," the signpost
that The Times's Web editors attach to the digital version of a
story after a formal correction has been published, is nowhere
to be found. In both cases, the record has been set straight, but
not at the spot where it went awry — nor with acknowledgment
that The Times was party to the divergence in the first place.

There are ways to correct this. Online and in archives, connect the second version of a story to the first. In print, take care
to insert the words "as reported in The Times yesterday" when
the cross-reference is germane. When appropriate, the insertion
of "mistakenly" or "erroneously" between "as" and "reported"
wouldn't be such a bad thing either. The paper that acknowledges its mistakes is going to retain the trust of readers longer
than the one that tries to pretend they never happened.

Now I'm going to pick on the worst habits of certain anti-
Times critics lurking on the Web. Last Sunday, an item
appeared on FreeRepublic.com under the headline "FReeper
Call to Action! Help make N.Y. Times correct the phony setup
outrage story of Bush ads." Posted by "Doug from Upland," it

exhorted readers of the self-described "Premier Conservative News Forum" to call Washington correspondent Richard W. Stevenson and demand that he "correct the record." Stevenson's apparent offense was a March 5 story he and Jim Rutenberg had written about negative reactions to Republican ads invoking the events of 9/11. Stevenson's telephone number was reproduced in the posting in large black letters.

Soon Stevenson's phone was ringing like an alarm clock, his voice mail filling up, he told me via e-mail, with "messages that impugned my professionalism and patriotism." Only one person, he said, bothered to leave a name and a phone number.

Had they all done so, Stevenson might have called them back and told them neither he nor Rutenberg had written what Doug from Upland had attributed to them. An Australian newspaper had run a story that included details from several different news services but left the Times writers' bylines in place. The material that provoked the posting and the calls had never appeared in The Times; informed that this was the case, Doug replaced his earlier exhortation with an apology to Stevenson.

I've been through several escapades like this one, launched from various ideological precincts scattered around the Web. They all conclude with the same lesson: It's all right to knock The Times. It's even your privilege to hate it. But it's always useful to read it first.

. . .

Education editor Suzanne Daley took strong exception to the section of this column about the Trinity-Dalton non-story, feeling particularly that her quotation, "Because we're a newspaper," was unfairly yanked out of the context of our lengthy conversation. I asked her to write, and I later published, a letter explaining her point of view (posting number 29 in my Web journal [@]). Jane Gross had a different objection, which I addressed at the end of my next column.

A couple of people at the paper asked why I mentioned Daley's deputy, Jack Kadden, by name. Over the months I went out of my way to interview, and to quote, many editors, and to mention their names in contexts both positive and negative. This was because, in the reader's mind, the writer—the byline—is the only known party, and therefore the responsible one. In fact, writers provide the crops, and even cook the meal, but editors put it on the table. The Times's Corrections column recognizes this: when a correction says "Due to an editing error," you can know it wasn't the writer's mistake. When it says nothing about an error's pedigree, blame it on the writer.

Shortly after this column appeared, Al Siegal announced a policy change: the initial version of a story eventually rowed back would be flagged in the electronic database with the notice, "clarifying article appended." Thus, readers of the original Jane Gross piece would be alerted to the later Tamar Lewin piece, and thereby get the whole story. It was a nice and noble idea, but really hasn't worked all that well. Not every follow-up story is a corrective; not every corrective addresses faulty reporting; and parsing every piece to see if it qualifies as a rowback would be a fulltime job. The good news is that electronic databases don't hide stories that you might not discover in a microfilm search: if you type "Trinity," "Dalton" and "anti-Semitic" into the search box at nytimes.com, you'll get Gross, you'll get Lewin—and you'll get Okrent, too.

The Privileges of Opinion, the Obligations of Fact

. . .

March 28, 2004

IT sounds like a simple question: Should opinion columnists be subject to the same corrections policy that governs the work of every other writer at The Times? So simple, in fact, that you must know that only an ornate answer could follow.

For the news pages, the rule is succinct. "Because its voice is loud and far-reaching," the paper's stylebook says, "The Times recognizes an ethical responsibility to correct all its factual errors, large and small (even misspellings of names), promptly and in a prominent reserved space in the paper." But on the page where The Times's seven Op-Ed columnists roam, there has long been no rule at all, or at least not one clearly elucidated and publicly promulgated. When I began in this job last fall, I was told The Times considered the space granted Op-Ed columnists theirs to use as they wish, subject only to the limits of legality, decency and publisher Arthur O. Sulzberger Jr.'s patience. Columnists decided when to run corrections, and where in their columns to run them.

But several days ago, editorial page editor Gail Collins handed me a memo in response to my inquiries. (You can read it in its entirety at www.nytimes.com/danielokrent; look for posting

No. 22.[@]) Less a formal statute than an explanation and justification of practice, the document lays out the position of both Collins and her boss, Sulzberger, who bears ultimate responsibility for hiring and firing columnists. Collins explains why columnists must be allowed the freedom of their opinions, but insists that they "are obviously required to be factually accurate. If one of them makes an error, he or she is expected to promptly correct it in the column." Corrections, under this new rule, are to be placed at the end of a subsequent column, "to maximize the chance that they will be seen by all their readers, everywhere," a reference to the wide syndication many of the columnists enjoy.

But who is to say what is factually accurate? Or whether a quotation is misrepresented? Or whether facts are used or misused in such a fashion as to render a columnist's opinion unfair? Or even whether fairness has anything to do with opinion in the first place? Can you imagine one of the Sunday morning television screamfests instituting a corrections policy?

In the consciously cynical words of a retired Times editor, speaking for all the hard-news types who find most commentary to be frippery, "How can you expect fairness from columnists when they make up all that stuff anyway?"

Of course they don't make the stuff up (at least the good ones don't). But many do use their material in ways that veer sharply from conventional journalistic practice. The opinion writer chooses which facts to present, and which to withhold. He can paint individuals he likes as paragons, and those he disdains as scoundrels. The more scurrilous practitioners rely on indirection and innuendo, nestling together in a bed of lush sophistry. I sometimes think opinion columns ought to carry a warning:

"The following is solely the opinion of the author, supported by data I alone have chosen to include. Live with it." Opinion is inherently unfair.

Columnists also attract a crowd radically unlike the audience that sticks to the news pages. Judging by my mail, the more partisan of The Times's columnists draw two distinct sets of fanatical loyalists: those who wish to have their own views reinforced, and those who enjoy the hot thrill of a blood-pressure spike. Paul Krugman, writes Nadia Koutzen of Toms River, N.J., "makes more sense (along with Bob Herbert) than anyone. He states irrefutable facts." Paul Krugman, writes Donald Luskin of Palo Alto, Calif., has committed "dozens of substantive factual errors, distortions, misquotations and false quotations—all pronounced in a voice of authoritativeness that most columnists would not presume to permit themselves."

For a wider audience, Luskin serves as Javert to Krugman's Jean Valjean. From a perch on National Review Online, he regularly assaults Krugman's logic, his politics, his economic theories, his character and his accuracy. (If you want to see what kind of a rumble can evolve from a columnist's use of a quotation, go to posting No. 23 of my Web journal to find a series of links relating to a recent charge against Krugman: can you figure out who's right?) Similarly, David Corn of The Nation has taken aim at William Safire, charging in one recent piece that "under the cover of opinion journalism," Safire is "dishing out disinformation." And Maureen Dowd is followed faithfully around the Web by an avenging army of passionate detractors who would probably be devastated if she ever stopped writing.

Anyone who calls the Internet's bustling trade in columnist-attack a cottage industry might more accurately liken it to the arms bazaar in Peshawar. Peace and calm were not enhanced a few weeks ago when Times lawyers took a legal sledgehammer to an imaginary Op-Ed Corrections column published by Robert Cox of the Web site The National Debate—but peace and calm rarely accompany arguments about political opinion in a polarized age.

This sort of contentiousness makes a clear, publicly stated corrections policy necessary, and finding a bright line in such murky precincts isn't easy. At the very minimum, anything that is indisputably inaccurate must be corrected: there is no protected opinion that holds that the sun rises in the west. Same with the patent misuse or distortion of quotations that are already in the public record. But if Safire asserts that there is a "smoking gun" linking Al Qaeda to Saddam Hussein, then even David Corn's best shots (which include many citations from Times news stories) aren't going to prove it isn't so. "An opinion may be wrong-headed," Safire told me by e-mail last week, "but it is never wrong. A belief or a conviction, no matter how illogical, crack-brained or infuriating, is an idea subject to vigorous dispute but is not an assertion subject to editorial or legal correction."

Safire good-humoredly (I think) asked me to whom he could complain if I quoted him out of context. I had a ready answer: "No one—I'm a columnist."

I generally don't like to engage in comparative newspapering, but I thought it was worth knowing what other papers do with (or to) their columnists. At The Boston Globe (owned by The New York Times Company), editorial page editor Renee Loth's practice is almost identical to the one now in place here; so is the policy of Paul Gigot, who presides over the opinion pages at The Wall Street Journal (definitely not owned by The Times).

The Los Angeles Times actually allows its readers' representative to participate in decisions on columnist corrections. (No thanks, I'd rather not.) At The Washington Post, if a columnist doesn't want to write a correction recommended by editorial page editor Fred Hiatt, Hiatt will put one on the op-ed page himself. At every one of these papers, the final arbiter is the editorial page editor.

Daniel Patrick Moynihan, who would have made an excellent editorial page editor if he could have put up with the meetings, once said that "everyone is entitled to his own opinion, but not his own facts." Gail Collins's determination that corrections will appear on their own at the end of a succeeding column, and not disappear into an unrelated digression, is on its own a significant piece of progress. But it's her assertion of responsibility that matters most. Critics might say her statement of policy is very gently phrased, but when I asked her if there was wiggle room, she was unequivocal: "It is my obligation to make sure no misstatements of fact on the editorial pages go uncorrected."

In the coming months I expect columnist corrections to become a little more frequent and a lot more forthright than they've been in the past. Yet the final measure of Collins's success, and of the individual columnists, will be not in the corrections but in the absence of the need for them. Wayne Wren of Houston, a self-described conservative and "avid reader" of National Review Online, expressed it with great equanimity in a recent e-mail message to my office: "If Mr. Krugman is making egregious errors in his Op-Ed column, they will catch up with him." Same goes for Brooks, Dowd, Friedman, Herbert, Kristof and Safire—and, most important, for The New York Times.

. . .

My March 14 column may have left some readers wondering why reporter Jane Gross didn't write the corrective follow-up to her story about an allegedly anti-Semitic incident at a private-school basketball game, an article that I criticized. Her editors say the task—the "rowback"—was assigned to another writer only because Gross had left for a long-planned vacation.

. . .

The origins of this column were rooted in an event that took place before I arrived at The Times, when Maureen Dowd quoted an excerpt from a George W. Bush speech but left out a sentence in the middle of it that affected its meaning. Dowd repeated the quotation in a subsequent column, this time with the missing sentence restored—but she failed to explain what had happened the first time.

The day I started in the public editor job, the Dowdophobes were waiting for me with hanging nooses in hand. Because Dowd's offense was committed before my time, I didn't pursue it. But the issue—essentially, the extent of a columnist's freedom to stack the deck to make a point—was inescapably an important one. After my piece ran, a retired masthead editor (the same one who had joked that columnists "make up all that stuff anyway") reported his astonishment that Collins had finally initiated a formal policy where none had existed before.

As it turned out, like the rowback clarification policy, it didn't really work. The majority of factual errors alleged by the columnists' various detractors were, in fact, interpretive disagreements, not matters of provable truth. Who was to say that Saddam's representatives didn't meet with al-Qaeda? Even if every known government commission looking into it failed to find evidence of such a meeting, no one could prove that it had not happened.

And when you're preparing to correct a columnist, proof is the only thing that matters. By any reasonable standard, a news story making the same assertion would be incomplete without at least mentioning the contrary view of others. But if you're going to have columnists, you're going to have to let them take outrageous positions.

Still, Moynihan's Rule should prevail, and what I (a veteran of the commentary-filled world of magazine publishing) was unable to accomplish, my successor (a hard-news guy who, for many years, had been the Al Siegal of The Wall Street Journal) achieved within weeks of assuming the public editor's post. Barney Calame persuaded Gail Collins that corrections should not be interred within the body of a columnist's piece, but should have their own, regular space on the opinion pages, where they are clearly the responsibility of the editors. I'll take credit for an assist on this one, but Barney put the puck in the goal.

The thing that most upset me while I was reporting the columnist piece? Discovering that the admirable Web site factcheck.org, sponsored by the Annenberg Public Policy Center at the University of Pennsylvania, uses the Moynihan quote as a motto—but renders it as "Everyone is entitled to *their* own opinion, but not *their* own facts." (My italics.) This could use some fact-checking. Brooks Jackson of the Annenberg Center assures me that this version of the quotation comes from the cover of the program for Moynihan's memorial service. Still, I think it's highly unlikely that Moynihan would ever have used the gender-neutral but grammatically egregious "their" in place of "his."

And if he in fact did? Well, I don't have to believe it if I don't want to.

The Juror, the Paper and a Dubious Need to Know

. . .

April 11, 2004

YOU know something strange has happened in journalism when, in a front-page article in The Times, a 79-year-old woman feels compelled to tell the world that every Christmas she tips the doormen in her apartment building. It's especially strange when the article's writer notes that this generosity runs "contrary to previous reports"—reports that first appeared in The Times itself.

No, I'm not going to start another rant about rowback, the technique that enables a newspaper to correct itself without ever acknowledging it might have erred. But The Times's wall-to-wall (and partly rowed back) coverage of the implosion of the Tyco trial provides an opportunity to see the newspaper doing the right thing, then doing the wrong thing, and finally provoking (for me, anyway) a reconsideration of a quarter-century of journalistic practice.

The adventure began on Friday, March 26, after Juror No. 4 in this long, arduous and finally wasted trial either did or did not flash an "O.K." sign toward the defense table. (Times reporters who witnessed it believed she did.) As reporters and editors worked on the story that afternoon and evening, disagreement broke out over whether to name the juror. One faction held that she had inserted herself into the news with her own behavior; the other, including reporter Jonathan D. Glater (a former lawyer), felt, as he said later, that "the news was the sign — not who she was."

Until the proceedings were over, Glater and others argued, her name should not be published. Business editor Lawrence Ingrassia, who was personally directing the trial coverage, conferred with managing editor Jill Abramson, and the juror's name was withheld. Readers of the next day's paper learned only some neutral details about the anonymous protagonist: she was a former schoolteacher who had graduated from law school in her late '50s and practiced briefly in a large firm. The best arguments of the two major New York–based dailies that published the juror's name have not remotely convinced me that their action provided the slightest benefit to a single reader, anywhere on the planet.

Except, perhaps, a concierge with an ungreased palm. This man entered the permanent archive of The New York Times on Monday, March 29, in a few shocking sentences at the end of an article headlined "Criminal Intent Seems the Focus of Juror's Doubt." The juror, readers learned, "lives on the Upper East Side of Manhattan, and on Friday people at her apartment building described her as standoffish. A concierge said she rarely spoke to the staff members except to give orders and, unlike other tenants, had never given a Christmas bonus to him or, as far as he knew, to the doormen." Another sentence read, "A former family friend said that Juror No. 4 was very intelligent but that once she made up her mind, she would not relinquish her opinion."

Now the reader had really learned something — several things, in fact. First, that this woman, whose name had just been published in two very large newspapers, was remote, cheap and stubborn. (Ingrassia does say that he regrets having published the Christmas bonus comment.) Second, that The Times is willing to publish negative comments, made by unidentified individuals, about someone who does not have the opportunity to reply. And third, that the paper conveniently knows how to retain its piety. Yes, The Times didn't disclose the juror's identity until the trial was concluded, but once it was revealed elsewhere, her name hung over the paper's reporting like the Cheshire Cat's smile. The Times doesn't live in a vacuum, but in this instance it pretended it did.

Wrote reader J. Allison Crockett of Brooklyn, "I now envision millions of New Yorkers rushing down to their lobbies to over-tip the building staff so that in the future, should they be jurors, The Times won't be able to slander their character."

The strange conclusion of this ill-starred trial eventually led me to a place distant from the conventional wisdom of the news business. Where I now differ from nearly all the reporters and editors with whom I've discussed the subject (including Glater) is in my newfound belief that even after a trial has ended, an individual juror's role in deliberations—arguments presented, behavior exhibited, votes taken—should remain private if the juror wishes to keep it private.

Most of those I spoke with were astonished to learn I was taking this position, so contrary is it to widely accepted practice. (Remember: nothing excites reporters more than a closed door.) Several were also surprised to learn that reporting on jury deliberations is in fact a fairly new phenomenon, and hardly one of the foundations of robust journalism. In 1978, a federal appellate court confirmed the right of reporters to interview jurors after a trial's conclusion. But it wasn't until 1982, when Steven Brill of The American Lawyer interviewed and wrote about the jurors in a major libel case, that this style of reporting began to approach common practice. It was in time rendered conventional by the trials of William Kennedy Smith, Leona Helmsley and O.J. Simpson, among others—people whose visibility was high enough, and their alleged crimes juicy enough, to give every juror coming out of such a trial a personal posse of reporters.

After the mistrial of investment banker Frank P. Quattrone last year, The Times published the names of the three jurors who had held out for acquittal. Two spoke willingly to reporters; one apparently did not, yet still her name was published. After the Tyco case, The Times named all the jurors, but allowed one to comment anonymously on Juror No. 4's behavior during the deliberations.

Nothing was gained in either instance, but consider the potential price: in press-worthy cases, will some jurors refrain from articulating their arguments for fear of public censure or harassment? Will they abandon sincerely held positions lest they become publicly known for, say, thwarting the conviction of a notorious defendant? To protect their privacy, will some try to avoid serving on juries altogether? We may soon find out: Quattrone's retrial begins Tuesday.

The arguments for disclosure are well established: Public actors in public life must be held accountable—which is why, for instance, newspapers try to report on cabinet meetings or closed-door legislative hearings. Only aggressive journalism can disclose potential misdeeds that occur in the jury room. From the beginnings of the Republic, jury verdicts achieved credibility because one's neighbors knew who had made the decision. Naming names makes reporting feel real.

Each of those arguments may be familiar, but none is persuasive: Jurors, unlike politicians, bureaucrats and even journalists, are involuntary participants in public life. Bad behavior in a jury room is subject to review if a single juror takes a complaint to the judge. The early Republic did not have to endure cable news, supermarket tabloids or interview wranglers from the morning talk shows. You can make reporting feel really real by describing someone's personal hygiene, but that's not conventionally part of the reportorial repertoire.

Jonathan Glater's comment about Juror No. 4 stays with me — the news was the sign she made (or didn't make), not who she was. Her actions were germane, her identity irrelevant. So it is, I believe, with jury deliberations. After a trial, newspapers can report the name of an individual juror, and report his or her actions, but it isn't fair to connect the two without the juror's permission. If you think about it, it's also close to pointless.

Another peculiar aspect of The Times's coverage of the Tyco jury was brought to my attention by reader Carl Cohen of Ann Arbor, Mich. After the mistrial was declared, the paper published a chart identifying each juror by name, occupation and race. "What difference does it make if one is a black food-chain manager or a white food-chain manager?" Cohen wrote, while noting that race was not even the slightest of factors in the trial. "A black former employee of Lehman Brothers or a white former employee of Lehman Brothers? Identifying by employment is sensible and helpful. Identifying by race is, I submit, inappropriate and uncalled for."

No argument here.

. . .

I'm proud of this one. I have no objection to reporters interviewing jurors, and in fact would be disappointed if a reporter working for me and covering an important trial failed to do so (after the trial's conclusion, of course). What goes over the line is publishing the name of a juror, and that juror's views, *without the juror's permission.* If this is considered fair matter for public discourse, then we might as well have juries conduct their deliberations live on cable TV.

Marcia Chambers, a former Times correspondent now affiliated with Yale Law School, objected to my assertion that interviewing jurors became common practice in 1982; in a letter published May 2, 2004, she said it was common practice when she arrived at The Times in 1973.

Paper of Record? No Way, No Reason, No Thanks

. . .

April 25, 2004

MY cellmate Arthur Bovino, who has at his fingertips data that could make a statistician weep, calculates that in the five months since the office of the public editor opened for business, we've received 589 messages that contain the phrase "paper of record."

Many readers summon up "All the News That's Fit to Print" (196 invocations to date) and "Gray Lady of 43rd Street" (80). But I've never been able to figure out whether "All the News" is a comment on the news itself or on the paper that contains it, and "Gray Lady," while geographically accurate, is both inapt and a cliché. "Paper of record" is easier to grasp: a compliment used as a cudgel. "If this is what passes as reporting in our national paper of record," wrote Jeff Kreines of Coosada, Ala., "no wonder this country is in the mess it's in." John E. O'Beirne of Yorktown Heights, N.Y., wrote to express his preference for one of The Times's competitors, which gets "much closer to the truth than the self-proclaimed 'paper of record.'"

Judging by both the progress of modern journalism (yes, there's been some, at least in the realm of self-knowledge) and an unscientific survey I recently conducted, I don't think too many people would want to work for a paper of record, which The Times once sort of was. Even fewer, I believe, would want to read it, as a few idle hours last week trying to keep awake over a Saturday Times of 40 years ago showed me.

For a dime, here's what a reader could have learned from The Times of April 25, 1964: The assistant commissioner of the Reclamation Bureau resigned to join the staff of Senator Carl Hayden. At the United Nations, the Special Committee on Colonialism heard a statement from "a Malta petitioner." The president of Algeria flew to Moscow, around the same time that the president of West Germany began a good-will tour of South America when "his Lufthansa jet airliner touched down at Lima's new international airport after a nonstop flight from Miami, where he spent the night." (A separate item attributed to United Press International read—in its entirety—"President Johnson's plane landed at Washington National Airport at 10:30 tonight.")

Congress watchers were provided a daily schedule of House and Senate hearings. A top-of-the-page headline revealed that five houses in Center Island and Mill Neck would be included in a tour sponsored by the Smith College Club of Long Island. The Women's Press Club was scheduled to meet that afternoon at the Statler Hilton. My personal favorite: Houston baseball officials gave pitcher Ken Johnson a $1,000 raise.

And that's just scratching a surface that stretched across a numbing collection of announcements, schedules, directories and transcripts: the appointment of two vice presidents at an auto parts company; the daily docket of bankruptcy proceedings in local courts; a listing (title, author, publisher, price) of every book published that day; obituaries of 24 luminaries of very faint wattage; a roster of the 35 ships that had sailed from the Port of New York since Thursday night, another of the 35 that had arrived.

Sure, there was a lot of wonderful work in The Times back then—on that same April 25, stories on more stimulating subjects bore the bylines of three young reporters named David Halberstam, J. Anthony Lukas and Gay Talese. But in many respects the paper-of-record Times had as much stenography as reporting, as much virtual reprinting of handouts (in the form of verbatim transcripts of unexceptional speeches) as provocative journalism. The leftist British journalist Robert Fisk said last fall that The Times should rename itself "American Officials Say." Forty years ago, that wouldn't have been so tendentious.

"Newspaper of record" did not originate with the editors. According to Times archivist Lora Korbut, the phrase first appeared in 1927, when the paper sponsored an essay contest to promote its annual index. Entrants were asked to elaborate on the contest's title, "The Value of The New York Times Index and Files as a Newspaper of Record." (This probably did not attract as many contestants as "The Apprentice.") Somehow what began as a promotion for an index service soon adhered to the skin of the paper itself, perhaps because the meticulous presentation of the acts of officialdom was long one of the ways The Times distinguished itself in an eight-newspaper town.

"Long ago," according to Bill Borders, a senior editor who's been with the paper for 43 years, "The Times used to feel an obligation to print lots of things that we knew no one much would read—the new members of the Peruvian cabinet, for example—just to get them on the record. Fortunately those days are over."

Judging by the responses I got from the 50 Times newsroom staff members to whom I put the question "Do you think The Times is the newspaper of record?" Borders is not alone in his gratitude. Several acknowledged the inspiration suggested by the loftiness of the phrase, but only a couple endorsed its literal meaning. With very few exceptions, the longer you've been here, or the higher you've risen in the organization, the less likely you are to believe The Times is, or should be, the paper of record. Metro columnist Clyde Haberman told me that in his 27 years at The Times, "I have never heard anyone inside the paper refer to it that way"; reporter Richard Pérez-Peña, an 11-year veteran, said, "I don't think I've ever heard my colleagues here use the phrase except rarely, in an ironic, almost self-mocking tone."

I think that's because they recognize both the impossibility of fulfilling the role and the deadening effect it could have on the paper. Katherine Bouton, deputy editor of the paper's Sunday magazine, said: "We understand now that all reporting is selective. With the exception of raw original source material, there really isn't anything 'of record,' is there?" Reporter Stephanie Strom noted that "we certainly aren't the paper of record for leaders of the African-American and Hispanic communities." Or, one could add, the Orthodox Jewish community or the Staten Island community or the lacrosse community or fill in the blank.

Here's another way of stating it: In a heterogeneous world, whose record is one newspaper even in the position to preserve? And what group of individuals, no matter how talented or dedicated, would dare arrogate to itself so godlike a role? If you rely on The Times as your only source of news, you are buying into the conceptions, attitudes and interests of the people who put it out every day. It cannot be definitive, and asking it to be is a disservice to both the staff and the readers. I mean no disrespect to The Times, but what discriminating citizen can really afford to rely on only one source of news? And can't all discriminating readers contextualize what their newspapers (or television stations or radio hosts or Web logs) tell them?

Another phrase often used to imbue daily journalism with a holy glow when in fact it's something of a put-down — "the first draft of history" — is far more appropriate. A first draft is definitionally imperfect, sometimes embarrassing and almost always needful of improvement. The crucial second draft consists of a paper's correction of errors, acknowledgment of omissions and, when the stakes are high enough, explanation of missteps. Even so, future generations will be unfortunate if their historians think there's only one source to turn to when trying to understand the past.

No one I queried nailed a plausible ambition for The Times more accurately than managing editor John Geddes: "I don't think there can be a 'paper of record.' The term implies an omniscient chronicler of events, an arbiter that perfectly captures the significance and import of a day in our lives. I don't work at that place. I work at a newspaper that exists in a world where there are constraints of time, resources and knowledge.

The wonder of the paper is that knowing the everyday limits to our ambitions doesn't prevent us from trying to exceed them."

It's the shape of the aspiration and the extent that it's achieved for which The Times should be held responsible. Readers who expect more will deserve what they get. Ask for the paper of record, and you will end up holding a catalog, a soporific or an apologist. Probably all three, in fact.

·　·　·

I sort of blew this one. I still think that the original meaning of POR is outmoded, and none of us would want to read a paper like the old, who's-the-new-Peruvian-finance-minister version of The Times. But what "paper of record" has come to mean, to many people, is "the paper that got all the facts, and reported them accurately."

As I write, I'm working on a book about the U.S. in the 1920s, consulting microfilm versions of several American newspapers, and finding I'm much more willing to believe something to be factually accurate if it appeared in The Times. If that's what makes something a "paper of record," I'm all for it.

There's No Business Like Tony Awards Business

·　·　·

May 9, 2004

UNLESS I acquire some unexpected clout around here in the next 48 hours, Times readers will wake up on Tuesday morning to read a prominent story announcing the nominees for an artis-

tically meaningless, blatantly commercial, shamefully exclu-
sionary and culturally corrosive award competition.

Let me put it another way: unless Times editors have over-
come several decades of their own inertia, readers on Tuesday
will find a prominent story serving the pecuniary interests of
three privately controlled companies whose principals have
earned the right to convene in what Damon Runyon once
called "the laughing room." That was Runyon's term for the
sound-proofed chamber where he imagined that the proprietors
of the "21" Club gathered to set the day's menu prices. Today's
version would be the sanctum where the men who run the
Shubert Organization, the Nederlander Organization and
Jujamcyn Theaters gather to toast The Times and its generous
support of their efforts.

Those are the three institutions that control Broadway and
in turn, along with the sponsors of touring productions of
Broadway shows, control the Tony Awards. The Oscars (or
Grammys or Pulitzers) of theater the Tonys are not. It may be
hard to defend the coverage of something as politicized, com-
mercialized and overhyped as the Oscars, but at least the
Academy of Motion Picture Arts and Sciences doesn't limit
entrants to films shown only in movie houses of a certain size
located in a single neighborhood.

The lengthy definition of eligibility in the Tony rules can be
summed up simply: a show qualifies if it's presented in a theater
with more than 500 seats, situated north of 40th Street, south of
66th Street, west of Sixth Avenue and east of 10th. Leave out the
Vivian Beaumont Theater at Lincoln Center and you could
change the northern boundary to 54th Street and the western
one to about a hundred feet past Ninth Avenue.

An even simpler definition: the awards are a real estate

promotion, restricted as they are to shows put on in the 31 houses owned or controlled by the Shuberts, the Nederlanders and Jujamcyn, plus another nine thrown in by accident of geography or affinity to the idea of the Big Musical (Clear Channel Entertainment, the dominant producer of national theatrical tours, owns the Ford Center; Disney owns the New Amsterdam).

Like the theaters, the voters themselves are to a large degree controlled by the Big Three and the touring company operators. Rocco Landesman, president of Jujamcyn, told me that nearly half the voters are connected to the tour producers. Because the only musical this year that looks as if it will work on tour is "Wicked," if it loses the Tony I'll eat my black satin jacket from the road company of "Jekyll and Hyde."

If you ask people what awards recognize achievement in live theater, few will cite any but the Tonys. But if a play or musical doesn't appear in one of the Tony theaters, it just doesn't count. Nothing from the various Off or Off Off Broadway houses, even though they launched all but one winner of the Pulitzer Prize for drama in the last decade (the exception originated in a nonprofit theater in Florida); nothing from the Brooklyn Academy of Music, which in most years presents the most challenging theater in New York. You could put Anton Chekhov together with George Gershwin to collaborate on a musical directed by George Abbott, but if the curtain rises in a theater on 37th Street, tough luck.

Unless the theater happened to be owned by Shubert, Nederlander or Jujamcyn. Given their near stranglehold on the Broadway business, they've got the throw weight to change the boundaries.

. . .

So how does a newspaper that prides itself on the independence of its editorial decision-making and its commitment to fit-to-print news treat this scam?

With trumpets. Tuesday's kickoff story will launch a parade of mentions — in the Weekend section, probably in the Boldface Names column, possibly in the daily Arts Briefing. If this year is like the last several, this will culminate in a panting orgy of Tony worship presented in a special takeout produced by the editors of the Arts & Leisure section, probably on the Sunday before the winners are announced. Last year, such a section devoted 18 separate articles, encompassing more than 20,000 words and acres of photographs, to all things Tony.

When I asked culture editor Steven Erlanger what justified this much noise, he told me the Tonys are newsworthy because Broadway itself is important to The Times and its readers. "It's part of our obligation," he said. "It doesn't mean we shouldn't be more skeptical about them, but the Tonys matter." The Times has published critical pieces about the extremely dubious Golden Globe film awards, he pointed out, but still the paper covers them.

Fair enough. But the Globes get an article or two each year, not the triumphal procession of Tonyness that marches through the pages of The Times. This may be good for the Times Company's operating statement (the ads surrounding all those articles are extremely succulent), but it's rotten for those readers of The Times who care about American theater. Tony worship means that excellent (but comparatively low-budget) works produced in small venues often don't get the attention they deserve. Off Broadway producers who think a show has a shot at a Tony and all the resulting publicity force small-scale works into inappropriately large houses (we'll soon see if the chamber musical "Caroline, or Change" can survive its recent transfer to Broadway). Nonprofit theatrical organizations that ostensibly exist to do innovative work instead chase the Tonys by acquiring eligible theaters, where vastly increased costs can only thwart innovation.

The Times has an interest in Broadway theater if only by proximity; 29 of the eligible houses are within five blocks of the chair I'm sitting in (put in a stage and the newsroom itself would qualify—not bad drama, either). The paper's financial interest is unquestioned: although I can't get a figure directly from The Times, Nancy Coyne of Serino Coyne, the largest of the city's theatrical advertising agencies, estimates that the industry spends $30 million to $40 million a year on ad space in the paper. You can bet that most of that doesn't come from the 199-seat theaters downtown.

But I doubt there's an editor or reporter in the Times Building who thinks advertising considerations should dictate news coverage. Nor do I think I could find one who would argue, say, that if the Oscars were for all practical purposes restricted to films produced by the three largest studios, they would still merit serious attention. Erlanger says that although special sections like those devoted to the Tonys exist partly because of advertising considerations, it's his job and his colleagues' to make sure the accompanying editorial content is up to Times standards. He thinks they do a good job of it. Perhaps so, but hanging this much theater coverage on the Tonys while many provocative Off and Off Off Broadway plays are pushed to the back of the bus is an insult to The Times's own ambitions.

As you may have guessed by now, I'm one of those Times readers who cares about live theater. Like many, many others, I count on The Times not just for world, national and local news, but for its attention to my special interests. It's one of the things that distinguish the paper; The Times has no one specialty, but at its best aspires to excellence in a collection of specialties. In some, it dominates. Everybody in the theater industry will tell you that in their business, The Times is the only voice that matters.

At the moment, The Times is on the brink of a long-planned, apparently expensive and unquestionably overdue renovation of its cultural report, scheduled to premiere in the fall. If its architects really aspire to excellent theater coverage, they will commit a retrogressive act: the appointment of a Sunday theater critic to enrich the discussion (an appointment, I should point out, endorsed by chief theater critic Ben Brantley). For decades, until 1996, the paper's daily critic wrote the review that appeared the morning after a show's opening night, and then a regular Sunday critic could address the same show in the next issue of Arts & Leisure. This provided a version of the stereophonic attention accorded important books by the daily reviewers and the Sunday Book Review—a balancing of perspective that can only be useful to readers.

Because in matters theatrical The Times speaks so loudly, amplifying that voice with the appointment of a Sunday critic would merit a standing ovation. In the meantime, squandering its voice—and its reputation for integrity—on a racket like the Tony Awards deserves nothing but boos.

.   .   .

Well, the "Jekyll and Hyde" jacket, accompanied by a side order of crow, wasn't very tasty. (There's more about my wrong call on "Wicked" below, in point number 5.) This piece wasn't nearly as important as many others, but I don't think writing any other gave me quite as much pleasure as this one did. Partly, that's because it came from my own gut; I had long bristled at The Times's insupportable devotion to the Tonys, and having a platform to state my case was something I didn't want to pass up. But there were plenty of other gratifying reasons, too:

1. The response was enormous. I heard from hundreds of people in New York's theater community, and just as many in New York's theater audience, who felt someone had said what they had long believed, but thought they could do nothing about. (This helped me get over any doubts I had about the propriety of taking on an issue that no reader had raised.)

2. It brought about some change: the piece that ran on Tuesday morning included a paragraph carefully explaining the limited scope of the Tonys, and their connection to the theater owners. Subsequent pieces that month and through the 2005 season did so, too; I'd like to think that it's become an institutionalized part of Tony coverage.

3. Bill Keller sent me an e-mail message: ". . . But what do you REALLY think? Seriously, it was a beating we deserved, and told me some things I didn't know. . . . I do think you'll see some changes." It's not that I lived to get approving messages from Bill Keller, but I'll confess that it went down very well with my morning coffee.

4. Those who disagreed with me did so very colorfully (see, in particular, theater owner Rocco Landesman's riposte, published May 23 and reprinted just below these notes). I was smacked around in Variety, insulted by one of the principals of the Shubert chain (he told a mutual friend that I knew nothing—*nothing*—about theater), and made

the butt of some pretty good jokes when "Wicked" lost
to the puppet musical, "Avenue Q."

5. In fact, at a goodbye dinner when I left The Times
    slightly more than a year later, Gail Collins thanked me
    for two things: helping to bring about a corrections poli-
    cy for Op-Ed columnists—and winning the Tony for
    "Avenue Q." I don't know whether my column truly
    shamed voters into bypassing "Wicked," but when the
    producers of "Avenue Q" decided to forgo a national
    tour and mount a permanent version of their show in
    Las Vegas, one out-of-town Tony voter told Michael
    Riedel of The New York Post, "If I had known they
    weren't going to tour it, I wouldn't have voted for it."

And Now for a Brief Intermission . . .

.   .   .

May 23, 2004

MY regular column isn't appearing today because I'm engaged
in a complex special project that I need another week to complete. So let me ask your forbearance.

In the meantime, I think it's worth relating the reaction to
my May 9 column on the Tony Awards. The response was surprisingly intense, and understandably divided.

Most people whose paychecks come from Broadway loathed
it. Most of the Off and Off Off Broadway world, as well as many
theatergoers and theater critics, loved it. Plenty of people without connections in either bloc not only didn't care about the

subject, but chastised me (that's a gentle way of putting it) for concerning myself with such trivia when the world is on fire.

This last group will not be interested in what follows. But for those who are, I'm turning the stage over to the president of Jujamcyn Theaters, one of the three major Broadway theater-owning groups:

To the Public Editor:
Your May 9 polemic, "There's No Business Like Tony Business," is priggish and overwrought. Please remember that the Tonys are more than our community's "recognition of excellence" in the theater; they are also an entertainment and a great game.

Once a year, producers compete publicly with each other, normally serious artists become humanized by their vanity and start behaving like the rest of us, and The New York Times reaps an advertising windfall. Theatergoers follow the nomination and awards proceedings as avidly as football fans follow the playoffs and the Super Bowl.

The Tonys celebrate Broadway, which has a roughly Midtown geography but more than anything connotes a certain scale. "Broadway" means that the orchestra will be a certain size, the production values at a certain level and the acting talent, occasionally including some well-known stars, noteworthy. And there has to be enough seating capacity to pay for it all. The Tony-eligible minimum is 500 seats.

As to your point that The Times looks at the Tonys uncritically, what can I say? You're the public editor, you read this newspaper. Nearly every year we complain bitterly that smack in the middle of the Tonys issue is an article by the chief theater critic about what a miserable season it's been on Broadway.

But enough about the Tonys. Did I mention that your argument for a Sunday theater critic was lucid, rational, logical and totally convincing?

ROCCO LANDESMAN
May 17, 2004

And another thing: In my Tony column, I wrote that the New Amsterdam Theater was owned by the Walt Disney Company. In fact, it is owned by the city and the state of New York; Disney holds a 99-year lease.

See you next week.

. . .

In my remaining year in the job, I never again wrote about a subject that had not been raised by readers; I'd had my fun. Next time out, in fact, I addressed the one subject that had caused more complaints, more outrage and more disappointment than any other.

Weapons of Mass Destruction? Or Mass Distraction?

. . .

May 30, 2004

FROM the moment this office opened for business last December, I felt I could not write about what had been published in the paper before my arrival. Once I stepped into the past, I reasoned, I might never be able to find my way back to the present.

Early this month, though, convinced that my territory includes what doesn't appear in the paper as well as what does, I began to look into a question arising from the past that weighs heavily on the present: Why had The Times failed to revisit its own coverage of Iraqi weapons of mass destruction? To anyone who read the paper between September 2002 and June 2003, the impression that Saddam Hussein possessed, or was acquiring, a frightening arsenal of W.M.D. seemed unmistakable. Except, of course, it appears to have been mistaken. On Tuesday, May 18, I told executive editor Bill Keller I would be writing today about The Times's responsibility to address the subject. He told me that an internal examination was already under way; we then proceeded independently and did not discuss it further. The results of The Times's own examination appeared in last Wednesday's paper, and can be found online at [@].

I think they got it right. Mostly. (I do question the placement: as one reader asked, "Will your column this Sunday address why the NYT buried its editors' note—full of apologies for burying stories on A10—on A10?")

Some of The Times's coverage in the months leading up to the invasion of Iraq was credulous; much of it was inappropriately italicized by lavish front-page display and heavy-breathing headlines; and several fine articles by David Johnston, James Risen and others that provided perspective or challenged information in the faulty stories were played as quietly as a lullaby. Especially notable among these was Risen's "C.I.A. Aides Feel Pressure in Preparing Iraqi Reports," which was completed several days before the invasion and unaccountably held for a week. It didn't appear until three days after the war's start, and even then was interred on Page B10.

The Times's flawed journalism continued in the weeks after the war began, when writers might have broken free from the cloaked government sources who had insinuated themselves and their agendas into the prewar coverage. I use "journalism" rather than "reporting" because reporters do not put stories into the newspaper. Editors make assignments, accept articles for publication, pass them through various editing hands, place them on a schedule, determine where they will appear. Editors are also obliged to assign follow-up pieces when the facts remain mired in partisan quicksand.

The apparent flimsiness of "Illicit Arms Kept Till Eve of War, an Iraqi Scientist Is Said to Assert," by Judith Miller (April 21, 2003), was no less noticeable than its prominent front-page display; the ensuing sequence of articles on the same subject, when Miller was embedded with a military unit searching for W.M.D., constituted an ongoing minuet of startling assertion followed by understated contradiction. But pinning this on Miller alone is both inaccurate and unfair: in one story on May 4, editors placed the headline "U.S. Experts Find Radioactive Material in Iraq" over a Miller piece even though she wrote, right at the top, that the discovery was very unlikely to be related to weaponry.

The failure was not individual, but institutional.

When I say the editors got it "mostly" right in their note this week, the qualifier arises from their inadequate explanation of the journalistic imperatives and practices that led The Times down this unfortunate path. There were several.

THE HUNGER FOR SCOOPS. Even in the quietest of times, newspaper people live to be first. When a story as momentous as this one comes into view, when caution and doubt could not be more necessary, they can instead be drowned in a flood of adrenalin. One old Times hand recently told me there was a period in the not-too-distant past when editors stressed the maxim "Don't get it first, get it right." That soon mutated into "Get it first and get it right." The next devolution was an obvious one.

War requires an extra standard of care, not a lesser one. But in The Times's W.M.D. coverage, readers encountered some rather breathless stories built on unsubstantiated "revelations" that, in many instances, were the anonymity-cloaked assertions of people with vested interests. Times reporters broke many stories before and after the war—but when the stories themselves later broke apart, in many instances Times readers never found out. Some remain scoops to this day. This is not a compliment.

FRONT-PAGE SYNDROME. There are few things more maligned in newsroom culture than the "on the one hand, on the other hand" story, with its exquisitely delicate (and often soporific) balancing. There are few things more greedily desired than a byline on Page 1. You can "write it onto 1," as the newsroom maxim has it, by imbuing your story with the sound of trumpets. Whispering is for wimps, and shouting is for the tabloids, but a terrifying assertion that may be the tactical disinformation of a self-interested source does the trick.

"Intelligence Break Led U.S. to Tie Envoy Killing to Iraq Qaeda Cell," by Patrick E. Tyler (Feb. 6, 2003), all but declared a direct link between Al Qaeda and Saddam Hussein—a link still to be conclusively established, more than 15 months later. Other stories pushed Pentagon assertions so aggressively you could almost sense epaulets sprouting on the shoulders of editors.

HIT-AND-RUN JOURNALISM. The more surprising the story, the more often it must be revisited. If a defector like Adnan Ihsan Saeed al-Haideri is hailed by intelligence officials for providing "some of the most valuable information" about chemical and biological laboratories in Iraq ("Defectors Bolster U.S. Case Against Iraq, Officials Say," by Judith Miller, Jan. 24, 2003), unfolding events should have compelled the paper to re-examine those assertions, and hold the officials publicly responsible if they did not pan out.

In that same story anonymous officials expressed fears that Haideri's relatives in Iraq "were executed as a message to potential defectors."

Were they? Did anyone go back to ask? Did anything Haideri say have genuine value? Stories, like plants, die if they are not tended. So do the reputations of newspapers.

CODDLING SOURCES. There is nothing more toxic to responsible journalism than an anonymous source. There is often nothing more necessary, too; crucial stories might never see print if a name had to be attached to every piece of information. But a newspaper has an obligation to convince readers why it believes the sources it does not identify are telling the truth. That automatic editor defense, "We're not confirming what he says, we're just reporting it," may apply to the statements of people speaking on the record. For anonymous sources, it's worse than no defense. It's a license granted to liars.

The contract between a reporter and an unnamed source — the offer of information in return for anonymity — is properly a binding one. But I believe that a source who turns out to have lied has breached that contract, and can fairly be exposed. The victims of the lie are the paper's readers, and the contract with them supersedes all others. (See Chalabi, Ahmad, et al.)

Beyond that, when the cultivation of a source leads to what amounts to a free pass for the source, truth takes the fall. A reporter who protects a source not just from exposure but from unfriendly reporting by colleagues is severely compromised. Reporters must be willing to help reveal a source's misdeeds; information does not earn immunity. To a degree, Chalabi's fall from grace was handled by The Times as if flipping a switch; proper coverage would have been more like a thermostat, constantly taking readings and then adjusting to the surrounding reality. (While I'm on the subject: Readers were never told that Chalabi's niece was hired in January 2003 to work in The Times's Kuwait bureau. She remained there until May of that year.)

END-RUN EDITING. Howell Raines, who was executive editor of the paper at the time, denies that The Times's standard procedures were cast aside in the weeks before and after the war began. (Raines's statement on the subject, made to The Los Angeles Times, may be read at [@].

But my own reporting (I have spoken to nearly two dozen current and former Times staff members whose work touched on W.M.D. coverage) has convinced me that a dysfunctional system enabled some reporters operating out of Washington and Baghdad to work outside the lines of customary bureau management.

In some instances, reporters who raised substantive questions about certain stories were not heeded. Worse, some with substantial knowledge of the subject at hand seem not to have been given the chance to express reservations. It is axiomatic in newsrooms that any given reporter's story, tacked up on a dartboard, can be pierced by challenges from any number of colleagues. But a commitment to scrutiny is a cardinal virtue.

When a particular story is consciously shielded from such challenges, it suggests that it contains something that plausibly should be challenged.

Readers have asked why The Times waited so long to address the issues raised in Wednesday's statement from the editors. I suspect that Keller and his key associates may have been reluctant to open new wounds when scabs were still raw on old ones, but I think their reticence made matters worse. It allowed critics to form a powerful chorus; it subjected staff members under criticism (including Miller) to unsubstantiated rumor and specious charges; it kept some of the staff off balance and distracted.

The editors' note to readers will have served its apparent function only if it launches a new round of examination and investigation. I don't mean further acts of contrition or garment-rending, but a series of aggressively reported stories detailing the misinformation, disinformation and suspect analysis that led virtually the entire world to believe Hussein had W.M.D. at his disposal.

No one can deny that this was a drama in which The Times played a role. On Friday, May 21, a front-page article by David E. Sanger ("A Seat of Honor Lost to Open Political Warfare") elegantly characterized Chalabi as "a man who, in lunches with politicians, secret sessions with intelligence chiefs and frequent conversations with reporters from Foggy Bottom to London's Mayfair, worked furiously to plot Mr. Hussein's fall." The words "from The Times, among other publications" would have fit nicely after "reporters" in that sentence. The aggressive journalism that I long for, and that the paper owes both its readers and its own self-respect, would reveal not just the tactics of those who promoted the W.M.D. stories, but how The Times itself was used to further their cunning campaign.

In 1920, Walter Lippmann and Charles Merz wrote that The Times had missed the real story of the Bolshevik Revolution because its writers and editors "were nervously excited by exciting events." That could have been said about The Times and the war in Iraq. The excitement's over; now the work begins.

· · ·

I've been told by several people that this was the most important column I wrote in my 18 months; I'm not so sure. What was important, if anything, grew out of the process of writing it. The many hours of interviews I conducted with people at (and formerly at) the paper did lead to some useful self-examination at The Times. Internal debate on the subject was advanced by management's awareness that I was planning on writing something on the subject, and Keller acknowledged he ran his Editor's Note when he did because he didn't want my words to be the first ones on the subject to be published in the paper. Most of all, there seemed to be a recognition, even among people who had opposed the creation of the public editor position, that publishing the critical comments of an independent voice could enhance the readership's faith in The Times.

Some readers wanted to know why I didn't name names—didn't single out specific editors as responsible for the most egregious of the stories and the prominence of their placement. Much as I tried, I couldn't nail down the specifics. No one I interviewed—not even those with axes to grind and a history of swinging them—could conclusively cite particular responsibility for particular pieces. But if the reader takes the absence of names to mean strictly "Howell Raines and his allies," the reader would be mistaken. As executive editor at the time, Raines bears ultimate responsibility—but the institutional failure required the complicity, or at least the complacence, of many people, including some of Raines's most outspoken detractors.

Internally, reaction to the column was largely positive. For months, various staff members—reporters, desk-level editors, bureau chiefs, two masthead-level editors—had urged me to take on the issue. Many of them felt that the W.M.D. coverage had disgraced the paper. Some said that they found their conversations with outsiders dominated by accusations that The Times was complicit in selling the Bush war plan to the American public. A few acknowledged that they wanted me (as one said) to "hang Judy out to dry."

It's not my job, or my wish, to defend Judy Miller. (The reference in the column to "unsubstantiated rumor and specious charges" concerning Miller was an allusion to ugly whispers about alleged sexual involvement with either her bosses or her sources. It's a hateful charge, unsupported by any evidence; I bring it up now only because it surfaced publicly during Miller's effort to avoid testimony before the grand jury in the Valerie Plame leak case.)* But in the months before and after I wrote this column, I was struck by how many people I encountered

---

* For readers who were living in caves in the summer and fall of 2005, or for those picking up a copy of this book from a remainder table in 2015, a brief version of the Valerie Plame case: Judith Miller was one of a small group of reporters who had learned that Plame, the wife of former Ambassador (and later Bush critic) Joseph C. Wilson IV, was a CIA agent. Although The Times never published this information, special prosecutor Patrick Fitzgerald, in an effort to learn who in the government had leaked Plame's covert identity, subpoenaed Miller, who refused to reveal her source. She subsequently spent 85 days in jail for contempt of court, and was released after she agreed to testify—with, she said upon her release, the approval of her source, vice-presidential aide I. Lewis "Scooter" Libby.

wanted to know why Miller was still working at the paper, given the quality of her W.M.D. reporting. When I asked what they found wanting, few could answer with specifics. Few, I believe, had in fact read the pieces that had aroused Miller's (and The Times's) critics.

But by the time this was published, Miller had become the symbol not just of The Times's missteps, but of the entire American press's failure to call the administration to account on its pre-war assertions. Even the Knight-Ridder chain, singled out by many as the only large media institution to see through the administration's W.M.D. assertions, published some articles fully as credulous as those that appeared in The Times and elsewhere. What many people forget is that nearly everyone—the media, the Democrats in Congress, much of the international community— believed Saddam Hussein had, and was capable of deploying, weapons of mass destruction.

So why Miller? Why did her name become the stand-in for this universal failure? First off, let's acknowledge that she did some very bad reporting, got many things wrong and defended her work far too long. But there were other reasons: for one, in her long career, the sharp-elbowed, hypercompetitive Miller had made many enemies, not least among her own colleagues. She was easy to demonize, and there were few who felt any urge to stand up on her behalf.

Crucially, when in the fall of 2003 Michael Massing in The New York Review of Books published a lengthy dissection of The Times's W.M.D. reporting (much of it Miller's), she responded with a letter, for publication, that cooked her goose. In essence, she said it wasn't necessarily her job as a reporter to challenge what she was told by her sources: "I wrote about the intelligence that was available from government and nongovernment sources."

From that moment forward, at a time when anti-war rage at the impotence of press and politicians became clamorous, the two words "Judy Miller" became a form of shorthand for a series of failures that reached way beyond her own very real errors. She hardly helped herself with her subsequent misadventures on television (see "Talking on the Air and Out of Turn: The Trouble With TV," on page 216), or her ill-conceived and eventually self-destructive posture as a martyr to the First Amendment in the Valerie Plame leak case. It had become much, much easier to spit out the epithet "Judy Miller" than to attempt to unravel the monumental and tangled failures of foreign intelligence, Congressional oversight, press complacency and public indifference that led to the war in Iraq.

Oddly, or maybe not, the person who seemed most angered by my W.M.D. piece was Patrick Tyler, who found my one-sentence criticism of his article on the putative link between Saddam and Al Qaeda an unwarranted attack on his integrity and his skills as a reporter. Concluding an increasingly volatile e-mail exchange, Tyler wrote, "God bless you, Dan. I thought you were going to be one of those people who could first, admit mistakes since that is your job in overseeing us for the readers, and secondly, someone who could see the nuances of journalism and help mediate the gulf between us and readers when the shrapnel is heavy and the horseshit thick. I was wrong."

In the penultimate line of the section headed, "The Hunger for Scoops," I meant to say that some of these stories remain *exclusives* to this day. And I should have said that the second half of the headline was borrowed from a song lyric by my pal Dave Frishberg.

An Electrician From the Ukrainian Town of Lutsk

. . .

June 13, 2004

I KNOW that's an odd headline, but it's not original with me. I lifted it from reporter Richard Bernstein's identification of an otherwise anonymous man he interviewed for an article published in The Times on April 25. This is not meant to criticize Bernstein: I don't know any electricians from Lutsk, but I would rather have one of them in my mind's eye than anyone identified as "an analyst," "an expert," "a lawyer involved in the case," "a senior State Department official," "a Democratic strategist" or any of the other standardized obfuscations that can make a morning with The Times so exasperating.

Last winter, I met Jason B. Williams, a New York University journalism student who was writing his master's thesis on unidentified sources in The Times. (I copped the idea for my headline from the title of his thesis, taken from another Times ID: "A Blue-Eyed Man With a Flowing Beard.") By reading every bylined A-section news story published in December 2003, Williams determined that 40 percent of the articles invoked at least one anonymous source, that the average day's paper brought 36 such sources into the reader's home and that more than half of these people were identified, at least in part, as "officials."

After The Times promulgated a revised policy on the use of
anonymous sources in February (it's a fascinating document—
read it at www.nytco.com/sources), I commissioned Williams to
conduct a similar study in April, to help me determine if the
new policy had had any measurable effect.

As it happens, the most important part of the new policy
involves something that cannot be checked independently: a
requirement that a ranking editor must know the identity of a
reporter's unnamed source. The one exception involves "crucial issues of law or national security in which sources face dire
consequences if exposed"; only executive editor Bill Keller can
waive the rule. (So far, Keller told me the other day, no one has
asked him for a waiver.) Allan M. Siegal, the paper's standards
editor, says that his frequent spot checks have detected "clear
improvement in the identification of sources to editors" since
the policy went into effect on March 1.

But Siegal also said, "I don't mind conceding that habits die
hard," which I regard as an explanation of why readers are still
being asked to do what they should never have to: take things
on faith. As the policy states, the use of unidentified sources
requires the paper to "accept an obligation not only to convince
a reader of their reliability but also to convey what we can learn
of their motivation."

Williams's numbers (which show a slightly greater rate of
anonymous quotation than his December study) and my own
reading of the paper tell me this obligation has not been met. In
April, barely 2 percent of stories citing anonymous sources
revealed why The Times granted the request for anonymity.
Only 8 percent of unidentified sources were described in a
meaningful fashion. ("Congressional official" is not meaningful; "Congressional staff member who works for the minority

leader" is.) Just last Monday, "The Split Between Disney and Miramax Gets a Little Wider," by Sharon Waxman and Laura M. Holson, was built on information provided by "close associates," "friends and executives" who had talked to Disney C.E.O. Michael Eisner, "two people who attended" a Disney board retreat, a "person who attended" a dinner with Eisner, "a senior Disney executive," "Hollywood experts" and "analysts."

I would love to know how much faith readers put into this kind of sourcing (and I have a feeling you'll tell me). Personally, I'm feeling pretty comfortable with the story, because neither Disney nor Miramax, which are not afflicted with timidity, has called me to say the story was factually wrong. But this doesn't do much good for the reader who is not granted the questionable privilege of daily contact with angry story subjects.

Electricians from Lutsk may be innocent bystanders, but most anonymous sources are not. They have many different motivations, but I doubt we'll ever see the paper cite what must be the most common one: deniability. If your name isn't attached to something that turns out to be wrong or embarrassing, you never have to take the heat for it.

Welcome, in other words, to Washington, where "senior State Department officials," "White House aides" and other familiar wraiths can say what they want without ever being held accountable for it. Their invisible domain extends overseas as well. Last Tuesday, in "Nine Iraqi Militias Are Said to Approve a Deal to Disband," by Dexter Filkins, one sentence began, "Two American officials, who spoke to a group of reporters on the condition of anonymity." This was no whispered conversation in some Baghdad back alley; Filkins told me there were roughly 40 people in the room when the officials spoke. All of them, of course, knew very well who the officials were. Their editors did, too. And there's no question the officials' colleagues in the government knew as well. In other words, everyone knew—except the paper's readers.

I can't find Filkins or his editors guilty for playing along with this dishonest practice; reporters must accept the rules to get the information. Times editors in fact tried to make an issue of such "background briefings" during the Clinton administration (Democrats are as adept as Republicans at this game). Andrew Rosenthal, the Washington editor at the time, instructed reporters to ask that everything be put on the record. When this request was invariably declined, the reporter was expected to ask why. The next part of the script had the reporter declare that The Times would therefore not participate in the briefing. "I dropped it after a while," Rosenthal told me last week, "because the rest of the press corps ridiculed our reporters." And because it just didn't do any good.

But The Times could do some good for its readers in other ways. For one thing, it oughtn't have to wait for me to whine about it to let readers know how official Washington plays its cynical game. The paper may have to play by the rules, but that doesn't mean these rules can't be explained to readers. They're the ultimate victims—citizens whom both the journalists and the officials presumably represent.

The paper could certainly make a stronger effort to explain sources' motivations. Why did all those mysterious people tell Waxman and Holson about Eisner's thinking? Were they floating balloons in his behalf? Were some of them winking at the Disney board, alerting them through The Times that Eisner might be susceptible to pressure on a deal? Did any have a personal interest in the Disney stock price?

The paper could also require its reporters to rephrase the

implicit contract with sources so that it says, "If you lie to me, I will no longer protect your identity." After I raised this idea in my May 30 column, I was asked whether it would be fair if sources didn't know this was the deal. Well, make it an explicit part of the deal—every anonymity deal—up front. And who's to say whether a comment is in fact a lie? This shouldn't be a problem: if I trust a reporter to protect my name in the first place, isn't it logical that I would trust her to make that determination as well?

The easiest reform to institute would turn the use of unidentified sources into an exceptional event. They're necessary, of course, in reporting on national security; they're inescapable in reporting on certain foreign policy issues (diplomats, being diplomatic, almost never allow their names to be used). I'll even grant that knowing what Disney is or is not doing with Miramax justifies reliance on unidentified sources.

But in last Tuesday's paper alone, anonymous testimony enabled readers to learn that senators examining the intelligence community intend to concentrate on looking forward, that no two large public events in Washington can be planned in the same fashion, that Barbra Streisand expects hoteliers to scatter rose petals in her bathroom and that many people inside government worry about political consultants becoming lobbyists.

I do not feel the earth shaking.

Finally, it's worth reconsidering the entire nature of reportorial authority and responsibility. In other words, why quote anonymous sources at all? Do their words take on more credibility because they're flanked with quotation marks? If Waxman and Holson had written their article in their own voice, eschewing all blind quotes and meaningless attributions and making only the assertions they were confident were true, we could hold someone responsible for the accuracy: not the dubious sources, but the writers themselves. Isn't that the way it ought to be?

Stay tuned; this is a complex issue, and I intend to explore it further in a future column.

. . .

This piece may have added only one more word to the industry's now-raging conversation on the topic of anonymous sourcing, but there's no question in my mind that this is the journalism conversation that matters more than any other these days. The Dan Rather report on George W. Bush's military record, the Valerie Plame leak case (and Judith Miller's subsequent jailing and The Times's subsequent flailing), the controversy over The Times's reporting on the NSA wiretap program—all of them hinged on anonymous sourcing. And all of them provoked discussion in newsrooms regarding when the practice is appropriate.

My summary view is that, in news reporting, the use of an anonymous source must pass two tests: Is what I've learned truly important? And, is there no other way—no on-the-record way—to convey it to my readers?

It's also worth bearing in mind the words of David Rosenbaum. Rosenbaum, a veteran Times reporter who was murdered in a Washington street robbery in January 2006, was as decent and generous a human being as one could possibly imagine; he also was an aggressive, determined reporter who broke many important stories throughout his long and distinguished career. Shortly after Rosenbaum's death, former Times Washington editor Adam Clymer told The New York Observer that Rosenbaum had come to believe that "promises of confidentiality were given much too casually. He said you needed to protect the City Hall janitor who exposes corruption, but not political gossips."

The Report, the Review and a Grandstand Play

. . .

June 27, 2004

SPORTS columnists have forever used the phrase "hitting to all fields" to introduce pieces that cover a variety of subjects. Unlike the best of them, who work a different story into every sentence, I can manage only three swings. Conveniently, I've aimed one to right field, one to left and one straight up the middle.

Stretching across four columns of the front page, the June 17 headline "Panel Finds No Qaeda-Iraq Tie; Describes a Wider Plot for 9/11" caused some readers, including Vice President Dick Cheney, to accuse The Times of "outrageous" (Cheney's word) distortion of the 9/11 commission's staff report. I don't buy "outrageous," but "distortion" works for me—specifically, the common newspaper crime of distortion by abbreviation. The staff report was largely concerned with attacks on United States soil, whereas the headline bore no such qualification. The headline also leaned on two of those words whose brevity makes them dear to all newsrooms: the resolute "no," and the imprecise "tie." Assistant managing editor Craig Whitney, who oversees the front page, argues that "tie" in the headline is "a correct shorthand summary" of the report's conclusion that there appeared to be no "collaborative relationship" between Al Qaeda and Iraq.

That's the problem with shorthand: If it's not written in your own hand, it's very hard to read. Headlines also pose two conundrums. The more complex the story, the more likely you are to get a headline that oversimplifies it. And the more complete the coverage associated with the headline, the less likely readers will find their own way to the gist of it. The main news section on June 17 contained eight separate articles on the staff report, consuming nearly 550 column inches. Unable to wander through all these glades and thickets of prose, many readers rely on headlines to provide as much of a summary as they are prepared to absorb.

While headlines may be short, their impact is large. Willful distortion? I don't see it. Misstep? Sure. Is an apology needed, as Internet columnist Bob Kohn, one of the paper's most forceful (and, often, most incisive) critics on the right, demanded by e-mail? No. Good reporting and careful presentation are what's needed. If out-of-tune headlines required apologies, the newspaper business would soon turn into a cacophony of confession.

Chief book critic Michiko Kakutani's review of Bill Clinton's "My Life," published in last Sunday's paper, was brutal. For any author, it would have been the review from hell, the one from which a career (much less the book at hand) could never recover. Of course, Bill Clinton isn't just any author, and early reports indicate that "My Life" might be the fastest-selling nonfiction book in United States history.

That a far more positive take on the book by novelist Larry McMurtry will appear in next Sunday's Book Review says more about reviewing than it does about "My Life." McMurtry and Kakutani didn't read different books; they're just different people, who appear to agree only on the book's sporadic wonkiness.

But Kakutani's review came first; it ran on the front page; and it featured a vocabulary of critical invective that might have knocked the breath out of even a Clinton hater.

Needless to say, Clinton supporters were displeased. Some wrote to say the review was another ambush in a Times anti-Clinton vendetta that began when "Whitewater" referred just to rafting conditions. Many wondered why Kakutani was allowed to include in a review her judgments not just of the book but of the Clinton presidency itself. Others chastised her for failing to mention the book's criticisms of The Times. And quite a few took her to task for the reference in the review's closing sentence to "Lies about . . . real estate." They argued that the failure of the Resolution Trust Corporation or the Office of the Independent Counsel to charge either of the Clintons with any Whitewater-related deceptions proves that the "lies" comment is a calumny.

I don't buy the vendetta charge; it suggests that the different parts of this newspaper operate in sync, when my seven months here have convinced me that the various departments are as carefully coordinated as Manhattan traffic in a thunderstorm. Kakutani herself doesn't seem party to any kind of Kill Bill campaign, as she demonstrated last year in her evisceration of Nigel Hamilton's full-frontal attack, "Bill Clinton: An American Journey." I can't for the life of me come up with a rule that would limit what a reviewer should be allowed to comment on in a review, and I can't imagine anyone who wouldn't keep personal opinions of a presidency in mind while reading the president's memoirs.

The other two complaints about Kakutani's review—failure to mention criticism of The Times and reference to real estate lies—would be absolutely appropriate to a news story. But critics exist to have opinions. Short of committing factual inaccuracy, libel or other major sins, they are free—must be free—to say what they wish. To my knowledge the R.T.C. and the O.I.C. never concluded that one or the other Clinton did not lie; the two offices found that they had committed no offenses that justified prosecution or taken any actions that would subject them to civil penalties. Thankfully, in the United States justice system, the threshold for establishing criminal behavior or a civil liability is much higher than the threshold for your opinion, my opinion or Michiko Kakutani's opinion.

But it was a different threshold that this review crossed: the sanctity of the front page as an opinion-free zone. Executive editor Bill Keller told me that "the voice of a brilliant critic was something we could add to the coverage that was uniquely ours." As far as I know, the only other time the paper put a book review on A1 was almost exactly a year ago, for Harry Potter. But Bill Clinton is no Harry Potter; his role in the ever intensifying political debate remains substantial, and in some ways might even be determinative. The front page is the home for news, and arguably for analysis, but if it's also the home for unbuckled opinion about figures on the public stage, then you could argue that editorials belong there, too. Managing editor Jill Abramson believes that the review "was every bit as interesting and newsworthy as the front-page stories disclosing its contents." But if Michiko Kakutani's opinions are news, it would be just as logical to write a story about them, or about especially strong columns by William Safire or Maureen Dowd. And that's a logical step too far for me.

I asked both Keller and Abramson whether they would have run the review on Page 1 had it been an unqualified rave, suspecting as I do that anything overly sunny and positive might seem almost promotional in so prominent a position; both said they would have.

I'm sure they believe it. I'm not sure I do.

Now, up the middle. In my June 13 column on anonymous sources, I ended with the admonition "Stay tuned; this is a complex issue, and I intend to explore it further in a future column."

"Complex" doesn't begin to describe it. Readers, journalists, interview subjects and one chronically off-the-record "senior aide" had much to say about the issue, and the gradations of their views are as finely calibrated as a microscope. I do plan to explore these complexities at some later date, but for now I'll stick to the one point on which there was near unanimous agreement: that "background briefings" of government and political figures are an affront to journalistic integrity and an insult to the citizenry. Even my senior aide (not in the current administration, nor particularly active in the current campaign, but a past master of the background briefing) doesn't like them very much.

So let me offer a blatant, grandstanding challenge to the five largest American papers and The Associated Press. Newspapers are by nature competitive rather than collaborative, but the very existence of the cooperatively owned A.P. demonstrates that concerted action can be good for journalism. Therefore: will the chief editors of USA Today, The Wall Street Journal, The New York Times, The Los Angeles Times, The Washington Post and The A.P. jointly agree not to cover group briefings conducted by government officials and other political figures who refuse to allow their names to be used?

If I hear from any of them, I'll let you know.

· · ·

Right field: Headlines, especially headlines about complex stories, especially those written under severe time pressure, are a bitch. So when I once sought to defend the paper by pointing out the difficulties to a reader in California who had complained about a headline on a story out of Jerusalem, I made the mistake of underscoring my point with a challenge: give yourself 10 minutes, I told the writer in an e-mail message, and see if you can do a better job in two lines of 27–30 characters each. The guy was back at me in about four minutes, with a headline far superior—in both accuracy and punchiness—to the one The Times had published. It wasn't a challenge I issued again.

Left field: I revisited the Kakutani-Clinton review twice—once in a correction (tagged on to my July 11 column, below), and again in "EXTRA! EXTRA! Read Not Quite Everything About It," on page 240.

Center field: as I would write in my September 12 column (p. 142), Ken Paulson of USA Today was the only editor who responded to my challenge. But the background briefing issue continued to bubble over the following months, and something resembling determination to end the practice broke out in many Washington bureaus. The key word, of course, is "resembling."

When I asked him about it in February, 2006, Washington Bureau Chief Philip Taubman said there had been "mild improvement. I can think of several occasions when briefings were put on the record after a number of bureau chiefs and editors objected in advance, and Scott McClellan at the White House has made an effort to put background briefings on the record." But, he concluded, "If the road ahead is 100 miles long, I'd say we've traveled 5 miles so far."

When the Right to Know Confronts the Need to Know

. . .

July 11, 2004

UNTIL 10 days ago all I knew about Tony Hendra was that he had been an editor of the original National Lampoon, played the band manager in "This Is Spinal Tap," wrote occasionally about wine and recently published "Father Joe," a best-selling memoir of his spiritual salvation through the counsel and friendship of a Benedictine monk.

Then, on Thursday, July 1, on the front page of the Arts section of The Times, I learned that Hendra may have committed the most unspeakable of acts. In "Daughter Says Father's Confessional Book Didn't Confess His Molestation of Her," by N.R. Kleinfield, he denied Jessica Hendra's accusation that he had sexually abused her when she was a child. But when I asked various Times readers over the next few days whether they had read the piece about Tony Hendra, they didn't say, "You mean the one in which he denied that he abused his daughter?" Of course: assertions linger; denials evaporate.

Many readers were shocked—some by Jessica Hendra's accusations, more because The Times published them. Carol Paradis of Brooklyn wrote to say she was "astonished that The Times would devote so much coverage, if any at all, to what is a private and obviously harrowing family dispute." A few suggested that even if the editors found the story newsworthy, running it at such great length—more than 2,500 words—lent it an air of conclusive judgment, despite Hendra's denials.

(Readers who objected to the subsequent appearance of the "Lives" column by Hendra that ran in The Times Magazine on July 4 should blame production schedules—the magazine is printed nine days in advance of the issue date—and the lack of coordination between the paper's various editorial units. Editors at the magazine did not know that an investigation of Jessica Hendra's charges was under way, and editors involved in the story about the charges did not know that the magazine planned to run an article by Tony Hendra.)

My own objection was, well I couldn't decide what I thought. Hendra isn't a politician, a teacher, a clergyman or otherwise in a position of authority over others, a conventional standard for public examination of otherwise private matters. But he did write a semi-confessional book about his own moral progress. It had also become a national best seller. Had his success, and the book's theme, made the most intimate details of his life a fair subject for public review? Let me amend that: not just intimate details, but unprovable allegations about despicable details?

According to culture editor Jonathan Landman, when editors learned of Jessica Hendra's charges, "we could have suppressed the whole thing in the name of taste or principle."

"Or we could check the facts as thoroughly as possible," he said, "and then make a morally complex decision based on those facts. That's what we did." The subject of Hendra's book and its success, Landman told me in an e-mail message, "were central to the newsworthiness of the daughter's accusation."

From my reconstruction of how this story made its way into print, I think The Times did it pretty much by the book. The paper did not begin by sifting through Tony Hendra's life, trying to find something that might taint the aura of virtue surrounding "Father Joe." Around June 20, after her father's book had already spent three weeks on the best-seller list, Jessica Hendra sent The Times's Op-Ed page an unsolicited essay containing her allegations. The page's editor, David Shipley, forwarded it to the newsroom with her permission, and soon Kleinfield was assigned the story.

This, too, was the right decision. Kleinfield is one of the paper's most capable reporters, a pro with more than three decades of experience. He spent a week on the story, and while it may appear that he called Hendra for his response rather late in the process, the article was not scheduled until after their last conversation. This wasn't an ambush interview—that deplorable tactic used by reporters who call the subject an hour before deadline and demand immediate responses to complex, often hostile questions.

Kleinfield says he first called Hendra the morning of June 29 and finally reached him late that afternoon. They spoke three times that day, the last time late that evening, and again on June 30. (I have not crosschecked this account with Hendra, with whom I have not communicated at all, but I've no reason to doubt its accuracy.)

Kleinfield also asked for the names of people Hendra would like him to speak with, presumably to support his denials. In an extensive e-mail message he sent me explaining the process of his investigation and his analysis of what he learned, Kleinfield made a crucially important statement. Based on his reporting, he wrote, "I concluded that she was molested."

Journalists often erect evasive defenses to justify publishing unprovable material; they say it's "plausible," or "worth airing" or "apparently credible." Kleinfield may be wrong about

Hendra, but his willingness to stand behind the story's dark implications is honest, and it's meaningful. This is not to suggest that the article was perfect. I wish it had included on-the-record testimony from people Kleinfield had not been directed to by the two Hendras. The vivid detailing of alleged sexual acts was unnecessary in some of its stomach-turning specifics. (The length, I believe, was appropriate: anything much shorter would have turned a complex situation into base gossip.)

But those issues bear discussion in another context. I'm trying to answer a different question: If I were an editor at The Times, would I have published an article containing grave allegations, buttressed by thorough reporting by one of my top people, about a man who had become a public figure specifically because of his assertions of moral growth?

I probably would have.

But I'm not a Times editor, and I don't know if it serves the paper or its readers if I try to think like one. This column should represent the views of readers, give them a fair airing and assess the validity of their criticisms. What did the Hendra article accomplish for readers, and at what potential cost?

I talked with a dozen or so Times editors and writers not involved in the article, and not one of them found the piece inappropriate. But I think it's noteworthy that among the readers who did object were several former newspaper journalists who could examine the newsroom ethos from a distance. "In 40-plus years of reading The Times I have not come across so scurrilous a piece," wrote Tom Zito, formerly of The Washington Post. "What possible purpose was served by running it, other than to perhaps make its subject consider suicide?"

Carey Winfrey, himself a former Times reporter, recalled a

comment made to him years ago by A.M. Rosenthal, at the time the paper's top editor. The most important lesson Rosenthal had learned from one of his predecessors was "Just because you have the power doesn't mean you have to use it."

This might have been one of those cases. Was the piece published because Hendra had had the good fortune of seeing a book originally issued in a printing of 15,000 copies (according to his publisher) become a national phenomenon? Because book buyers should be warned that "Father Joe" may be disingenuous at the least, and perhaps dishonest? Or because of the public's broad right to know?

Plausible reasons, each of them. But what if the charge is false? And even if the preponderant evidence indicates it's true, doesn't the small chance that it's false outweigh the value of giving readers access to the private miseries of the Hendra family? Either way, Tony Hendra will bear the scars of this article forever. People who did not write a book claiming spiritual salvation will suffer as well: his three young children from his second marriage, for instance. In the face of this risk, what do readers of The Times (or of "Father Joe") gain by believing Hendra guilty of abuse? There's a difference between the right to know and the need to know, and in this case, the need escapes me.

I don't mean in any way to diminish the gravity of Jessica Hendra's charges; I can't imagine an accusation more serious, a transgression more detestable. If her story is true, Tony Hendra deserves punishment far greater than humiliation in the pages of The Times. As an editor, the verities of the profession might have led me to publish this article. But as a reader, I wish The Times hadn't.

· · ·

In my June 27 column, I described Nigel Hamilton's "Bill Clinton: An American Journey" as a "full-frontal attack." This characterization came from my reliance on a review by critic Michiko Kakutani. She may be right, but given that I've never read the book, it was stupid of me to characterize it with such glib surety.

. . .

This one split readers almost evenly; for each one who excoriated me for cruel indifference to what Jessica Hendra had suffered, someone else thanked me for calling The Times to account (in truth, given my equivocation in the piece, that was something I hadn't really thought I had done).

From newspaper reporters and editors, though, I received almost universal disapproval. Times reporter Nina Bernstein was particularly eloquent in her defense of Kleinfield's piece, and I posted her comments on my Web journal. (See entry number 32 [@].) A year and a half later, I'm still not sure how I feel—ask me two days in a row, and I may not give you the same answer. But I do believe that if a piece like this one belongs in the newspaper, Kleinfield and his editors handled it as well as it possibly could have been handled. And maybe that's why they are newspaper editors, and I am not.

Bill Keller raised an especially provocative point: "The only tangible consequence I can see of The Times killing the story is that you'd have been writing your column upside down—was The Times right to sit on the story?—and ending up with your inner reader and your inner editor reversing places."

Is The New York Times a Liberal Newspaper?

. . .

July 25, 2004

OF course it is.

The fattest file on my hard drive is jammed with letters from the disappointed, the dismayed and the irate who find in this newspaper a liberal bias that infects not just political coverage but a range of issues from abortion to zoology to the appointment of an admitted Democrat to be its watchdog. (That would be me.) By contrast, readers who attack The Times from the left—and there are plenty—generally confine their complaints to the paper's coverage of electoral politics and foreign policy.

I'll get to the politics-and-policy issues this fall (I want to watch the campaign coverage before I conclude anything), but for now my concern is the flammable stuff that ignites the right. These are the social issues: gay rights, gun control, abortion and environmental regulation, among others. And if you think The Times plays it down the middle on any of them, you've been reading the paper with your eyes closed.

But if you're examining the paper's coverage of these subjects from a perspective that is neither urban nor Northeastern nor culturally seen-it-all; if you are among the groups The Times treats as strange objects to be examined on a laboratory slide (devout Catholics, gun owners, Orthodox Jews, Texans); if your value system wouldn't wear well on a composite New York Times journalist, then a walk through this paper can make you feel you're traveling in a strange and forbidding world.

Start with the editorial page, so thoroughly saturated in liberal theology that when it occasionally strays from that point of view the shocked yelps from the left overwhelm even the ceaseless rumble of disapproval from the right.

Across the gutter, the Op-Ed page editors do an evenhanded job of representing a range of views in the essays from outsiders they publish—but you need an awfully heavy counterweight to balance a page that also bears the work of seven opinionated columnists, only two of whom could be classified as conservative (and, even then, of the conservative subspecies that supports legalization of gay unions and, in the case of William Safire, opposes some central provisions of the Patriot Act).

But opinion pages are opinion pages, and "balanced opinion page" is an oxymoron. So let's move elsewhere. In the Sunday magazine, the culture-wars applause-o-meter chronically points left. On the Arts & Leisure front page every week, columnist Frank Rich slices up President Bush, Mel Gibson, John Ashcroft and other paladins of the right in prose as uncompromising as Paul Krugman's or Maureen Dowd's. The culture pages often feature forms of art, dance or theater that may pass for normal (or at least tolerable) in New York but might be pretty shocking in other places.

Same goes for fashion coverage, particularly in the Sunday magazine, where I've encountered models who look like they're preparing to murder (or be murdered), and others arrayed in a mode you could call dominatrix chic. If you're like Jim Chapman, one of my correspondents who has given up on The Times, you're lost in space. Wrote Chapman, "Whatever happened to poetry that required rhyme and meter, to songs that required lyrics and tunes, to clothing ads that stressed the costume rather than the barely clothed females and slovenly dressed, slack-jawed, unshaven men?"

In the Sunday Styles section, there are gay wedding announcements, of course, but also downtown sex clubs and T-shirts bearing the slogan, "I'm afraid of Americans." The findings of racial-equity reformer Richard Lapchick have been appearing in the sports pages for decades ("Since when is diversity a sport?" one e-mail complainant grumbled). The front page of the Metro section has featured a long piece best described by its subhead, "Cross-Dressers Gladly Pay to Get in Touch with Their Feminine Side." And a creationist will find no comfort in Science Times.

Not that creationists should expect to find comfort in Science Times. Newspapers have the right to decide what's important and what's not. But their editors must also expect that some readers will think: "This does not represent me or my interests. In fact, it represents my enemy." So is it any wonder that the offended or befuddled reader might consider every-thing else in the paper—including, say, campaign coverage—suspicious as well?

Times publisher Arthur O. Sulzberger Jr. doesn't think this walk through The Times is a tour of liberalism. He prefers to call the paper's viewpoint "urban." He says that the tumultuous, poly-glot metropolitan environment The Times occupies means "We're less easily shocked," and that the paper reflects "a value system that recognizes the power of flexibility."

He's right; living in New York makes a lot of people think that way, and a lot of people who think that way find their way to New York (me, for one). The Times has chosen to be an unashamed product of the city whose name it bears, a condition magnified by the been-there-done-that irony afflicting too many journalists. Articles containing the word "postmodern" have appeared in The Times an average of four times a week this year—true fact!—and if that doesn't reflect a Manhattan sensibility, I'm Noam Chomsky.

But it's one thing to make the paper's pages a congenial home for editorial polemicists, conceptual artists, the fashion-forward or other like-minded souls (European papers, aligned with specific political parties, have been doing it for centuries), and quite another to tell only the side of the story your co-religionists wish to hear. I don't think it's intentional when The Times does this. But negligence doesn't have to be intentional.

The gay marriage issue provides a perfect example. Set aside the editorial page, the columnists or the lengthy article in the magazine ("Toward a More Perfect Union," by David J. Garrow, May 9) that compared the lawyers who won the Massachusetts same-sex marriage lawsuit to Thurgood Marshall and Martin Luther King. That's all fine, especially for those of us who believe that homosexual couples should have precisely the same civil rights as heterosexuals.

But for those who also believe the news pages cannot retain their credibility unless all aspects of an issue are subject to robust examination, it's disappointing to see The Times present the social and cultural aspects of same-sex marriage in a tone that approaches cheerleading. So far this year, front-page headlines have told me that "For Children of Gays, Marriage Brings Joy" (March 19); that the family of "Two Fathers, With One Happy to Stay at Home" (Jan. 12) is a new archetype; and that "Gay Couples Seek Unions in God's Eyes" (Jan. 30). I've learned where gay couples go to celebrate their marriages; I've met gay couples picking out bridal dresses; I've been introduced to couples who have been together for decades and have now sanctified their vows in Canada, couples who have successfully integrated the world of competitive ballroom dancing, couples whose lives are the platonic model of suburban stability.

Every one of these articles was perfectly legitimate. Cumulatively, though, they would make a very effective ad campaign for the gay marriage cause. You wouldn't even need the articles: run the headlines over the invariably sunny pictures of invariably happy people that ran with most of these pieces, and you'd have the makings of a life insurance commercial.

This implicit advocacy is underscored by what hasn't appeared. Apart from one excursion into the legal ramifications of custody battles ("Split Gay Couples Face Custody Hurdles," by Adam Liptak and Pam Belluck, March 24), potentially net-tlesome effects of gay marriage have been virtually absent from The Times since the issue exploded last winter.

The San Francisco Chronicle runs an uninflected article about Congressional testimony from a Stanford scholar making the case that gay marriage in the Netherlands has had a deleterious effect on heterosexual marriage. The Boston Globe explores the potential impact of same-sex marriage on tax revenues, and the paucity of reliable research on child-rearing in gay families. But in The Times, I have learned next to nothing about these issues, nor about partner abuse in the gay community, about any social difficulties that might be encountered by children of gay couples or about divorce rates (or causes, or consequences) among the 7,000 couples legally joined in Vermont since civil union was established there four years ago.

On a topic that has produced one of the defining debates

of our time, Times editors have failed to provide the three-dimensional perspective balanced journalism requires. This has not occurred because of management fiat, but because getting outside one's own value system takes a great deal of self-questioning. Six years ago, the ownership of this sophisticated New York institution decided to make it a truly national paper. Today, only 50 percent of The Times's readership resides in metropolitan New York, but the paper's heart, mind and habits remain embedded here. You can take the paper out of the city, but without an effort to take the city and all its attendant provocations, experiments and attitudes out of the paper, readers with a different worldview will find The Times an alien beast.

Taking the New York out of The New York Times would be a really bad idea. But a determination by the editors to be mindful of the weight of its hometown's presence would not.

With that, I'm leaving town. Next week, letters from readers; after that, this space will be occupied by my polymathic pal Jack Rosenthal, a former Times writer and editor whose name appeared on the masthead for 25 years. I'm going to spend August in a deck chair and see if I can once again read The Times like a civilian. See you after Labor Day.

· · ·

Oh my oh my oh my. This one landed, as I should have expected, with an explosion. That Sunday morning, one of my dearest friends sent me an e-mail expressing how appalled she was that I had taken this position, that I was only feeding red meat to the right. An old colleague—a gay man—couldn't even bring himself to complain to me; he wrote to my wife to ask how I could be so cruel as to take this position.

Problem was, the position they were talking about was my

position on same-sex marriage—both of them felt I had tried to discredit it, when it's in fact something that I support. Their reaction almost proved my point: we read the way we read, and write the way we write, because of the intricate complexes of personal history, experience and attitude that make us who we are—no less among The Times's readers than among its writers.

At The Times, many who had grown concerned about this general issue (not gay marriage, but ingrained institutional perspective) thanked me for having written the piece. Most, though, wished I hadn't written a headline and lead sentence that were so inflammatory, and could be so readily repeated. Within days, TimesWatch.com added the headline and lead (with appropriate attribution) to the top of a page that bore the site's official slogan, "Documenting and Exposing the Liberal Political Agenda of The New York Times." A group opposed to gay marriage encouraged its members to send me thank you notes.

They, too, brought their intricate complexes of personal history, experience, and attitude to their reading of my column. Who could blame them for reacting as they did? Who could be blamed for making it so easy?

Only me, only me. As I've said, headlines are a bitch.

Q. How Was Your Vacation? A. Pretty Newsy, Thanks

. . .

September 12, 2004

NINE months into an 18-month appointment, with enough history to look back on and more than enough journalistic mud wrestling to look forward to, it's time for the public editor to sit for another interview. All questions below are exactly the sort of softballs you'd toss if you were interviewing yourself.

Q. So how was your vacation?

A. Wonderful and weird. Wonderful because vacations are inherently wonderful, but weird because every single day a certain familiar newspaper found its way into my hands—yet by the end of the first week it looked very different from the paper I'd encountered as public editor.

Q. Sunstroke?

A. No—role reversal. I'd found myself once again able to read The Times like a civilian, instead of like an auditor from the inspector general's office or the presiding official at an auto-da-fé. As in my innocent, pre-P.E. days, I would turn first to the obits and then the sports section, and not to the corrections on A2. I read the book reviews as if I were interested in the books under discussion, not in the motivations, inclinations or parentage of the discussants. I gobbled up the extensive coverage the Arts section gave to the downtown Fringe Festival. I didn't read World Business, or the fashion supplement to the Sunday magazine. It almost made me feel like a real person.

Q. What about the political coverage?

A. Sure, I read it. In fact, the day I hit my deck chair, I decided to spend August getting all my news only from The Times. I wanted to see whether total reliance on the paper would enable me to emerge into September with a view of the campaigns that accorded with reality.

Take, for instance, the Swift Boat dust-up. Instead of considering the hundreds of messages from irate readers that accumulated while I was gone, instead of interviewing editors and writers involved in the story, I simply read what was in the paper. I didn't read every word of the voluminous coverage (who reads every word, except a public editor chained to his desk or a Times hater looking for desecrations?), but I read about as much as any normal human might.

Here's what I learned: In a series of ads, a group of Vietnam veterans who served with or near John Kerry in the Mekong Delta charged him with several deceptions about his war service. The ads were financed and produced by a number of people, many of them Texas Republicans, with a connection to President Bush or his associates. One key figure, however, was a political independent who voted for Al Gore in 2000 and has been challenging Senator Kerry's post-service condemnations of certain American practices in Vietnam for three decades.

From what The Times's news coverage told me, official records contradict the central charges leveled in the ads. However, it is not accurate to say, as Senator Kerry has, that he spent Christmas 1968 in Cambodia.

If my summary is wrong, The Times erred. If it's accurate, the paper did a fine job. If my description offends you because you dislike Kerry, or because you think the extent of The Times's Swift Boat coverage lent credence to false charges, this tells me more about you than it does about The Times.

Q. That sounds pretty peevish. Is there more to it?

A. Well, yes. I concluded July with a column ("Is The New York Times a Liberal Newspaper?") that caused several readers to assail me for making a case against gay marriage, and even more to accuse me of giving aid and comfort to supporters of the Federal Marriage Amendment by criticizing The Times's coverage of the issue. I really don't think I did the former, but judging by the enthusiastically supportive mail (including more than 400 identical—and proportionally discountable—postcards from one conservative group), I certainly appear to have ladled out the aid and comfort.

Q. Are you sorry about it?

A. As a supporter of gay rights, sure—but as public editor, not for a second. A political reporter with any claim to honesty can't ignore a story like the Swift Boat controversy, and a public editor with any aspiration to fair-mindedness can't be afraid to agree with people who might well disagree with him on everything else.

I just wish that my allies of convenience would attribute my views to me personally, and not by inference to The Times institutionally. Any sentence that begins, "As The Times's own Daniel Okrent says," should be immediately euthanized. I don't speak for the paper, and if I'm The Times's "own" anything (except, maybe, The Times's own nuisance), I'm clearly failing at this job.

Q. Any results from your challenge to the editors of America's five largest papers, asking them to refuse to report on news briefings conducted by officials who insist on anonymity?

A. Only heard from one of them. Ken Paulson, the editor of USA Today, wrote to say that his paper, in conjunction with The Associated Press, has frequently objected to the anonymity rules of background briefings. However, when his paper's objections are dismissed, it nonetheless feels required to report on the briefings because, Paulson said, "our primary obligation is to keep our readers fully informed." He concluded: "You may want to rephrase your challenge to America's newspapers. Instead of walking out, are they ready to speak up?"

I didn't hear a peep from the editors of The Wall Street Journal, The Los Angeles Times, The Washington Post or The New York Times. Regarding the first three, I'm with the old

Lindy's waiter: "Not my table." But in the months ahead I plan to annoy the last of the four on the anonymous sources issue, both in print and in person. Here are two of the questions I'll ask him: When officials who demand anonymity call a news briefing because they wish to get their story out, but are unwilling to be held accountable for it, why is The Times obliged to be their messenger? How is this different from publishing an unattributed and unsubstantiated rumor?

O.K., Keller—consider yourself asked.

Q. What else do you plan on addressing in your last nine months?

A. The list is long—corrections policy, book reviewing, the use of "experts," loaded language, Middle East coverage, honesty in photographs, what the editors mean by "news analysis" (not to mention "White House Letter," "Political Memo" and various other ways they say "not a news story").

And then, of course, there's that Godzilla hulking outside my window, campaign coverage. Just before Labor Day, I started to get my clipping fingers in shape for the coming ordeal, and by last Thursday I'd already built up an impressive collection of calluses. My colleague Arthur Bovino tells me that while I was away, many readers urged me to write about election coverage sooner rather than later, "while it still might make a difference," as several put it. My take is just the opposite: actor friends tell me that knowing the critics are in the audience will bring out their best performances, whereas the review that finally gets published is often just something to disagree with.

Q. Of course, actors don't like critics very much. How are you getting along with people at The Times these days?

A. Far better than you might imagine, or than I had predicted. I don't want to get into the racket of criticizing other papers (this one keeps me busy enough), but at least one recent report on how I've been received here may have left the wrong impression. Early on, there was exactly as much defensiveness, hostility and contention as you might expect from a large body of people (Times news staff) that suddenly found itself invaded by a mutant virus (me). But since late spring, it's been entirely different: the body has adapted and apparently finds the virus tolerable, if not exactly pleasant. Overwhelmingly—only one truly excruciating exception comes to mind—the writers and editors I deal with are both responsive and courteous. They may not (I could say "do not," but let me hold on to my illusions) care for what I write, but they aren't letting this get in the way of how they deal with me.

I'm grateful for it, and I respect them for it. And I'm almost ready to say this job has almost gotten to be almost fun.

. . .

Q. How stupid is Okrent?

A. Exceptionally stupid.

This last Q&A is extracted from an essay by Bob Somerby, on his Web site, The Daily Howler. Somerby, whose blog has a following on the left, didn't like me, the way I did my job, the way I wrote, the way I thought, or the way I took vacations. You can read his complete prosecution here [@], and from within it you can link to an earlier one, devoted to my "Is the New York Times Liberal?" column.

One failure I'll cop to was not being more careful in spelling out the reason for my only-The-Times regimen in August. When I wrote this column, of course I didn't know whether The Times's coverage was accurate: that was the point. I meant to indicate what a typical reader of The Times might have gleaned from its pages had he relied on it as his only source on this issue. If my description was wrong, then The Times got it wrong. You decide.

I'll grant Somerby his point about the political independent who *claimed* to have voted for Gore (not, as I wrote, voted for Gore). He's right: no one could know but the man himself whether he indeed voted for the Democratic candidate in 2000, and I failed to make the distinction. But people who don't read newspapers for a living, or who don't devote every available hour to stoking a raging blog, might have emerged from that August's coverage with the same conclusion. Sometimes what we read in newspapers isn't exactly what we think we've read, and there's a lesson in that, too.

Of the items on my list of planned columns, the only one I didn't get around to was book reviewing. At some subconscious level, I likely recognized that someone who writes books for a living might not want to dine on the hand that could someday feed him.

The "recent report" about how The Times was getting along with its public editor appeared in the Wall Street Journal on July 12, 2004, under the headline "Paper Trail: New York Times Finds Its Watchdog Has a Strong Bite," and is available to Journal subscribers (or those who would pay for a single download) at www.wsj.com. Every word in it was accurate—but every example of stress and strife cited by the author, James Bandler, had occurred months before, when the going was still pretty rocky. Keller was very angry with Bandler's piece, which did leave an impression somewhat at variance with what had by then become the rather humdrum reality of my working life.

Corrections: Eccentric, Essential and Ready for an Upgrade

. . .

September 26, 2004

FEW things irritate (or amuse) readers of The Times more than the corrections that appear daily on Page A2. The runic syntax, the elliptic references, the straight-faced earnestness of a prose style that has acquired the gloss of self-parody—they may offer their own eccentric delights, but they don't necessarily give readers, or bruised story subjects, what they want.

To the editors, the corrections reflect the paper's determination to convince its readers that it takes accuracy seriously. To critics, though, they establish the opposite: a smokescreen of trivia intended to obscure serious transgressions that the paper chooses to ignore.

That's nonsense. Even though many corrections seem no more important than a hiccup, you might not feel that way if it's your name The Times has misspelled. I can tell you from my near daily involvement with them that assistant managing editor Allan M. Siegal and senior editor William Borders, who oversee the corrections process, take this responsibility seriously, play it straight and do not win popularity contests at 229 West 43rd Street. In my experience, for every reporter who welcomes a substantive correction of his or her work there's another who grabs onto the nearest counterargument with the claws of a cat, and then starts hissing like one, too.

With a few exceptions, the reporters most willing to see their work corrected are the paper's most respected journalists, who in many cases attained that status partly by being so consistently accurate in the first place. Reporters' openness to corrections also enhances their credibility among those of us who monitor their work.

The week before last, Robert Strong, a former Texas National Guard officer, wrote me to say he had been grievously misquoted in "CBS Defends Its Report On Bush Military Record" (Sept. 11); he insisted he had said that he was not skeptical that Lt. Col. Jerry B. Killian had access to an I.B.M. Selectric typewriter with special characters in 1972, not that he was skeptical, as reporter Ralph Blumenthal had had it. Earlier that week, Blumenthal had instantly acknowledged another interviewee's complaint that he had truncated a quotation, and readily accepted a correction; in this instance, though, he held his ground and told his editors, and me, that he had detailed notes indicating Strong had said what he was quoted as saying. No correction ran.

Blumenthal's record was excellent, his internal logic consistent, his openness to corrections proven just days before. Strong (whose own internal logic seemed fine, too) stuck to his position. Al Siegal, speaking with the wisdom (and the sigh) acquired during his 27 years of toil in the vineyards of corrections, told me after we had struggled through this one, "Situations like this tend to have very unsatisfactory outcomes."

For Robert Strong, that's putting it mildly. For complainants who have not had the privilege (if that's what it is, given the outcome) of having their grievance aired on Page 2 of the Week in

Review section, it's no doubt even more discouraging. The apparent standoff is not a tie game at all, but a shutout: New York Times 1, Complaining Interviewee 0.

Worse, I don't know how it can end up any other way. I've played with the idea of creating a forum on my Web site where the aggrieved could register unrequited complaints, but it does not take a Diogenes to see the opportunity for mischief and deceit that washes so widely over the Web. Although the letters column on the editorial page is not generally a forum for challenges of fact or fairness, it does accommodate the occasional formal demurrer; separate letters columns in the various Sunday sections often contain claims of mistreatment from parties of interest. Certainly the editors could provide more space for this sort of thing on nytimes.com. They might also consider appending those challenges that do merit publication to the electronically archived version of the article in question, just as they do now with corrections. Like a point of personal privilege offered under Robert's Rules of Order, they ought to be acknowledged, if not necessarily heeded.

But even in the circumscribed realm of the current corrections policy, there's room for improvement on the form established 32 years ago, when A.M. Rosenthal, then the managing editor, first set aside correction space adjacent to the daily News Summary. Eleven years after that, Rosenthal introduced the Editors' Note, a form devoted to remedying, as The Times's stylebook puts it, "lapses of fairness, balance or perspective— faults more subtle or less concrete than factual errors, though often as grave and sometimes graver." Errors are honest mistakes; the "lapses" addressed in Editors' Notes are usually bad journalism.

Through Thursday, The Times had published nearly 2,300

corrections this year, but only 35 Editors' Notes. The rarity of Editors' Notes underscores their gravity. Contrarily, the soil that yields corrections is so fertile it becomes easy to ignore large parts of the crop. Correcting the misspellings of proper names is a nice gesture, especially for people who may never be mentioned in The Times again. And letting the world know that the "beachfront complex of bars along the Florida-Alabama border that was damaged" by Hurricane Ivan "is Flora-Bama, not Floribama" is. . . well, it isn't a bad thing to do. But this sort of underbrush obscures corrections of real consequence.

For instance, on Thursday, one correction indicated that an Iranian official had not warned that his country might produce "highly enriched uranium, which is used in nuclear weapons," but might "resume suspended efforts to produce enriched uranium, the form that can power nuclear reactors." The mistake may have been as innocent as the Flora-Bama fumble, but relative to a reader's understanding of the original story, the difference between reactor-grade uranium and weapons-grade uranium is more serious by a factor of, oh, several million. Not nearly as serious, but also meaningful to a reader's comprehension, the same Corrections column noted that the rate of New York City children hospitalized for asthma in 2003 was 6.5 per 1,000, not 6.5 per 100,000. That's a difference with a distinction.

Mistakes like these—as unwitting as the misspelling of names, and in no way triggered by malefactions like those that beget Editors' Notes—deserve a category of their own. If Caroline Smith DeWaal does not go by the name Caroline S. DeWaal, or if "Georges Bataille's Story of the Eye" was produced not by ARM/Cinema but by ARM/Cinema 25 (both facts noted in that same Thursday's paper), let the record show it. But readers deserve to have mistakes like the misidentified uranium and the miscounted asthma attacks brought to their attention in an arena less crowded (and less stylized) than the Corrections column.

Let Editors' Notes remain Editors' Notes, let Corrections remain Corrections—but give substantive (if innocent) errors their own place on the page, under their own heading. I haven't any idea what to call this new format I'm recommending, so let's kick off Public Editor Readership Contest No. 1.

Send entries to public@nytimes.com, and I'll paste the winner on Al Siegal's door.

Unattributed Source Watch: Two especially tasty descriptions of why people are allowed to speak anonymously in the pages of The Times showed up recently. In "Familiar Democratic Faces, but New Duties in Kerry Camp" (Sept. 16), David M. Halbfinger quoted "one senior Kerry aide," "one senior adviser," "one official who attends strategy sessions," "a Democratic operative" and, by paraphrase, "other senior campaign aides." They were all granted anonymity, Halbfinger wrote, "because the campaign bars aides from discussing its internal workings." In "CBS Says Producer Violated Policy by Putting Source In Touch With Kerry Aide" (Sept. 22), Jim Rutenberg and Bill Carter provided an even more delicious explanation for the timidity of their anonymous sources: "several people at the news division," they wrote, "insisted on anonymity because they had been told not to talk to reporters." Any impulse I had to chastise Halbfinger, Rutenberg and Carter was substantially mitigated by their bringing to the readers' attention pols who apparently break specious rules they write themselves, and news officials who tell their reporters not to talk to reporters.

Finally, readers (especially readers who are also journalists) offended by the willingness of news organizations to play along with Washington's bad habit of "background briefings" might want to check out the public service that columnist Jack Shafer of Slate is offering to perform, with me as his co-conspirator. You can read about it in "Outing the Anonymice," at [@].

. . .

Not a week after this column appeared, Al Siegal announced a change in the corrections policy. The heading "Corrections" would be reserved for substantive rectifications (concerning matters like the Iranian nuclear program, or the New York City asthma rate); a new category, "For the Record"—Siegal won the naming contest by blitzkrieg—would be reserved for Flora-Bama, Caroline Smith DeWaal, and the like.

It turned out that I hadn't been so persuasive; Siegal had apparently been contemplating such a change, and my piece simply nudged him into action. Immediately, reporters who had once argued, grumbled and wheedled to keep their mistakes out of the original Corrections column now turned their attention to arguing about how their new goof-ups should be classified, always preferring a five-yard penalty (For the Record) to a 15-yarder (Corrections). I should add that in the months ahead my assertion that the most respected reporters were most amenable to corrections sadly proved to be an overstatement; some of the writers I most respect turned out to be as defensive about their errors as I probably am.

My friend Steve Adler, then a deputy managing editor at The Wall Street Journal and now the editor-in-chief of Business Week, inadvertently made it clear he wasn't reading every word of my column when we went to the theater with our wives a few

days later. "Did you see that ridiculous thing they've done with
the Corrections column?" Steve asked. "Whose idea was that?"
I blamed Siegal.

How Would Jackson Pollock Cover This Campaign?

. . .

October 10, 2004

SEPTEMBER 26, re "Kerry as the Boss: Always More
Questions": Faith C. McCready thinks "the Kerry campaign
ought to be paying The Times a consultant/advertising fee" for
the article. Scott Libbey of Chevy Chase, Md., calls it "another
negative article on Kerry," and concludes: "I don't know how
you guys can look at yourselves in the mirror anymore. I really
don't."

October 5, regarding a few stories: From Michael Malone of
Darien, Conn., "I know that many of the Times reporters and
editors are breathlessly trying to get Kerry elected." And from
John Owens of San Francisco, "I often won't read your paper
because of the relentless pounding on Kerry."

Al Markel of San Francisco asks why The Times hasn't
reviewed the anti-Kerry "Unfit for Command" while Samuel
Leff of Manhattan wonders why Justin Frank's critical psycho-
analytic study, "Bush on the Couch," has been ignored by the
Book Review editors. Francis Moynihan of Avon, Conn., con-
gratulates The Times's Web site for "finally, a headline critical
of Kerry" that uses the word "pander"; John Owens objects, saying that "a comparable headline about Bush would read

'. . . according to the poll Americans find Bush to be a liar and an idiot.'" I'm tempted to refer all these correspondents, and the many hundreds of others they represent, to my colleague Mike Needs, ombudsman of The Akron Beacon Journal. "On Monday and Tuesday," Mike wrote in an e-mail last week, "my calls were all from conservatives saying the paper leaned left."

"On Wednesday, Thursday and Friday," he continued, "my calls were all from liberals saying the paper leaned right. But I did have one caller who said we were getting the balance just right. I discounted that one."

A definition of irony: what an ombudsman or public editor must appreciate to survive this campaign.

I've been reading The Times's campaign coverage like any other interested (and, by now, exhausted) citizen for months, but with special care, a pair of scissors, two marking pens and three other papers to use for comparison since Labor Day. Along the way, my own research has been richly amplified by reader mail, the buzzing of the blogs and the occasional complaint registered by party officials. Two readers generously provided me exhaustive analyses of the photographs of each candidate published in The Times (and came to opposite conclusions).

I will stipulate here that I'll be voting for John Kerry next month and will further admit that I have bent over backward to listen to pro-Bush complaints, in a conscious effort to counterbalance my own prejudices. I don't buy the argument a couple of Times editors have made, that because charges of bias come from both liberals and conservatives, the paper must therefore be doing things right. This makes as much sense as saying that a man with one foot on a block of ice and the other on a bed of hot coals must feel just fine.

In fact, I can find many things to criticize in The Times's election coverage. I'm as interested in the inside baseball of campaigns as the next politics nerd, but the paper's obsessive attention to backroom maneuvers and spin-room speculation obscures, rather than enhances, my understanding of the candidates. Much seems directed not at readers but at the campaign staffs and other journalists. The chronic overreliance on anonymous comments from self-serving partisans in news stories is equally maddening. (I prefer the pieces tagged "News Analysis" or "Political Memo," where at least we can hear the sound of the writer's own voice, and take into account the writer's apparent views.) And why the paper would ask a reporter to provide "real-time analysis" online during the debates is beyond me. The very phrase is an oxymoron; analysis requires reflection.

But there are plenty of press critics in print and on the Web, so I'll cede the general criticism to them. Here's the question for a public editor: Is The Times systematically biased toward either candidate?

No.

So farewell, legions of the left and armies of the right—all of you who have been faithful supporters when I've endorsed your various positions in past columns, but who will believe I have either lost my mind or sacrificed my credibility. I'm grateful for your close attention and your stimulating company, and I admire your passionate commitment.

But passion is a distorting lens that makes it hard to perceive the shape of things. Partisans will see the depredations committed against their man, but won't notice similar articles or headlines or photographs that may damage the other guy. Readers outraged by the Sept. 26 piece on Kerry's decision-making style ask when The Times will do a similar piece on Bush apparently because they didn't notice the one that ran Aug. 29 ("Bush Takes On Direct Role in Shaping Election Tactics").

A Bush-hater will see a front-page picture of the confident president greeting enthusiastic crowds and shout "Bias!" much more quickly than he will remember the nearly identical photo of Kerry that ran the day before. Republicans who object to the play given a recent story about scientists campaigning against the president are unaware of the Democrats' cries of bias after The Times failed in June to report on an anti-Bush statement signed by 27 retired diplomats.

If there's a commissariat at The Times ordering up coverage to help or hurt a specific candidate, it's doing a lousy job; close reading shows bruises administered to each (and free passes handed out) in a pattern adapted from Jackson Pollock. Many people want to know why the other guy's position is in the first paragraph of a story, and their side doesn't weigh in until the sixth; they don't notice when it's the other way around. Sherrie Sutton of Manhattan, who describes herself as "the only possible Bush vote on the Upper West Side," asked why Times headlines consistently use "attack" when Republicans criticize Democrats, but not when Democrats criticize Republicans. Intrigued, my associate, Arthur Bovino, determined that in the past year, headlined Republicans attacked Democrats 12 times and Democrats attacked Republicans 22 times. Ms. Sutton replied: "Statistics don't lie, and you've got 'em. Interesting, that in the face of facts, I could still feel unsatisfied that campaign coverage by the NYTimes is balanced."

Interesting, and honest, and for most of us, inevitable as well. Conservatives thought Cheney won the vice-presidential debate; liberals thought Edwards did. I can look at pictures of my children and see that they are flawless; you will see them differently (even though they are, of course, flawless). Write a book, get a lousy review—it's happened to me several times—and you challenge the reviewer's judgment, not your own. We see, and we are more vulnerable to, those things that matter most to us.

Unquestionably, individual articles, headlines or photographs do cast one or another candidate in a colored light, either rosy or dark. Headlines are especially toxic because of their reductive nature. Eric Kessin of Scarsdale, N.Y., wrote to say that the Friday, Sept. 2, headline "Jobless Figures Could Emphasize Bush's Big Weakness" might as easily have read "Jobless Figures Could Emphasize Bush's Claim of Economic Growth." He was right and, in fact, the Saturday story was headlined "Job Figures Help President Promote Economic Record."

That was accurate, but it, too, was not without its own coloration. Nothing is, especially when removed from the context of the long slog of the campaign and The Times's extended coverage. If The Times fails to give prominent space to a candidate's speech because it's a repeat of yesterday's, the paper is helping the opposition; if it does cover it, it's promoting the interests of the repetitive candidate. Show me an interesting photograph, and I'll show you an opinion. (I can't wait to hear what readers think of the Kerry portrait today on the cover The New York Times Magazine, much less the article itself.) (Check that: Yes, I can.)

Those readers who long for the days of absolutely untinted, nothing-but-the-facts newspapering ought to have an Associated Press ticker installed on the breakfast table. Newspapers today and especially this newspaper are asking their reporters and editors to go deep into a story, and when and where you go deep is itself a matter of judgment. And every judgment, it appears, offends someone.

It is axiomatic that the facts or characterizations a journalist chooses to include can tilt a reader's impression. So can the choice of articles, the prominence they're given, the immense weight of the entire, cumulative chronicle of a too-long campaign.

But it is equally axiomatic that the reader who has already tilted toward a particular candidate or position will instinctively view the world and The Times from his or her own personal angle.

This piece turned out to be more of a rant than I intended, but given the vicious nature of some of the attacks levied against certain reporters, I wasn't inclined to be temperate. There are many critics of The Times's election coverage who are measured and reasonable, and their views—very different from my own—will be represented in this space next week. I also don't wish to discourage readers who in good faith find errors, misrepresentations or unfair characterizations. They may occur randomly, but their frequency is disappointing, and I'll continue to forward meritorious complaints to the appropriate editors and reporters. Many will find expression in the Corrections column, or in this one.

But before I turn over the podium, I do want you to know just how debased the level of discourse has become. When a reporter receives an e-mail message that says, "I hope your kid gets his head blown off in a Republican war," a limit has been passed.

That's what a coward named "John Smith," from San Francisco, wrote to national political correspondent Adam Nagourney several days ago because Nagourney wrote something Smith considered (if such a person is capable of consideration) pro-Bush. Some women reporters regularly receive sexual insults and threats. As nasty as critics on the right can get (plenty nasty), the left seems to be winning the vileness derby this year. Maybe the bloggers who encourage their readers to send this sort of thing to The Times might want to ask them instead to say it in public. I don't think they'd dare.

. . .

This column generally got the reaction one would expect: a mixture of polite agreement, polite disagreement, ranting rage and dismissive grunts. The following week I presented in my space two columns taking issue with mine: one by Times critic Bob Kohn, representing the right, and one by Columbia Prof. Todd Gitlin, representing the left; they're reproduced below. What I didn't expect, but should have, was the reaction to the shirttail— the last two paragraphs. See my notes after the correction (following the two columns of Kohn and Gitlin) published on October 24.

The dismissive grunts came from those Republicans who believe that The Times's news staff is a cabal of Democratic Party functionaries. I wish I could get them to re-read the news pages of The Times during the last Democratic administration. Most Republican Times-bashers either have forgotten the paper's very aggressive coverage of the Clinton years—particularly its dogged pursuit of the Whitewater affair—or they must have ascribed it to the paper doing what Republicans think any worthwhile paper would do: pulling unrelentingly on any thread that might lead to unpleasant disclosures about a Democratic administration.*

When I wrote this column, I wish I had had at hand a story that would appear in The Times more than a year later, in January 2006. It ran in the Science Times section, and it reported on a study of how the politically partisan respond to certain stimuli: "Using M.R.I. scanners, neuroscientists have now tracked what happens in the politically partisan brain when it tries to digest damning facts about favored candidates or criticisms of them. The process is almost entirely emotional and unconscious, the researchers report, and there are flares of activity in the brain's pleasure centers when unwelcome information is being rejected. 'Everything we know about cognition suggests that, when faced with a contradiction, we use the rational regions of our brain to think about it, but that was not the case here,' said Dr. Drew Estheimer, a psychologist at Emory and lead author of the study. . . ."

The Kerry profile in the Sunday magazine, "John Kerry's Undeclared War," characterized the candidate as uncertain about foreign policy; the cover photograph was even less flattering.

* During the Republican hegemony in place during my tenure, the only remnant of Clinton coverage that floated past me was brought to my attention by a woman named Marcia Lewis, who happened to be Monica Lewinsky's mother. Why, she wondered, did The Times insist on referring to the "Monica Lewinsky scandal"? Her daughter, she pointed out, was an intern in her early twenties; the person with whom she had become involved was the most powerful man in the world. "Whose scandal was it?" she asked. This two-time Clinton voter thought she had a point.

Political Bias at The Times? Two Counterarguments.

. . .

October 17, 2004

LAST week, I argued in this space that The Times is not systematically biased in its campaign coverage—a position that necessarily invites rebuttal. I consequently asked two prominent critics of The Times to take a whack at it. Leading off, Todd Gitlin, a professor of journalism and sociology at Columbia University and the author most recently of "Letters to a Young Activist"; batting second, Bob Kohn, a California lawyer and the author of "Journalistic Fraud: How The New York Times Distorts the News and Why It Can No Longer Be Trusted."

By TODD GITLIN

THE Times is not pro-Bush in the way that The Washington Times is pro-Bush, slamming John Kerry with Vietnam falsehoods week after week.

But The Times's decorous approach to the news has often helped President Bush in three significant ways: by equating his gross deceptions with Mr. Kerry's minor lapses; by omitting or burying news of administration activities and their consequences; and by missing the deep pattern of Mr. Bush's prejudices and malfeasances.

First of all, The Times's news columns are loath to call untruth untruth. (Space being short, I will skip over the nice question of when Mr. Bush is knowingly lying, when he is half-lying, when he is clumsily improvising, when he is deluding himself and when he is asserting what a reasonable person would know to be untrue.) Stenography often substitutes for research. Look at The Times at its most pungent—a rare roundup piece that landed on Page A19, Oct. 8, headlined: "In His New Attacks, Bush Pushes Limit on the Facts."

The article explains that "the White House has charted new ground with the sweep of its negative campaigning," taking its "attacks to a blistering new level," so that, "several analysts say, Mr. Bush pushed the limits of subjective interpretation and offered exaggerated or what some Democrats said were distorted accounts."

New level? Pushed the limits? What some Democrats said? The authors, Adam Nagourney and Richard W. Stevenson, offer evidence that President Bush exaggerated and distorted what Mr. Kerry meant by pre-emptive attacks' passing a global test. Then why mince words?

The Times's generosity toward government claims about Al Qaeda–Saddam connections and Iraqi W.M.D. has been amply documented, even, belatedly, in The Times itself. But on other fronts as well, The Times cuts Mr. Bush plenty of slack. One reason is that The Times, like other top media, scants the substance of the candidates' views in favor of their tactics and strategies. But when the president is a serial obfuscator and fabricator—not to say flip-flopper—this inside-dopester coverage works to his advantage.

Consider the disproportion between The Times's attention to Mr. Kerry's Vietnam battles and its inattention to Mr. Bush's business career of failing upward: improving his fortunes while his companies failed. How did he succeed in making big money when his oil company, Harken Energy, nearly collapsed? Too often, as the president himself might say, Mr. Bush can run, and The Times lets him hide.

So can Vice President Dick Cheney. Though Mr. Cheney has denied it, Halliburton, during the years he headed it, did $73 million of business with Saddam Hussein. The Washington Post looked into the story thoroughly. Over the past four years, The Times hasn't once done so in its news pages. Would The Times have let Bill Clinton get away with trading with tyrants? Wouldn't such a story have been at least as newsworthy as the disastrous Whitewater investment that the paper examined endlessly on its front page?

Indeed, The Times frequently buries revelations of administration malfeasance. Coverage of declining environmental standards is spotty, though sometimes extensive. The subject of climate change has made the front page seven times in the past two years; some will think this more than enough, but if the issues are really as grave as most scientists believe, it's the least a serious newspaper ought to do.

Third, The Times leaves dots unconnected. The Republican Party doesn't incidentally or occasionally stoop to please big corporations. It does so systematically. The administration and its Congressional allies regularly permit lobbyists to write the regulations by which they themselves are to be regulated. Last May, The Denver Post reported: "President Bush has installed more than 100 top officials who were once lobbyists, attorneys or spokespeople for the industries they oversee." But the infrequent Times article citing examples of such foxhenhouse cohabitation in coal, say, does not refer to examples from drug, hospital, utility, oil and gas and other sectors (as did The Post).

It was refreshing, nevertheless, to see The Times last week devoting front page space to the Senate's $136 billion corporate tax cut. Where are the similar rundowns of who benefits from other government policies? True, an on-again, off-again watch-dog is better than no watchdog at all. But Times readers should not have to settle for a watchdog with laryngitis.

By BOB KOHN

IS The New York Times systematically biased against President Bush? Of course it is.

I was recently introduced to a radio audience as someone who hates The New York Times. Hate was too strong a word; I love this newspaper, and if you are reading this, you love it, too. To love this paper is to care what happens to it. We want it to be there for us—always—especially every Sunday morning with that cup of coffee, and we hope to hand the experience down to our children, so that they too may be informed and delighted by its pages.

Several weeks ago, Daniel Okrent, this paper's public editor, courageously stated the obvious: of course The New York Times is a liberal newspaper. And he wasn't just talking about an edi-torial page he finds "thoroughly saturated in liberal theology" or the Sunday carvings of Frank Rich, who "slices up" President Bush and friends in the Arts & Leisure section.

More incisively, the public editor demonstrated how The Times—in its purportedly objective news pages—leans left on the social issues, showing by example how The Times presents same-sex marriages in a tone that approaches "cheerleading." Now, turning to politics, the public editor would have us believe there is no systematic bias against either presidential candidate.

This divide-and-conquer approach—separating The Times's advocacy of liberal causes from its campaign coverage—masks the powerful means this paper employs to undermine the Bush campaign.

Same-sex marriage, abortion, stem-cell research, gun control, environmental regulation, capital punishment and faith-based initiatives—are these not issues in the presidential election? Hoist with his own petard, the public editor has already demonstrated how The Times, by advocating its liberal social agenda, systematically slants the news against President Bush.

Now, let's assume that what the public editor asserted here last week is correct—that The Times's campaign coverage, viewed in its entirety, is providing a fair presentation of President Bush's views. What does such fairness mean when the very same news pages are advocating the opposite?

To readers, it means that President Bush is wrong, not only because the editorial page of The Times says he's wrong, but because the president's views fly in the face of what are being presented as objective facts. No technique of bias is more powerful—more useful as a means of influence—than presenting a candidate's unadulterated views through a prism of advocacy passed off as hard news.

And the practice is by no means limited to the social questions. The justification for the Iraq war, now John Kerry's top campaign issue, provides a poignant backdrop for how The Times systematically uses its front page to undercut President Bush's credibility. In fact, the bias against Bush on Iraq has become so acute that two of the paper's own Op-Ed columnists have established a virtual annex to the public editor's office.

When The Times in a banner headline this summer declared "Panel Finds No Qaeda-Iraq Tie," William Safire fired back: "All wrong." While Republicans charged The Times with bias, Safire blamed the Sept. 11 commission. I would have gone along with Safire had the paper's editors corrected the story in a typeface as large as the one they had used to distort it. They haven't. Not even in small type.

When The Times front page recently proclaimed, "U.S. Report Finds Iraqis Eliminated Illicit Arms in 90s," David Brooks, referring to the general media coverage, came unglued: "I have never in my life seen a government report so distorted by partisan passions." Despite Mr. Brooks's efforts, a report that made it "crystal clear" why Saddam Hussein had to go instead became a talking point for Kerry—courtesy of The New York Times.

What kind of newspaper will we leave to our children? If you still don't believe it's the wrong kind, put yourself in my slippers: imagine how your Sunday morning coffee encounters with The Times would sour if the front page of the Arts & Leisure section were turned over to, say, Ann Coulter. Is that the kind of paper you want? That's the paper you have.

A Correction

. . .

October 24, 2004

MANY people were distressed by my mention of various readers' names in my Oct. 10 column, and particularly by my singling out one who had sent an especially vituperative message to Times reporter Adam Nagourney. My policy: I consider all messages sent to me, or forwarded to me by Times staff members, to be public unless the writer has stipulated otherwise.

Every message sent to my office gets an instant response asking if the writer wishes his or her name to be withheld. No signed comments are published without confirmation of authorship, either by telephone or e-mail.

I published the name of the man who wrote to Nagourney for the same reason that newspapers publish the names of people who commit other grievous acts. The man who vandalizes a church, say, doesn't want his name in the paper either. But I don't think his wishes should protect him from public responsibility for what he has done.

Same goes for public editors: I was wrong to call the reader a coward; that was engaging in the same debased discourse that I condemn. I apologize.

. . .

Of course, "John Smith" was not the name of Nagourney's correspondent from San Francisco—the original column, as published, had his real name, which apparently led to his being subjected to anonymous threats and harassment, and this in turn led to an outpouring of anger that still hadn't entirely abated more than a year later. Critics said I had no right to mention the name in print, especially when the writer had specifically asked me not to (my office had been in touch with him to verify his authorship—a standard procedure for anyone who publishes reader letters). I had used the power of an enormous institution to crush a helpless individual. The message—forwarded to me by Adam Nagourney—hadn't even been addressed to me. "Smith was an individual engaged in a private correspondence," wrote a woman on a Web site called "The Common Ills." Mike Peterson, a journalist from upstate New York, wrote that I had misused the "disproportionate amount of power" that automatically accrues to someone writing for a newspaper. Even my old friend Peter Applebome, a Times metro columnist, thought I had stepped over a line.

Perhaps I did—but I still have this nagging feeling that people ought to accept responsibility for their actions. Smith's message wasn't a piece of mere nastiness; it was hateful and vile. (Smith had not told Nagourney, that "he hoped his son got drafted," as one Web poster put it.) I deleted the man's name from this version of the column, and this account of the controversy, not because anyone told me to but because my point has been made, and I've no reason to afflict him any further. Neither was I "censured" by The Times for having published the name, as some bloggers, including Sam Seder of Majority Report Radio, have reported.

Seder (who wrote in his blog that I should feel free to mention his name) launched his piece about my transgression with the headline "Fuck You Nagourney and Fuck You Okrent." A few lines later he called Nagourney a "piece of cowardly shit," while I was a "cowardly piece of shit." I still don't understand the difference.

Analysts Say Experts Are Hazardous to Your Newspaper

. . .

October 31, 2004

ANY reader of this newspaper knows how The Times likes to invoke the wisdom of people identified as "experts" or "analysts," but until I counted their presence the other day I had no idea how crowded with expertise the paper was. On Tuesday alone, such seers and sages were rolled out 33 times. In a few cases they even added useful wisdom or perspective. In many others, though, their presence may have achieved the opposite of what the writers intended: they made readers wonder whether they were being conned.

I'm not talking about the partisan political operatives whose apparent license to spin, sneer and smear devalues so much political reporting. I'm concerned with those experts rolled out to explain or contextualize complex matters (as reporters who use them would argue) or to confirm what the reporter already thinks (as far too many readers believe). There are a lot of issues that connect to this subject—including the Godzilla of journalism issues, objectivity. But today I'll stick to two: establishing the credibility of named experts, and obliterating the very presence of the unnamed kind.

Bad reporters find experts by calling up university press relations officials or brokerage research departments and saying, in effect, "Gimme an expert"; some academic publicity machines send out rosters, complete with phone numbers, e-mail addresses and areas of expertise, so that the lazy journalist doesn't even have to make that first call. Really bad reporters, paradoxically, work a little harder: knowing the conclusions they want to arrive at, they seek out experts who just happen to agree with them. Give me a position, and I'll find you an expert to support it—and not just an expert but one with an institutional affiliation sounding so dignified it could make a nobleman genuflect. Give me a Center for the Study of . . . , an Institute for the Advancement of . . . , or an American Council on . . . , and often as not I'll give you an organization whose special interests are as sharply defined as its name is not.

Good reporters work a beat hard, talking constantly to people who can speak authoritatively, and over time find those who can be trusted to speak honestly as well. Business reporters, confronted with brain-numbing columns of numbers, turn to equity analysts to lead them to the light. Reporters on the health and drug beats, charged with picking their way through the competing claims of drug companies and advocacy groups or sorting out the contradictory results of different clinical trials, seek out experts to provide clarity and balance.

Finding truly disinterested parties is difficult, and often the most informed experts can be intimately connected to the matter under consideration. With the notable exception of the Prudential Equity Group, which does not allow its analysts to talk to the press, most investment banks and brokerages have reason to think that press appearances make for good publicity (except, of course, when the appearance occurs in a courtroom). According to Times business columnist Gretchen Morgenson—I'm entitled to my expert, too—"far too many Wall Street analysts are megaphones for corporate management" yet they're "trotted out in far too many stories, mouthing what management said about the quarterly performance, adding little value." And all too often touting a stock they own, or knocking one they're selling short.

At least Times policy for business reporters requires disclosure of conflicts when quoting self-interested analysts. (I just wish the policy were followed more consistently.) A recent memo to his staff from the business editor, Lawrence Ingrassia, reminded reporters and editors that it should be "standard operating procedure" to tell readers if someone quoted in an article has a self-interest in play. On the science desk, all reporters received an eight-point memo this past August articulating rules and regulations designed to ensure that similar disclosure occurs in that department.

The long-overdue science policy may be the reason why I've been hearing less often lately from Merrill Goozner of the Center for Science in the Public Interest. For months, though, Goozner and his colleagues at the nutrition research and advocacy group have brought to my attention comments in The Times from experts about drugs marketed by companies who have paid them consulting fees on other projects. You might think the solution would be some more aggressive hunting for disinterested experts. But pure science is hard to find these days. In 1980, private industry financed 30 percent of all clinical drug trials; two decades later, federal funding has not kept pace, and the drug companies and associated businesses are today responsible for well over 60 percent of this sort of research.

Not surprisingly, they tend to finance the most competent of the researchers, which poses a conundrum for the science editor, Laura Chang. She notes: "The potential for conflicts of interest among scientists are real and growing in the current research structure, and we make a point to ask about such conflicts. But sometimes scientists who receive drug company money do useful, sound research." The Center for Science in the Public Interest maintains a Web site that provides details on various researchers' connections to specific sponsors, but Times reporter Gardiner Harris says, "I keep intending to ask that they put together a Web site of experts who are free of conflict."

Because it's as hard as it is to find the truly independent scientist, it's important for the paper to tell its readers about any and all conflicts. Reporters fear that complex disclosure statements might soil their prose. But at the very least, editors could make a habit of inserting a parenthetical statement informing readers that full details on possible conflicts appear on The Times's Web site. Alternatively, readers might make a habit of wondering why they don't.

That would be futile, though, when we don't know which analysts are doing the analyzing, or which experts are providing the expertise. On Tuesday, 17 of those 33 articles cited the wisdom of "experts," "industry experts," "military budget experts" and the like, but failed to name—or even describe—a single one.

In "Discord on North Korea as Powell Finishes East Asia Trip," Steven R. Weisman, The Times's chief diplomatic correspondent, wrote of current negotiations that "the impasse is not likely to be broken soon, many experts say, at least until the American presidential election is over." When I asked him about his posse of experts, he acknowledged that "you caught me using some lazy writing, probably because I was on deadline and exhausted from jet lag."

I'm grateful for Weisman's honesty, and would like to think I'd get similar responses from writers who in just a few days last week told Times readers what "political analysts say" about declining crime rates, "industry analysts" about Internet marketing of car parts and "analysts in Damascus" about the Syria-Iraq border. I'd have much more faith in assertions attributed to these ghosts if they were instead made in the authors' own voices. Weisman, who's been writing about international affairs for more than 20 years, told me that he felt confident that his North Korea characterization was accurate, and that he should have written a phrase like "the impasse appears unlikely to be broken soon."

Fine with me; one reason I read a paper with ambitions like The Times's is because I want the expertise of its writers to lead me through complex matters. The contrary argument holds that, absent attribution, the writer is only providing an opinion, but attribution to unnamed experts is no attribution at all. When a writer offers an interpretation in his own voice, he's putting his own reputation behind it. Writers (and newspapers) who are often wrong may soon lose their reputations. But writers (and newspapers) too timid or too disingenuous to assert what they know to be true may not deserve those reputations in the first place.

I know this view may be at odds with conventional views of journalistic objectivity, so I'll address those in my next column—unless I'm distracted by disputed coverage of, say, a disputed election.

Unattributed Source Watch: Last Sunday, in "Scenarios: What if They Lose? Calls to Reinvent a Party," Adam Nagourney wrote that Howard Dean "is said to have told associates that he believes an antiwar candidate would have fared better against Mr. Bush." Dean wrote me to insist he has not said anything of the sort to associates; Nagourney told me he relied on "Dean associates who said they heard Dr. Dean express this feeling."

Without a name attached to it, this just isn't news.

. . .

Mixed reaction on this one within The Times, beginning with anger from the reporter who had relied on "analysts in Damascus." Although I hadn't cited his name, or even the date or headline of his piece, he wrote to say that it was difficult enough to report in the Middle East without being stabbed in the back from home. Others said they'd love to be able to drop the invisible analysts and experts, but their editors wouldn't let them. Usually, I was told by more than a few reporters, editors said readers were entitled to know how reporters knew what they knew. As if "analysts said" told the readers anything at all.

I don't think this is a battle that will ever be won, but I do sense an increased willingness on the part of some reporters to state in their own voices what they know to be true—and, apparently, a growing willingness on the part of editors to let them do it. Obviously, it's easier to get away with this sort of thing in a columnist's voice: as far as I know, my assertion that private funding for drug research had doubled since 1980 didn't lead anyone to squawk about my failure to cite a source. If you trust the columnist, you trust his facts. (*Q.v.* Paul Krugman, about whom more later.)

But news reporters should have no problem speaking with authority—if, of course, they have earned authority. Once again I turn to the example of the late David Rosenbaum. In a tribute to Rosenbaum published on nytimes.com, deputy national editor David Firestone wrote this:

"One of his greatest lessons was reminding his colleagues that they had brains and memories and should not be afraid to use them. Because he had seen so much and understood it all, David could confidently make assertions in his stories and Q-heds [the insider's term for a piece slugged "News Analysis"] that made weak-kneed editors blanch. Here's a classic from 2003:

"'When all the proposals are tallied in the budget President Bush submitted today, they amount to the most ambitious changes in government operations that any president has put forward in decades.'

"Another reporter might have felt obliged to get someone at Brookings to make that statement. But he saw no need to clutter bald truths with needless attributions."

It's Good to Be Objective. It's Even Better to Be Right.

. . .

November 14, 2004

IN my Oct. 31 column, I took a crude hatchet to The Times's wimpy reliance on "experts," "analysts" and other commentators whose words may decorate a given article but often provide neither coherence nor much more than the illusion of balance.

Surprisingly, I didn't hear from any experts determined to defend their positions in the address books of Times reporters. Maybe that's because some of them have established impregnable beachheads: Prof. Stephen Gillers of N.Y.U. has made 24 appearances in The Times so far this year (five under his own name, the rest in pieces by Times writers); Tom Wolzien of Sanford C. Bernstein and Company has shown up 28 times; and the inevitable Gene Russianoff has appeared fully 46 times, in pieces by 23 different writers. Russianoff is a "staff lawyer for the Straphangers Campaign, a transit advocacy group," a label The Times has slapped on him the way Homer glued "gray-eyed goddess" to Athena.

Russianoff has been the Oracle of the Subways since . . . well, almost since there were straps for straphangers. (New to the city 35 years ago, I thought the word was pronounced "straffengers," with a soft g.)

Times reporters assure me that he is reliable, honest and well informed. I believe this to be true, as I'm confident it is of Gillers and Wolzien as well, and maybe even of Hall of Famer Norman Quotestein, a.k.a. Ornstein, of the American Enterprise Institute.

But if I believe these experts are all good and wise, it's because I believe the reporters who tell me so. Why, I wonder, do I need the analysis of an expert or the expertise of the analyst, when it's the writer I'm finally compelled to rely upon in any case?

In fact, there are often good reasons to turn to experts — for instance, when the desk dumps an assignment in your lap three hours before deadline, on a subject you know little about. But there's also the need to protect that precious piece of the journalistic ethos, objectivity — in the words of one deputy news editor, Philip Corbett, "not only a worthy goal, but probably our most important one: the goal that underpins most of our other ideals, like fairness and accuracy." And reporters think that getting an "expert" to comment adds the aura of objectivity.

In recent years, though, the concept of objectivity has taken a bit of a beating. Some journalists (and critics of journalists) argue that it is in fact unachievable; we all bring our experiences, sensibilities and innate prejudices to the door, and even the act of attempting to leave them on the stoop will alter our approach.

Besides, you can't police objectivity simply by scouring an article for evidences of bias, imbalance or other taints. Try starting with the headline writer, who is inherently constrained by space yet charged with distilling essences from what is often an extremely complex stew — a necessarily reductive act that can't help but deform nuances. Then there's the editor who determines placement: "Ex-C.I.A. Chief Nets $500,000 on Talk Circuit" would have been interesting on A26 last Thursday; on A1, it carried a suggestion of scandal.

And before an article finds its way into the paper—sometimes long before—the decision to assign it is itself influenced by personal predisposition. "In Health Care, Gap Between Rich and Poor Persists, W.H.O. Says," also in Thursday's paper, was a discretionary choice. It made it into print on one desk editor's watch, but could have been just as plausibly ignored had someone else, with even a slightly different worldview, been sitting in the same chair that day. As for major investigative pieces, they generally start not because they are propelled by a piece of news but because a reporter or an editor determines—often out of white-hot passion—that "This is important. This is something we must do." Most investigations, by nature, carry a point a view.

When it comes to objectivity, then, the determinative factor is who's doing the determining. In any enterprise, there are few decisions as important as whom you hire and promote; in a newspaper, where every choice has meaning, it's virtually the only thing that matters.

The historical roots of objectivity as a journalistic ideal suggest there's more to it than parking one's opinions at the curb. Before it was applied specifically to journalism, the idea of objectivity grew out of a variety of early 20th century intellectual movements recognizing that somewhere in the swamps of conscious and unconscious thought, people could be biased without knowing it. By the 1920s Walter Lippmann and others were arguing that reporters could combat unconscious bias by applying scientific method and its "sense of evidence" to journalistic inquiry. Only by the rigorous testing of hypotheses could the investigator—the journalist—reach reliable, bias-free conclusions. The key word, and the one that has disappeared from the definition over several generations, is "conclusions." Fairness requires the consideration of all sides of an issue; it doesn't require the uncritical reporting of any. Yet even the best reporters will sometimes display a disappointing reluctance to set things straight.

That's why I was so exasperated last June, shortly after Ronald Reagan's death, to see a classic balancing statement pop up and sit there unchallenged, in an article by Robin Toner and Robert Pear. "Critics See a Reagan Legacy Tainted by AIDS, Civil Rights and Union Policies" (June 9, 2004) included this: "Gary Bauer, Mr. Reagan's domestic policy adviser for the last two years of his administration, countered that spending on AIDS research rose under Mr. Reagan." Bauer's comment may have balanced what Reagan's detractors had to say, but the writers' failure to challenge it denied readers an objective truth: AIDS funding couldn't help but rise under Reagan, because there was no AIDS funding before Reagan—in fact, there was no AIDS before Reagan.

I suspect that when writers don't comment on specious statements, it's usually because they worry that any challenge might itself seem tendentious. And it's true that many readers do find conclusive statements objectionable. Reporter Jodi Wilgoren provoked a flood of complaints when she described John Kerry in April as "a social loner" without attributing her characterization to anyone—as if her own experience covering the senator, and discussing him with scores of his friends and associates, were not evidence enough. Similarly, readers complained when

Neil Lewis, in "Mixed Results for Bush in Battles Over Judges" (Oct. 22), followed a description of the president's early judicial appointments with this: "There could have been no clearer signal that Mr. Bush intended to follow the pattern set by his father and President Ronald Reagan of shifting the courts rightward and reaping the political benefit of pleasing social conservatives." Those who objected argued that it was the writer's opinion, and improper—even though, as one acknowledged, it was undeniably true.

But haven't we reached the point where denying the reader what a writer knows to be true is far more unfair than including it? I was delighted when, in "After 6 Months, Tyco Prosecutors Close Case Against Ex-Officials" (March 18), Alex Berenson described the prosecutor's case as "bewildering," "tedious" and having "rarely been presented in a straightforward way"—a vision of the trial that would have been utterly unavailable had Berenson not dared to offer conclusive characterizations based on his own observations. On a much larger scale, I was dismayed when a reporter for The Wall Street Journal in a letter to friends (later passed around the Internet) described the horrors of life in Baghdad, and was criticized in some quarters for thereby jeopardizing her impartiality. But what she described was based on indisputable first-hand experience. If there was a journalistic offense here, it was that readers of The Journal had been denied knowledge of what this reporter knew to be true. Whom did that serve?

I shouldn't knock The Journal, which admirably allows its reporters far more authority to make assertions in their own voices than most American dailies, and which hasn't asked me to be its public editor. My beat's here on West 43rd Street, where some of the very best journalists in the country keep what they know off the page because they've been tied up by an imprecise definition of objectivity. I'm not calling for unsupported opinion, but for a flowering of facts—not just those recorded stenographically or uttered by experts, but the sort that arise from experience, knowledge and a brave willingness to stand behind what you know to be true.

. . .

There's no question that discussion of what constitutes objectivity, whether it's attainable and whether it's even desirable is growing more and more common among journalists. This is inescapable in a changing media world in which predisposition and opinion are the starting points for the news and information sources that many Americans are increasingly turning to—namely, the blogosphere. The best characterization of the distinction between the much-reviled "mainstream media" and most online-only media is one I first heard used by Newsweek columnist Jonathan Alter: what we old farts are aiming for (if not always achieving) is "fact-based journalism," while much of what the Web values usually begins with opinion. Whether we mainstreamers achieve our goal may be arguable, but of the Web's attainments in the realm of opinion there can be no doubt. As Christopher Hitchens has said, "People increasingly prefer their bias to be straight."

I don't know whether the piece won over very many journalists who continue to use objectivity as their standard, but it wasn't very useful for the notoriety of Stephen Gillers and Tom Wolzien: for what it's worth, in the 12 months after the column ran, Gillers was quoted only six times (compared to 24 in the previous year), Wolzien only four (compared to 28). The indispensable Gene Russianoff—and a reporter and a columnist both insisted to me that he was indeed indispensable—saw his quote count drop off much less sharply, from 46 to 35.

I know that I said in the essay that opens this book that David Cay Johnston's attack over my outside affiliations caused my worst day as public editor. Three others could have been contenders:

- The day I received a nine paragraph e-mail message alleging factual errors, false charges and conflict of interest in a book review—from Jayson Blair. As it happened, the review did have two factual errors in it, and The Times promptly published a correction.
- The day that I had to acknowledge that the film-making bully Harvey Weinstein was right about a complaint.
- And the day after this column was published, when newscaster Lou Dobbs, in the midst of his frenzied campaign against outsourcing, called to let me know how much he liked it.

One source who deserved citation in this piece but did not receive it was Tom Rosenstiel, director of the Project for Excellence in Journalism, who gave me a quick lesson in the origins of the idea of objectivity; my apologies.

Arts Editors and Arts Consumers: Not on the Same Page

. . .

November 28, 2004

IT landed on my desk a few weeks ago with an echoing thump that could have awakened Brooks Atkinson. On the cover it said

"Save the Listings: Restore the 'Arts & Leisure Guide' to the Sunday New York Times." Inside, 615 pages carried 5,000 Internet-gathered signatures, many of them accompanied by bits of testimony variously beseeching, enraged or tearful.

Just a few weeks earlier, The Times had tossed the venerable columns of agate type that had filled so many pages of the Arts & Leisure section for so long, with as many as 300 cultural events acknowledged, however briefly, in a single edition. In what seemed to be their place, a single page featured slightly more than 20 cultural items, tucked in and around some less than enlightening photographs, under headlines so opaque as to be incomprehensible. Down the side of the page, in very large type, marched the days of the week. The items aligned next to each described a few events or productions scheduled for those particular days, but in several cases they were events that could also be enjoyed (or endured) on many other days. To many readers, this was not just confusing; it was replacing a symphony with a jingle.

Editors reacted to the petition, I soon learned, the way editors almost always react when readers rise against a long-planned, well-intended innovation: a little dumbfounded, a little defensive, a little dismissive. I sort of understood. The replacement of the old listings with "The Guide," as the new feature was unfortunately titled (the name was too similar to the one it had replaced, suggesting that it was the original's equivalent), has been but one part of a mammoth remaking of the cultural coverage of The Times. The editors' exasperation brought to mind a favorite quotation, from the British psychoanalyst Wilfred Bion: "Why do you hate me? I haven't done anything to help you."

In this case, the editors had helped more than enough to

earn the readers' disapproval. At a time when most American newspapers are slashing arts coverage (according to a study conducted by the National Arts Journalism Project at Columbia, from 1998 to 2003 the space given to cultural coverage in major American papers dropped by roughly 25 percent), The Times had gone in the opposite direction. The revamped cultural report now included more than seven additional pages per week. Twenty staff positions were created to produce the new content and improve the old. Full-time reporters had been put on the architecture, classical music and theater beats, and additional reporters will soon supplement the art, movie and television groups. Critics have been newly assigned to experimental arts, the Internet, and "nonart museums and exhibitions" (there must be a better phrase than that), and some lustrous new hires—notably Manohla Dargis on movies and Charles Isherwood on theater—have brought an added gleam to existing positions.

But all that the readers seemed to notice was what was gone.

There's an unfortunate tendency in the newspaper business to disparage a petition like this one as an "organized" effort, as if only random, disconnected cries of pain from despairing readers should be heeded. I've also heard this particular protest dismissed as "commercially inspired" by self-interested arts presenters and promoters who are worried that the box office will suffer, and have disingenuously conspired to rouse the masses. This glib dismissal suggests that the people who buy tickets are unwitting suckers, seduced by scoundrels. It doesn't recognize a basic market reality: if people show up to pay for a ticket, it's presumably because there's something in it for them.

Inside The Times, there were several knocks on the old listings: They were dull. They were so absent critical judgment that readers, said Arts & Leisure editor Jodi Kantor, were "lost in a sea of names and titles." Culture editor Jonathan Landman believed they were "cryptic and hard to use for all but highly expert arts consumers." Kantor, Landman and others assert that because much of the information was available elsewhere, the old listings were redundant, and therefore vestigial.

There may be something to these criticisms (I'll certainly go along with the dullness charge), but each bears the scent of journalistic arrogance. Journalists like to do journalism; they're much less excited by the compilation of largely uninflected data. The old listings required great care, but they called for neither enterprising reporting nor graceful style nor, really, for critical judgment. Kantor told me that "we find it hard to believe that those listings, so skimpy they didn't even list prices, created much of an audience for events." But that "lost in a sea of names and titles" argument is refuted by the results. If the listings didn't create much of an audience, why are audience-chasing producers so upset that they'd join, or even inspire, an organized protest effort?

Landman's only-for-experts argument is simply condescending. It also sounds like the view of someone who's not a terribly avid arts consumer. Sure, the average reader could stumble through much of the listings pages puzzled by references to obscure painters or outré theater companies or little-known dance troupes. But that same "inexpert" reader could open the paper on a Sunday morning, see a reference to a Chopin recital at a church in Murray Hill that afternoon, and extract a very pleasant day from it. Additionally, what Landman imprecisely calls "highly expert arts consumers" are not such rare creatures in New York. If you've already made the commitment to peruse the jazz listings, then it's likely you already know quite a bit about George Coleman and Lou Donaldson and Steve Turre. That doesn't take an expert; that takes a fan, and this city—cultural capital of the nation—is home to thousands upon thousands of fans.

Culture is "an area of coverage in which our role is very nearly unique," executive editor Bill Keller wrote to a protesting reader. "Nobody," he added, "comes close to the range and ambition of what we do—hip-hop and the Philharmonic, television and opera, Hollywood and Broadway, books, painting, dance." In fact, he might have added, if you're sitting in any New York concert hall or theater, the people around you are bound together not just by their interest in what's on stage, but by their readership of this newspaper. Maybe Kantor or Landman would like to tell my 74-year-old friend Schulte, a lifelong Times reader and stone-cold vocal music maniac, that he ought to be planning his week in the pages of Time Out New York instead.

Here's the good news, Listings Protesters of America: uncharacteristically for an institution that is slow to change and usually inflexible once it has done so, the editors are prepared to alter their course. Bill Keller says, "We are listening hard to readers who still prefer the old system in hopes of finding a compromise that suits their needs." Landman and Kantor are directing a serious re-examination of the new listings, and working with their colleagues to improve them.

Particular attention is being paid to the extensive listings in the Friday Weekend section. Editors saw these as the primary substitute for, and improvement over, the old Sunday listings; they're based on reviews written by staff critics, they're highly informative, and they offer substantive judgments. They're also devoted to productions that take place on weekends (logically enough) and that have already opened and been reviewed. Weekend editor Myra Forsberg says she and her colleagues are working to find ways to accommodate midweek events and to preview one-night and short-run productions.

They're looking to find room for more, too. I gather that individual listings will soon be shorter, creating room for events that can't now make the cut. No one could have enjoyed reading all that agate type in the old listings, but comments in the petition and my conversations with readers suggest that most culture consumers would exchange a little eyestrain for news of more events. And at least two full Sunday pages are ready to be conscripted for the cause. If the old listings were dull compilations, duplicative of information available elsewhere, how can The Times possibly justify the chicken-scratchings that fill Friday's full-page "Movie Clock"?

Then there's The Guide—well intended, and somewhat improved with each passing week, but nonetheless an ill-conceived failure. Kantor says the range of items included "is a testament to the richness of New York's cultural life." But it's also testament to a narrowing down so severe, and so individualistic, that its arbitrariness is unnerving. I've got nothing against Choire Sicha, the author; the enormous range of arts events in New York filtered through the sensibility of a single individual wouldn't be any more useful if the sensibility was Edmund Wilson's. Interesting, sure, but it's simply wrong-headed to represent it as useful. And for a newspaper that considers itself the leader in cultural coverage, "useful" is an admirable goal.

. . .

Nothing I wrote in 18 months made Bill Keller angrier than this piece did (so far as I know: while he might have kept his anger to himself over other columns, he let me have it with both barrels on this one). I think this was partly because Keller and the other masthead editors had already been pretty badly beaten up by complaining readers, staff members, and—yes, inescapably— advertisers. It was also because, during my reporting, Jonathan Landman and I had gotten into a pretty nasty e-mail exchange, and Keller became convinced that I had used the column to retaliate.

He may have been right, at least in the sense that my language might have gotten ramped up because Landman and I had—not for the first time—raised our voices at each other (if you can raise voices in e-mail). But I believe the substance of the piece was absolutely on target. So did many members of the culture department—by midweek, quite a few of them, including three of the paper's first-string critics, had called or written me to express their gratitude.

Within a few months the revised Friday listings included many more items and covered the entire week ahead, and "The Guide" was replaced by a useful subject-by-subject preview of the week by Times critics.

I addressed my unfortunate use of deprecatory language in my next column, but it's worth relating a conversation I had with Keller after the storm had passed. In our original post-column exchange, he had excoriated me for being "fundamentally unfair"; said that my treatment of Landman and Jodi Kantor had been "the cheapest of cheap shots"; and complained that I had not given the editors credit for the extensive changes in arts coverage, thereby "render[ing] the rejuvenation of culture coverage a net failure." To this last point, I had replied, essentially, "go back and look at the fourth paragraph."

Keller, in turn, said that I had thrown in an ostensibly balancing

paragraph that was "grudging at best." When we discussed it calm-
ly and collegially several weeks later, I asked how often he had
heard the same complaint from story subjects displeased with the
paper's treatment of them and unmollified by the carefully placed
paragraph acknowledging the complainant's side of the story. I
doubt either of us could possibly count that high.

Now It's Time for The Times to Talk About The Times

. . .

December 12, 2004

TWO weeks ago, my column on The Times's arts listings
brought gratitude from those who agreed with me and anger
and derision, leavened with a few reasonable points of argument, from those who did not. I wouldn't expect it any other
way. But among those who pounced on me here at the paper
were some who were provoked by my use of "glib," "arrogance"
and "condescending" to portray the attitude of the culture
editors.

Those who took me to task included some Times editors and
writers who agreed with my position on the listings changes, but
found my choice of words indelicate. They may be right. If I
were a better writer I would have followed the ancient dictum
"show, don't tell"—let readers come to their own conclusions
instead of leading them with my own loaded characterizations.
(While I'm in garment-rending mode, I want to correct a mistaken impression I may have left: when I wrote that "at least two
full Sunday pages are ready to be conscripted for the cause" of

revised listings, that was and is my opinion, and not the position of the editors.)

Sometimes, though, telling can be better than showing, especially when the showing comes as a shock—for instance, when the editors make major changes in what they've been giving readers for decades, and explain neither what they're doing nor why. Instead, angry readers inspire a public editor to take their side, and he (according to the culture editors, at least) proceeds to misrepresent the paper's intentions.

Here's an idea: if the editors did the explaining themselves, maybe I wouldn't have to do it for them.

For decades, the Fraternal Order of Falsely Modest Newspaper People has marched under an indelible banner: "We're not the story," it says. "The story's the story."

While I was reporting the listings column, culture editor Jonathan Landman acknowledged that this might not be the most effective of attitudes. "We tend to shy away from self-promotion in these matters," he wrote in an e-mail message, "preferring to let the paper speak for itself. In the case of the changes in cultural coverage this may be O.K. in the long run, but it was clearly inadequate in the short."

I suppose the speak-for-itself trope made sense back when the image of the American newspaper was embodied in a freckled newsboy tossing a rolled paper onto a porch hung with geraniums. But in an age when the press is so widely regarded as a predatory and uncontrolled beast, the failure to allow readers a view inside the cage can only aggravate their worst suspicions.

This doesn't apply just to format changes, like the culture listings. Not a week goes by when mail from readers doesn't contain earnest queries about any number of practices and standards that a little explaining could make glowingly clear.

Some newspapers do a very good job at this. James H. Smith, the executive editor of The Record-Journal in Meriden, Conn., often uses his biweekly column to explain his paper's practices: why, for example, it doesn't go out of its way to concentrate on "good news" or why it often includes unsavory details about someone's past in its obituaries.

Mike Pride of The Concord Monitor in New Hampshire has told readers why certain particularly raw photographs were published, and how his editorial board goes about the process of deciding on political endorsements ("Readers Didn't Like These Calls" [@] and "Lynch's Entry: A Governor's Race Between Millionaires Is Not a Good Sign" [@]"). And it's not just small papers that do this: when The Washington Post issued a new set of policies regarding its journalistic practice last March, executive editor Leonard Downie Jr. explained them to readers on Page 1 of the Sunday opinion section. Several years ago, Downie published a step-by-step recounting of his paper's decision to publish a story on the sexual transgressions of Senator Bob Packwood.

At The Times, there have in fact been a few recent instances when information about what the paper is up to has made it into print. Publisher Arthur O. Sulzberger Jr. and chief executive Russell T. Lewis wrote a piece for the Op-Ed page in October ("The Promise of the First Amendment") explaining why the paper supported reporter Judith Miller's refusal to reveal the names of sources to a federal grand jury. In an "Editorial Observer" column just last Sunday ("A Soldier's Story: The Curious Transformation of a Son of Dynasty"), editorial board member Lawrence Downes forthrightly acknowledged that no one on the board had a close relative on active duty in Iraq. Both Op-Ed editor David Shipley ("And Now a

Word From Op-Ed") and letters editor Thomas Feyer ("The Letters Editor and the Reader: Our Compact, Updated" and "To the Reader") in the past year wrote useful articles explaining their policies and practices.

It's no coincidence that each of these examples appeared on the paper's two opinion pages, which by design accommodate personal expression, colloquy with readers and the unembarrassed use of those news-averse words "I" and "we." But at a time when news reporters appear regularly on television talk shows, and editors answer frequent inquiries from other news organizations, they are already acknowledging that some things do need further explaining.

And, sometimes, they admit that a paper that speaks for itself can speak in error. Times reporters and editors often respond to readers who make individual inquiries, frequently acknowledging that, yes, an article missed a nuance, or used phrasing that left an erroneous impression, or otherwise got something wrong—not a correctable fact, perhaps, but an implication or interpretation. The recipient of such a note ends up both grateful and edified, and that is swell for him or her, but doesn't provide any enlightenment for the several hundred thousands of others who may have read the initial story and been misled by it.

Radical notion: why not provide an arena on The Times's Web site where reporters could voluntarily provide this sort of corrective amplification? Some reporters I've raised this with have offered several reasons why this might not work: peer pressure (or, worse and much more likely, pressure from bosses) could make it voluntary in name only; reporters might use the forum to pin blame on editors (or vice versa); the failure of a critical number of staff members to make use of it could make the paper appear even more remote than it already does.

Maybe. But even without erecting this online confessional, The Times's editors could render an enormous service (and save themselves a world of grief) by finding ways to speak directly to the paper's entire readership. The horrifying picture on Page 1, the news story that may seem months old but suddenly appears in print just before a national election, the longstanding Sunday feature that overnight mutates into something else—their impact would be enhanced, not diminished, by candid explanation. Check out posting No. 37 on my Web journal [@] for reporter Richard W. Stevenson's account of how and why The Times seemed to botch the story on Treasury Secretary John Snow's nonresignation last week, and you'll see what I mean.

I think executive editor Bill Keller sees it, too. He told a colleague after the debut of the new listings, "I wish we had taken a block of space in Arts & Leisure the day we moved the listings, and run a 60-point Apocalypse Bold headline: 'Where the hell are my listings!?' over an explanation of the relocation to Friday and the introduction of capsule reviews." I may not have the authority to order up Apocalypse heads, but I do own a block of space, and I use it only three weeks out of every four (two for columns, one for letters). If Keller doesn't call me arrogant, condescending or glib—actually, even if he does—I'm ready to let him rent that last slot.

· · ·

This column was more closely related to the arts listings column than I realized at the time I wrote it. For deciding whether to address readers directly is simply the flip side of determining to what degree a newspaper should *listen* to readers.

I've known few editors who believe that if readers ask for

something, they should be given it; if editors always complied, we might have a popular press that looks very much like a mushrooming portion of the popular press we have: increasingly obsessed with celebrity and self-help, and increasingly devoid of substance. There's also the instinctive response that many editors have to the loud complaints of organized groups: the editors believe (often correctly) that responding to pressure of that nature can often mean sacrificing what is right for what is commercially or politically expedient, so they *really* dig in their heels. (This is a reality that some of those groups who lead periodic boycotts of The Times—most commonly, organizations offended by the paper's Middle East coverage—might bear in mind.)

But in closing your ears to complaint, even to complaint that comes from the well-organized, the threatful or the odious, you build a cocoon that separates a publication not only from a portion of its readership, but from reality as well. A regular column from the editors to the readers might not only address many of the complaints thrown at the establishment press, but might very well forestall them, too.

We're probably never going to see a collection of individual editors' or writers' acknowledgments of error or failure linked to nytimes.com's home page. But if I were appointed public editor again tomorrow,* I would include all of those I received in a special section of my own portion of the Web site. Jim Roberts, the national editor during my tenure, was quick to defend his department when he thought it merited defense, but also willing to acknowledge mistakes. For example, this reply to a reader complaint I had forwarded to him in March 2004:

"I don't know where the 'analysts say' comes from. The writer

---

* Relax—they wouldn't offer, and I wouldn't accept.

is right in pointing out that none are quoted. And the language about tax cuts in 'welfare-type programs' is woefully inexact. The language in the tax cut sentence is also too vague. And while I think it's safe to say the bulk of benefits in the Bush tax cuts went to people making 'higher incomes,' it's way too inexact on a subject that prompts so much political debate.

"In other words," Roberts concluded, "that story should not have appeared that way. I'll share this with other editors on my desk."

I received comments like this one regularly from the more forthright (and less defensive) of Times editors, and would forward them to the readers who had complained. These readers were invariably grateful for both the candor and the care that Roberts demonstrated. A newspaper that publishes a million words a week, as The Times does, can't help but publish stories that could have been better—and saying so is a wonderful way to build up trust with readers. I only wish I had thought to share comments like Roberts's more broadly with readers when I was public editor.

First of All, There's the Continuing Daily Miracle

. . .

December 26, 2004

I REALLY hadn't planned on doing this. Several weeks ago I decided that I'd write a year-end column enumerating a bunch of The Times's crimes and misdemeanors over the past 12 months—the ones I never got around to writing about because

they seemed of insufficient interest to support an entire column, or because they were replays of transgressions I had
already addressed. Or because articles I'd clipped, notated and
misplaced months ago suddenly showed up in my sock drawer.

Then I read "Changing Senate Looks Much Better to
Abortion Foes," by Robin Toner (Dec. 2). This led me to decide
that providing a catalog of sins would be churlish, not to mention unseasonable—and that a very different sort of column
would not only be seasonable, but what I wanted to write.

Toner's piece was a straightforward report illuminating the
potential effect of Republican election victories on forthcoming
abortion-related legislation. Nestled in that sentence are three
words that get right to the core of The Times's mission:
"straightforward," "report" and "illuminating." The piece wasn't
perfect. Toner at one point invoked the speculation of "many
analysts," and I have more tolerance for head lice than for face-
less analysts, but her article did exactly what newspaper journalism is meant to do.

It addressed an extremely contentious issue without betray-
ing the writer's own views. It avoided the euphemistic use of
those specious and self-serving slogans "pro-life" and "pro-
choice," and instead used "anti-abortion" and "abortion rights"
to describe people who are, as it happens, against abortion or are
supporters of abortion rights. It explained the nature of abortion-
related legislation to be debated in the coming Congressional
session, examined the strategies apt to be employed and weighed
the likelihood of passage. People on each side of the issue were
given a fair hearing. From reading Toner's piece, I learned much
about an important public issue.

It was, in this regard, like many, many articles published in
The Times every day. If public editors were assigned the

responsibility of ferreting out the good work done here, The Times would need an army of them. I couldn't even begin to list the paper's major 2004 successes in this space, much less the daily accomplishments of so many. (Still, I can't help mentioning three recent first-magnitude triumphs: Dexter Filkins's gripping and intimate coverage of the battle of Falluja; C.J. Chivers's horrifying account of the slaughter of innocents in Beslan; and Jonathan Franzen's lapel-grabbing review of Alice Munro's new collection of stories.) (Nor could I list the failures, but in just the last two weeks I was led to wonder why on earth the paper would publish a pointless and, to many readers, offensive article on a dog's "bark mitzvah," or a vaguely sourced, piling-on piece about Bernard Kerik's love life, or why, on one day, the paper put four reporters—four!—on the story of an evicted bird.) (O.K.! Enough parentheses! Back to the point!)

The point: beyond the continuing daily miracle of well-considered, well-executed articles, photographs and graphics on every subject under the sun (including, inevitably, a few subjects some of us might do without), The Times this year has done a number of things that affirm its bond with readers. One, I flatter myself to think, is that the editors haven't yet padlocked my office door or given over this space to the Neediest Cases appeal. In fact, executive editor Bill Keller confirmed last week that when my term expires in May, the experiment of a public editorship will move a step closer to permanence with the appointment of a successor, probably to a term longer than my 18 months.

But what the editors and writers and photographers have done themselves is, of course, what's really important, some of it behind the scenes and some in plain sight on the page. For instance:

- The Op-Ed columnists for the first time operate under a formal corrections policy, and if you haven't been seeing tons of corrections on the page, it may be for the best of reasons: judging by the shrinking volume of complaints I receive from readers, columnists' errors have become much less frequent.

- The science desk has instituted a policy of full disclosure of potential conflicts of interest among individuals cited in articles. Execution hasn't been perfect, but it's getting there.

- Those damnable anonymous sources—or "anonymice," in the term coined by my partner-in-whine, media hound Jack Shafer of Slate.com— haven't begun to disappear in meaningful numbers, but at least they've begun to scurry toward the exits. Far fewer are being cited to support matters of small consequence. Additionally, the effort to explain why anonymity is granted to certain sources is accelerating, though I do think the rimshot "because of the sensitivity of the topic" is close to useless—especially when the real reason is "because the White House imposes a gag rule on staff" or "because the senator doesn't want anyone in his office mentioned in the press except himself" or "because the board member wants to advance his own agenda without paying a price for it."

- Recognizing that much of the country doesn't look the way it may sometimes appear from West 43rd Street, the paper assigned reporter David D. Kirkpatrick to cover political and social conservatives. (I will not deny that there is a certain irony in what may seem an affirmative action effort aimed at the political right.) And I'm absolutely convinced that the national desk has been making a clear and increasingly effective effort to scrub stories for evidence of bias.

- Assistant managing editor Allan M. Siegal believes that communication with readers has improved: "I think desks and many individuals are less likely to disregard reader complaints, or to procrastinate in replying, because 'he sees you when you're sleeping, he knows when you're awake, he knows if you've been bad or good, so be good for goodness' sake.'" You're welcome.
- In one small victory for a vocal readership (but a giant leap for the idea of responsiveness), the editors of the Book Review, actually heeding a chorus of complaints, will be dropping their recently instituted "Contributors" box next Sunday and returning writer ID's to the place they belong—on the same page where the writer's review appears.
- Many reporters, most notably those covering extremely sensitive beats, have engaged fruitfully with partisans and other critics. I especially want to single out Jerusalem bureau chief Steven Erlanger, whose every word is strip-searched for nuance and implication by thousands, but who yet shows a willingness to listen; his colleague Greg Myre; and most of the reporters in the Baghdad bureau, whose responsiveness to reader inquiries while they labor under frightening conditions is truly astonishing.

The last development I'll cite is still gestating, but potentially more important than all the others. At the instigation of Bill Keller and under the direction of Al Siegal, several working groups have begun to examine issues at the very heart of journalistic practice: how to improve communication between readers and the editors; whether and how to cut down on the use of anonymous sources and how to justify their use when it's deemed unavoidable; how, in the words of one internal document, to create "a shield against bias"; and how to ensure accuracy.

I can imagine a critic of The Times (or a critic of committees) blowing this off as a public relations dodge, or as a futile exercise doomed to a slow death-by-bureaucracy. But I can tell you that many of the paper's finest and most honorable journalists are engaged in this effort, and the existence of various press reports about it (including, I hope, this one) means that they are to a certain extent doing it in public. I've reprinted the memo that announced the committee's formation on my Web journal (posting No. 40 [@]). Readers should expect results three or four months down the road; if you don't see them, demand them.

And let us all have a fair, accurate and responsive new year.

. . .

I suppose I should not have been surprised when some of my most insistent critics flipped out over this one. One fellow on the right (a borderline sociopath who seems to know no greater pleasure than seeing his name in print, which means you won't see it here) went nuclear; by complimenting The Times in any way at all, he said, I had demonstrated my gross unfitness for my job.

The report of Siegal's new committee was issued in the spring of 2005 [@], and it was a remarkable document: nearly every one of its recommendations addressed an effort to bring the paper closer to its readers; to make it more open to its readers; and to connect the paper more intimately to the world it covers. As of this writing, only a few of its recommendations have been acted on, but they include some very important initiatives:

- Much more effective limits have been placed on anonymous sourcing, and much more effective procedures established for policing it. "A year from now," Keller wrote in a June 2005 memo to the staff, "I would like reporters to feel that the use of anonymous sources is not a routine, but an exception, and that if the justification is not clear in the story they will be challenged." He also said he expected "care in the use of anonymous sources to be one of the criteria used in evaluating the work of reporters and editors."

- Serious restrictions have been placed on which television shows reporters are allowed to appear on.
- Classes on biased and tendentious language are now being given to all new editors and writers (alas, the classes are strictly elective for veterans).
- A formal effort is being made to further diversify the staff. Wrote Keller, "The point is not that we should begin recruiting reporters and editors for their political outlook; it is part of our professional code that we keep our political views out of the paper. The point is that we want a range of experience."
- As I write, a system that would finally enable readers to write directly to every reporter was, I was told, "about to be turned on."

Despite these advances, in a couple other areas openness has taken it on the chin. When Times columnists—not just those on the Op-Ed page, but throughout the paper—were segregated behind a members-only wall at nytimes.com, e-mail access to them was denied to anyone who was neither a subscriber to the print edition nor a paid-up member of the web service. Most disappointingly, despite Keller's assurance that senior editors (including Keller himself) would make appearances "every other week . . . for Q & A forums on our Web site," as of early March 2006 nothing at all had happened on that front. Keller did tell me, though, that he was still planning to do it.

I gather that a few of the committee's other recommendations (posting of staff e-mail addresses; clearer graphic delineation between news pieces and analyses, commentaries and the like) are, as I write, still in the works.

No Picture Tells the Truth. The Best Do Better Than That.

. . .

January 9, 2005

TWO Mondays ago, the scale of the Indian Ocean catastrophe was just emerging from the incomplete earlier reports (from a Times article the day before: a tidal wave had "killed more than 150 people in Sri Lanka"). By the 4:30 Page 1 meeting, picture editors had examined more than 900 images of devastation to find the one that would stretch across five columns and nearly half the depth of Tuesday's front page. Into a million homes came a grieving mother crouched beside the lifeless bodies of tiny children, and perhaps more horrifying, three pairs of feet extending from beneath a white sheet in an upper corner, suggesting the presence beyond the frame of row upon awful row of the tsunami's pitiless toll.*

Many readers and at least a few members of The Times's newsroom staff considered the picture exploitative, unduly graphic, and by its size and placement, inappropriately forced upon the

Gautam Singh/Associated Press

This photo that appeared on the front page of The Times on Dec. 28 shocked or offended many readers.

* All photographs discussed here and accompanied by [@] can be linked to from the online version of this article.

paper's readers. Some felt it disrespectful of both the living and the dead. A few said The Times would not have published it had the children been white Americans. Boaz Rabin of Weehawken, N.J., wrote, "Lead with letters the size of eggs, use any words you see fit, but don't put a nightmare on the front page."

I asked managing editor Jill Abramson why she chose this picture. She said in an e-mail message that after careful and difficult consideration, she decided that the photo "seemed to perfectly convey the news: the sheer enormity of the disaster, as we learned one-third of the casualties are children in a part of the world where more than 50 percent of the population is children. It is an indescribably painful photograph, but one that was in all ways commensurate to the event." When I spoke with director of photography Michele McNally, who believes the paper has the obligation "to bear witness" at moments like this, she had a question for me: "Wouldn't you want us to show pictures from Auschwitz if the gates were opened in our time?"

The surpassing power of pictures enables them to become the permanent markers of enormous events. The marines planting the flag at Iwo Jima, the South Vietnamese general shooting his captive at point-blank range, the young John F. Kennedy Jr. saluting his father's passing coffin: each is the universal symbol for a historical moment. You don't need to see them to see them.

But in every case, someone needs to choose them. Photo editors (The Times employs 40) and their colleagues make hundreds of choices a week. Stories may whisper with nuance and headlines declaim in summary, but pictures seize the microphone, and if they're good, they don't let go. In most cases, a story gets a single picture; major stories may get more, but usually only one on the front page itself—and that becomes the picture that stands for the event.

This won't make every reader happy. From last year's mail:

- "The picture hardly reflects the regular Turkish population." [@]
- "I have never been a particular [fan] of Richard Grasso, but The Times should not prejudge his lawsuit by publishing photos that portray him as a monster." [@]
- "I find it appalling and disgusting that you would print an Iraqi holding up the boots of one of our dead soldiers." [@]
- "Why are we shown the pictures of tragically mutilated U.S. civilian contractors but not slain Iraqi children?" [@]

One reader felt that a picture of a smiling Jesse Jackson next to George W. Bush made it appear that Jackson had endorsed the president [@]. Another believed that a photo of a dead Palestinian child in the arms of a policeman looked staged, as if to resemble the Pietà [@].

Richard Avedon once said: "There is no such thing as inaccuracy in a photograph. All photographs are accurate. None of them is the truth." In this Age of Fungible Pixels, when not every publication, political campaign or advocacy organization follows the Times policy prohibiting manipulation of news photographs, I'm not even sure about the accuracy part. But the untruth—or, at least, imperfect truth—of any single photograph is inescapable. Some readers object to the way a picture is cropped, arguing that evidence changing its meaning has been sliced out of the frame. But meaning is determined long before that. A photographer points the camera here, then turns three inches to the left and snaps again: different picture, maybe a different reality. A photo editor selects from the images the photographer submits (should the subject be smiling? Frowning? Animated? Distracted?). The designer wants it large (major impact) or small (lesser impact). The editor picks it for Page 1 (important) or not (not). By the time a reader sees a picture, it has been repeatedly massaged by judgment. But it's necessarily presented as fact.

Last May, for an article considering whether Brazilian President Luiz Inácio Lula da Silva had a drinking problem, editors selected a seven-month-old file photo showing the president hoisting a beer at an Oktoberfest celebration [@]. It may have been a sensible choice; drinking was the subject, and a picture of the president standing at a lectern would have been dull and disconnected. But any ambiguity in the article was steamrolled by visual evidence that may have been factual (da Silva once had a beer), but perhaps not truthful.

Even in the coverage of an event as photographically unpromising as a guy in a suit giving a speech, pictures convey judgment. When George J. Tenet resigned as C.I.A. director in June, a front page shot showed him looking down, biting his lip, possibly near tears [@]; according to Bruce Mansbridge of Austin, Tex., at other moments during the broadcast of Tenet's speech, "he appeared quite upbeat." When Donald H. Rumsfeld visited Abu Ghraib in May, The Times showed him flanked by soldiers, striding through the grounds of the prison [@], as if (wrote Karen Smullen of Long Island) "Karl Rove must have said, 'What we really need now is a photo of [Rumsfeld] leading soldiers and looking earnest and determined and strong.'" Did Rumsfeld pause at any point and laugh at a joke told by a colleague, or bark at a reporter who asked him a difficult question?

Did any of these pictures tell the whole story, or just a sliver of it?

Mix a subjective process with something as idiosyncratic as taste and you're left with a volatile compound. Add human tragedy and it becomes emotionally explosive. The day The Times ran the picture of the dead children, many other papers led with a photograph of a grief-racked man clutching the hand of his dead son. It, too, was a powerful picture, and it's easy to see why so many used it. But it was—this is difficult to say—a portrait of generic tragedy. The devastated man could have been in the deserts of Darfur, or in a house in Mosul, or on a sidewalk in Peoria; he could have been photographed 10 years ago, or 10 years from now. His pain was universal.

Arko Datta/Reuters

But the picture on the front page of The Times could only have been photographed now, and only on the devastated shores of the Indian Ocean. My colleague David House of The Fort Worth Star-Telegram says, "In this instance, covering life means covering death." The babies in their silent rows were as real, and as specific, as the insane act of nature that murdered them. This picture was the story of the Indian Ocean tsunami of December 2004—not the truth, but a stand-in for the truth that will not leave the

Ombudsmen and public editors at papers that ran this photograph reported receiving very few objections.

thoughts of those who saw it. The Times was right to publish it.

Speaking of pictures: In my Oct. 10 column, I distorted reality by not mentioning the researchers who had conducted detailed studies of The Times's photo coverage of the presidential candidates. Belated thanks to Josh Hammond and Tom Holzel.

. . .

I have to admit it: the picture that stays with me from the tsunami is the one I called generic; the one The Times ran is vaguer in my memory, and when I recently looked for it on the Web I realized that the image in my mind was in some respects not the same as the one that ran in the paper. This brings up the issue that has been causing arguments between photo editors and their bosses since the time of Mathew Brady: the photo editor wants the graphically strongest photograph, and the boss wants the one that conveys the most information.

As it happened, Abramson and McNally were in agreement on the photo of the dead children, and the way it was used followed a dictum imparted to me by Dick Stolley, a former editor of Life magazine and the founding editor of People: "If the picture isn't great, run it really big." That unquestionably had a lot to do with the initial impact of the photo The Times used, but in the mind's eye it gets smaller and smaller with time.

In recent years—since the otherwise troubling editorship of Howell Raines, who engineered vast improvement in The Times's use of photographs—graphic impact has become as important to the paper as the conveyance of information. Were I in the business of complimenting the editors of The Times (other than during the holiday season), I'd give them credit for this trend almost daily.

Numbed by the Numbers, When They Just Don't Add Up

· · ·

January 23, 2005

SOME people in the newspaper business—including, I suspect, a few sitting upstairs from me, in the New York Times Company's corporate offices—were displeased by a story that ran on Jan. 10, "Your Daily Paper, Courtesy of a Sponsor." The article, by Jacques Steinberg and Tom Torok, was a pretty sharp pin stuck into the circulation numbers of many American newspapers, revealing how subscriptions paid for by advertisers are delivered to readers who haven't asked for them.

I fielded a couple of days' worth of objections from the newspaper industry, and while I concluded that the piece was largely fair and entirely accurate (if somewhat overstated), I do think it could have been more candid about The Times's own practices. Readers who wanted to know how The Times fitted into this story didn't find out until (more likely, "unless") they made it to the 30th paragraph; the practices at The Boston Globe, owned by The New York Times Company, were unveiled in Paragraph 27. Even then the article was slightly less than forthcoming. By studying circulation patterns of Sunday papers, the article made The Times appear less reliant on these advertiser-subsidized subscriptions than it would have if the comparisons had been based on weekday circulation.

In fact, one could say there's a stark difference: according to the most recent available numbers, the quantity of the paper's third-party-paid subscriptions on a given weekday is 79 percent higher than the comparable Sunday number.

This sounds very ominous. It sounds somewhat less ominous when you realize that these same third-party-paid subscriptions account for 1.4 percent of Sunday circulation, and 2.5 percent of weekday circulation. And it sounds not even worth noting (take a deep breath here) if you consider that the difference between the number of weekday subsidized copies and Sunday subsidized copies is 0.4 percent of weekday circulation, and 0.27 percent of Sunday circulation.

Set aside the question of whether The Times should have stated its figures higher and more completely in the piece. (No, let's not set it aside: Caesar's wife should speak early and loudly.) There's another issue rolling around all these numbers — namely, numbers. Do you have any idea which of the figures I've cited, all of them accurate, are meaningful?

Neither do I.

One of the appealing things about the complaints I receive about innumeracy at The Times is their ecumenical origin; when it comes to how it handles numbers, The Times is an equal opportunity offender. Like a bad cough that spreads its germs indiscriminately, numbers misapplied and ill-explained irritate the sensibilities of the right and the left, the drug company official and the animal rights activist, the art collector and the Jets fan.

Number fumbling arises, I believe, not from mendacity but from laziness, carelessness or lack of comprehension. I'll put myself in the latter category (as some readers no doubt will as well, after they've read through my representation of the numbers that follow). Most of the journalists I know who enter the profession comfortable with numbers write about sports, where debate about the meaning of statistics is a daily competition, or economics, a field in which interpretation of numbers will no more likely produce inarguable results than will finger painting.

So it is left to the rest of us who write for the paper to stumble through numbers, scatter them on the page and hope that readers understand. Does it matter if many of these figures are meaningless symbols serving the interests of the parties that issue them? Take a variety of reports on some recent lawsuits: A man is suing the city for $20 million arising from charges, eventually dismissed, brought against him for kidnapping and sexual abuse. The mother of the football player Derrick Thomas, who died in 2000, is suing General Motors for $75 million. Villagers on an Indonesian island are suing Newmont Mining Corporation for $543 million. Not one of these numbers is grounded in anything more substantial than the imagination of a plaintiff's lawyer, but each is given the authority of print.

No different, really, was Wednesday's assertion that Bernard J. Ebbers, if convicted of all charges in the MCI-WorldCom accounting scandal, "could be sentenced to as much as 85 years," a formulation that bears no relationship to any conceivable outcome yet serves the prosecutor's public case very nicely.

Numbers issued by those measuring criminal enterprise ("In Mexico, drug trafficking is a $250-billion-a-year industry") or the economic impact of a new stadium ("Bloomberg said that he expected the arena to generate about $400 million a year through various economic activities") don't deserve to be published without challenge; it doesn't serve agencies who want to fight drug trafficking to underestimate the problem, nor can any politician support a development project without hyping its potential benefit.

Still, The Times persists. In November, when New York City Comptroller William Thompson released a study purporting to show that New Yorkers purchase more than $23 billion in counterfeit goods each year, The Times repeated the analysis as if it were credible. Quick arithmetic would have demonstrated that $23 billion would work out to roughly $8,000 per city household, a number ludicrous on its face. (In the Web version of this column, I've linked to an excellent dissection of Thompson's report, by freelance journalist Felix Salmon [@].)

Last Sunday, an article on the city's proposed $1.1 billion investment in three stadium projects cited the assertion by the president of the city's Economic Development Corporation that "for every dollar invested by the city in the three projects, taxpayers would get a return of $3.50 to $4.50 over 30 years." It didn't say that the same $1.1 billion invested in a 30-year Treasury bond would return $4 for every dollar invested, and a lot more reliably, too. (Credit where it's due: reporter Charles V. Bagli did note that the $1.1 billion could pay for 25 schools housing 600 students each.)

Sometimes the absence of a number is as deflating to an article's credibility as the presence of a deceptive one. Few articles noting that President Bush received more votes than any candidate in history also mentioned that more people voted against him than any candidate in history. Quoting Michael Moore's assertion that standing ovations in Greensboro, N.C., proved that "Fahrenheit 9/11" is "a red state movie" disregards the fact that metropolitan Greensboro has over 1.2 million people; you could probably find in a population that large enough people to give a standing O for a reading of the bylaws of the American Dental Association.

Of course both Moore and the reporter who wrote that piece operate in the movie business, where records are about as meaningful as promises. "Shrek 2" is not, as an article in The Times Magazine had it in November, "the third-highest-grossing movie of all time"; if you consider inflation, it's not even in the Top 10 (and "Titanic" is far from No. 1). This record-mania has spread everywhere. "Record-high gas prices" summoned up last year weren't even close; at its summer peak, gas cost 80 cents a gallon less than it did in 1981. Says economics reporter David Leonhardt, "Treating 2004 dollars the same as 1981 dollars isn't much different from treating dollars the same as rupees. The fact that 10 is a bigger number than 9 doesn't make 10 rupees worth more than $9; nor does it make $10 from 2004 worth more than $9 from 1981." Inflation isn't the only culprit stalking the record books: "Record deficits" may not be records when they're expressed as a percentage of gross domestic product, a far more reasonable measure than any raw number.

Numbers without context, especially large ones with many zeros trailing behind, are about as intelligible as vowels without consonants. When Congress allocated $28.4 billion to the National Institutes of Health, was that a lot or a little? I'd certainly begin to have a sense of it if I knew that this came to 3 percent of all discretionary spending. When John Kerry proposed tax cuts of $420 billion over 10 years, was that a meaningful number? Tell me that it amounts to about $150 per person per year, and I can grasp it. When Harvard announced that it was allocating $2 million more to financial aid for poor students, bringing the total to $82 million a year, was it really being generous? Well, in 2004, $82 million was about six days' income from the

Harvard endowment, and the heralded $2 million increase that prompted this fairly prominent article was the equivalent of what the endowment earned every 3 hours and 36 minutes.

If all these numbers make your eyes roll, then you're finding yourself in the same position as a lot of readers, and apparently a lot of reporters and editors as well. (I haven't even gotten into deceptive stats that have the patina of authority, like those three all-time champs, the Dow Jones Industrial Average, the unemployment rate and batting averages; if you're interested, I take a few swings at them in my Web journal, in Posting No. 42 [@].)

Although everyone who writes for The Times is presumably comfortable with words, every sentence nonetheless goes through the hands of copy editors, highly trained specialists who can bring life to a dead paragraph or clarity to a tortured clause with a tap-tap here and a delete-insert there. But numbers, so alien to so many, don't get nearly this respect. The paper requires no specific training to enhance numeracy, and no specialists whose sole job is to foster it. David Leonhardt and Charles Blow, the deputy design director for news, have just begun to conduct occasional seminars on "Using and Misusing Numbers," and that's a start. But as I read the paper and try to dodge the context-absent numbers that are thrown about like shot-puts, I long for more.

In "Floater," his 1980 novel about life at a newsweekly, Calvin Trillin introduced the Rhymes-With man—a mysterious character locked in a padded room who is allowed out only to provide readers with parenthetical clues to the pronunciation of foreign words, like ratatouille ("rhymes with lotta hooey"). Maybe The Times could sign up several Number-Means people to help the staff—and the readers—through the sticky digits.

Chief database editor Tom Torok was mightily displeased by this column—not by its general argument, but by my using a story he co-wrote in the lead. Even though I wrote that the piece "was largely fair and entirely accurate," Torok felt that putting it at the head of a story about innumeracy convicted it by association (see "When the Readers Speak Out, Can Anyone Hear Them?," on page 222, for more about Torok's complaint).

I was dismayed by that, because only the rather tortuous length of my lead led me to feel I had to mention Torok and his co-author, media reporter Jacques Steinberg, by name. Throughout the rest of the piece, I took quick shots at 14 separate articles, but named none of the writers and editors (except, I now realize, Charles V. Bagli, whom I paused to praise in a parenthetical aside). I chose to protect these apparent malefactors for the same reason you don't put the names of jaywalkers in the paper: virtually everyone misuses numbers. Innumeracy is a nearly universal affliction among journalists, not just at The Times but throughout the industry.

No one in management with whom I discussed the issue objected to the notion of hiring a few Number-Means people (you'd need more than one if you wanted to have a number specialist present every day). But these sad days for the newspaper business, when fewer people are stretched to do more and more work, are not conducive to creating new positions. This is a shame. In the days after my column ran, I heard from three people who said they wanted to apply for the job; the paper would be better if it hired them.

Talking on the Air and Out of Turn: The Trouble With TV

· · ·

February 6, 2005

LAST Sunday, Times reporter Judith Miller appeared on MSNBC's "Hardball With Chris Matthews" to discuss the Iraqi elections. In the course of the conversation Miller said sources had told her the Bush administration "has been reaching out" to the Iraqi political figure Ahmad Chalabi "to offer him expressions of cooperation." She continued, "According to one report, he was even offered a chance to be an interior minister in the new government." This led Matthews to interrupt Miller, exclaim "Wait a minute!" and press her to elaborate.

Now, Matthews is the sort of television host who will interrupt a guest about as often as he blinks, and his reliance on exclamation is roughly equal to his reliance on breathing. But to anyone who has tried to follow the jagged contours of Ahmad Chalabi's connections to the Bush administration, Miller's statement was a shocker. This piece of news hadn't appeared in The Times that morning; it didn't appear in The Times the next morning; as I write this column, on Friday, it still hasn't appeared. A lengthy analysis of the election aftermath by reporter Dexter Filkins, published Tuesday, didn't even hint of any current contact between Chalabi and the Bush administration.

But if you watched "Hardball" on Sunday night, and saw

Judith Miller identified as a reporter for The New York Times, you would have every reason to think she was speaking with the authority of the paper. That, presumably, is why television news and talk producers ask Times reporters to appear on their programs; that, presumably, is why The Times's publicity apparatus books broadcast appearances for as many as 12 different reporters in a typical week. Yet Miller's revelation—Jack Shafer of Slate.com called it "the second biggest Iraq story of the day (after the successful election)"—was fit to be broadcast on television, even if not fit to print. Why the difference?

Let me make a few things clear before going forward. First, I don't believe Miller's appearance on Matthews's show has anything to do with the current contempt citation hanging over her, the one resulting from her refusal to reveal sources to a federal grand jury. I believe she is right to resist the subpoena; that her apparent willingness to go to jail to protect her sources is admirable; and that The Times is right to defend her unflinchingly.

Second, hers isn't the only byline from The Times to appear on the bottom of the screen when you're watching "Hardball"; I've been on the show myself, sneezing through my makeup. I also appear regularly on a local Times-produced show here in New York, and occasionally on various other broadcast outlets whose producers are looking for a talking head to take a shot at The Times, defend The Times or bloviate about the state of American journalism. I disclose all this unexceptional and uninteresting information as a preface to my argument that reporters—not columnists or critics, only reporters—should appear on television news programs rarely, on talk shows even less often and on programs dominated by interrogators as insistent and adept as Matthews not at all.

There are many, many reasons why newspaper people would want to appear on television. There's vanity, of course, and the ensuing cheap thrill of having someone stare at you on the subway, trying to figure out who you are. There's the admirable desire to help promote the paper you work for, and the less admirable one to promote your own career. There's the—well, I can't actually think of any others. But I can give you several reasons why it's bad for reporters, and bad for The Times.

Judging by their absence from the paper, one must conclude that either Miller's Chalabi revelations were wrong or unsubstantiated or that The Times is suppressing an important piece of news. If the first, the paper has suffered a blow to its credibility: Matthews introduced Miller as "an investigative reporter for The New York Times." The ID on the screen said "Judith Miller, 'The New York Times.'" At five separate points in the show Matthews invoked her connection to The Times, as any host would.

If there's an act of suppression going on, the price is of course incalculable. But I don't remotely think that is the case. I've been able to determine with a very high degree of confidence that editors in the two departments most likely to have an interest in Miller's Chalabi assertions were unaware of them. (Miller was away from New York this week, and did not respond to messages I left on her office phone, her cellphone and on e-mail. Executive editor Bill Keller declined to discuss the matter. "I'm sorry to be unhelpful on this one, but Judy faces a serious danger of being sent to jail for protecting a confidential source," Keller told me in an e-mail message. "I think this is not the time to be drawn into unrelated public discussions of Judy.")

Newspapers are different from talk shows. In the best circumstances, what appears in the newspaper is the collaborative product of reporter, editor, copy editor, desk or department head, and sometimes, the anointing ministrations of a masthead editor. What emerges from most television talk programs—in fact, what makes them interesting—is unedited, at times lightly considered, often impulsive. Yet those letters at the bottom of the screen ("Reporter, The New York Times") weld everything that's said to the paper's credibility.

Miller dodged the second danger lurking in the television studio, when she wouldn't take Matthews's bait and tell him whether she thought the elections, as he put it, "prove President Bush right, yes or no, about Iraq." But in the real-time, high-speed badminton match of a television interview or debate, opinions (or at least characterizations) that would never appear in the paper emerge. At several points during last year's presidential campaign, readers complained that one or another of The Times's political writers, appearing on TV, had said something that indicated they were biased for or against (in fact, almost always against) one of the candidates, and should therefore be disqualified from further coverage. This is not what you want your readers to think.

In the privacy of a one-on-one, off-camera interview, some print reporters will extract the information they're looking for with smiles and flattery; others will try pounding and intimidation. I know one magazine reporter who can switch between the two modes (and various others) so fluently you'd swear you were watching one of those one-man shows where a single actor plays a dozen roles. But both cajolery and aggression (not to mention their less glamorous teammates, patience, determination and shoe leather) are tactics informed, and justified, by a noble strategy: gathering the information that will enable readers to understand the events, personalities and issues of the day. So long as legal and ethical lines aren't breached, what matters is not the method of reporting but the results.

On television, dogged questioning can appear to be oppositional, even harassing. When White House correspondent Elisabeth Bumiller served as a panelist in a televised debate during last winter's primary season, some readers were convinced that her aggressive questioning of John Kerry and a head-to-head scrap with Al Sharpton demonstrated hostility. The same questions and the same attitudes deployed in a private interview could have produced answers that, in the paper, would have seemed absolutely proper and appropriate. But television can transform and distort reality; thinking you know a reporter from what you see on TV can be like thinking you know an actor from the way he behaves on stage.

I don't think any of my cavils pertain to columnists or critics, who make their livings peddling opinion. They are their own brand names. When David Brooks appears on one show and Maureen Dowd on another, their diverging viewpoints do not demonstrate contradictions at The Times; they demonstrate the views of David Brooks and Maureen Dowd. (I'll leave it to you to determine whether a public editor falls into this category.)

But reporters represent the standards of the entire paper's news gathering effort. It would be overkill for The Times to keep its reporters off television in all circumstances, but surely the top editors understand how publicity that can undermine reader trust is the worst kind of publicity a newspaper can get. They need to enforce a policy ensuring that no staff member will "say anything on radio, television or the Internet that could not appear under his or her byline in The Times."

Should be easy: those words are directly from the paper's "Ethical Journalism" handbook. But mild admonition is no insurance against reporters' getting ambushed, flattered or flustered into saying something an editor would strike in an instant. The only way the Times is going solve this problem is by making it a practice to regulate its reporters' appearances, and letting the paper—the reason everyone's here—speak for itself.

. . .

The buried lead in this column is the paragraph in which I comment, very briefly, on the contempt citation against Judy Miller, and The Times's unflinching defense of her. I was waiting for the case and the crisis to gel before writing about it—which didn't happen until after I had left The Times, Miller had gone to jail, Miller had emerged from jail, and Miller and The Times had gone through their unpleasant public divorce.

In the fourth paragraph—those few sentences that touched on Miller's contempt case—I got one fact wrong and expressed two ill-advised opinions. The fact: Miller's appearance on Matthews's show did indeed have something to do with the contempt citation. Further reporting led me to discover that The Times was pushing Miller forward very aggressively in those months, hoping that frequent public appearances would have an effect on public opinion. The Times may not have wanted her on "Hardball" to talk about Ahmad Chalabi, but she was on "Hardball" at least in part because The Times wanted her out in public.

The regrettable opinions are, in hindsight, obvious: Miller was not right to resist the prosecutor's subpoena to the extent that she did, and The Times's unflinching defense could have benefited from a flinch or two. If Walter Pincus of The Washington

Post—no reporter on national security affairs is further beyond reproach—found a way to limit his testimony and not compromise a source against the source's wishes, then surely Miller could have done the same, as it became clear after she ultimately agreed to testify. The Times had hired a First Amendment lawyer, fought the case on extremely questionable First Amendment grounds, and lost; The Post had hired criminal lawyers, who kept the most volatile issues contained and negotiated a satisfactory settlement with the prosecutor's office.

The resulting train wreck of October 2005 could have, and should have, been avoided; that it wasn't ended up embarrassing The Times needlessly. Worse, the failure of the paper's Horatio-at-the-Bridge legal strategy has surely emboldened prosecutors who itch to get their hands on other journalists' notes.

And I still think news reporters shouldn't go on talk shows.

When the Readers Speak Out, Can Anyone Hear Them?

. . .

February 20, 2005

A FEW days after publication of my Jan. 23 column on innumeracy ("Numbed by the Numbers, When They Just Don't Add Up"), Tom Torok, The Times's chief database editor, expressed his strong objections to what he perceived to be a damaging portrayal of his work.

I had opened the column with a brief discussion of a story carrying the bylines of Torok and reporter Jacques Steinberg, and then leapt into a discussion of the misuse of numbers elsewhere in the paper. Torok believed, as he said in an e-mail message, that I used their piece "as the lead example of number fumbling," and that he and Steinberg had been "harmed" by it.

Being a newspaper journalist—for now, at least—I went immediately into a spasm of defensiveness. I don't think there was anything wrong with Torok's and Steinberg's numbers. I hadn't said there was. I had even called their piece "entirely accurate."

But there was the headline; there was the piece's larger context; and there was Torok's question, "Do you simply want to ignore the effects of such a column if they unfairly harm someone?" Which suggested a larger question encompassing the pleadings of hundreds of others who, like Torok, have come to my door bruised or angry: "What recourse do I have if I've been misrepresented, mischaracterized or maligned by The Times, especially if the editors disagree?" And the question even larger than that, at least in terms of the number of readers who have raised it: "Why can't I criticize The Times in the pages of The Times?"

The cheap answer would be, "Because that's my job." The pertinent answer—the one newspaper people have been using since Gutenberg—is, "Write a letter to the editor." But the unsung coda, in the overwhelming preponderance of cases, is familiar: "even though there's almost no chance it will be published."

The Times needs to find an alternative ending for this depressing tune. Certainly the numbers are impossible. The letters department receives 1,000 messages every day, and publishes 15. Beyond that, many of the paper's readers find certain practices and policies regarding letters either dumbfounding or objectionable. Chief among these is the paper's general hesitance to publish letters that make accusations against The Times, criticize writers or editors, or otherwise call into question the newspaper's fairness, news judgment or professional practices.

As letters editor Thomas Feyer points out, The Times does occasionally print correspondence of this sort. But he also notes his unwillingness to publish criticisms of individual writers, and a reluctance to publish letters that suggest bias. "Such letters," he says, "seem to impute motives to reporters or to The Times that the letter writers have no way to know."

Similar practices are in place in the various Sunday sections that publish their own letters. (The exception is the Book Review, where the letters page can sometimes resemble the Battle of the Marne.) Over the months, many readers have brought to my attention instances when they were asked to remove negative references to The Times if they wished to have their letters published.

Patricia Grossman of Brooklyn had a letter published last August, but only after she agreed to delete her accusation that a Times headline had maligned protesters at the Republican convention. (Feyer, who was on vacation at the time, told me that it's possible the deletion was made for space, but that he also believed Grossman "was imputing a political view to The Times that wasn't warranted.") Gary Sheffer of General Electric's public relations staff was told his letter would be published only if specific references to what he considered inadequate reporting were deleted. (Sunday Business editor Jim Impoco told me, "We prefer letters that address the issue, rather than just take shots at the reporter," and that certain factual references in Sheffer's letter were incorrect.) Last spring, Scott Segal, representing an electric power industry trade group unhappy with an article about federal environmental policy, was asked to delete from his letter the suggestion that I had endorsed one of his points (which I had, in a letter to him); editors told Segal he couldn't use it because he had quoted "selectively from a letter that largely defends the piece." (This was basically correct, but to the point at hand not especially relevant.)

A little defensive, hmm? I understand the policy that keeps out assaults aimed at specific writers; as Feyer says, "a news article is the product not only of the reporter whose name is on it, but The Times as a whole: the senior management and the desk editors, the copy editors and the headline writers." I also agree with assistant managing editor Allan M. Siegal's response when I asked why those responsible for errors are not identified in the Corrections column: "Public humiliation is neither appropriate discipline nor a good teaching tool." (I'd make an exception for columnists, who pick their own fights.)

But allowing the subjects of stories and other readers— including, perhaps, self-examining Times writers—to criticize The Times as an institution for its reporting or its headlines, its news judgment or its preconceptions, its prose style or its public editor is something the paper is strong enough to withstand. What's difficult is figuring out how to do it given the limitations of space and staff, and the risk of degeneration into charge, countercharge, imprecation, untruth, calumny and libel.

Two answers: the Web, and editing.

Here's what you can do on the Web. You are not limited to three slender columns of the right side of the editorial page; nytimes.com stretches from here to the horizon. In the electronically archived version of articles—the ones that exist for the ages—you could move letters from their own ghetto and append them to the articles they address; that's the way that corrections are handled. In fact, even in the print edition, it makes sense to move letters about news coverage away from the editorial page, where they reside in inappropriate proximity to ideological arguments about editorials and columns, and to a space of their own, perhaps on Page A2. If the news pages and the opinion pages are truly separate, then truly separate them and give news editors, not opinion editors, responsibility for letters relating to news stories.

The better use of the Web site could also give readers the chance to see letters from The Times. One of the great frustrations of my job is seeing the thoughtful letters that go out from Times reporters to readers who have taken issue with something they've written. Why frustration? Because one reader gets the benefit of the thoughtfulness (and, sometimes, the writer's candid acknowledgment that he or she might have done something better), and a couple of million others who might appreciate it do not.

There are many at The Times who really dislike some of these ideas. Al Siegal understandably worries that the paper's authority, the staff's morale and the honest pursuit of truth could be severely undermined by deceitful or disingenuous attacks on specific articles by interested parties. And some reporters are very wary of posting for the millions their own letters to individual readers, fearing they would soon be forced (by editors, by competitive reporters, by me) into an endless public confessional.

The argument that all this would be too hard to monitor, that expanded Web forums would require too much staff attention to keep from degenerating into a free-fire zone of mudslinging, rumor-spreading or character-bashing, is a strong one. Even now it's a problem, as some of the current forums at nytimes.com can be so unruly and digressive that they've lost their intended value. It will take some very serious editing resources to make certain that every Web-posted letter passes reasonable standards to prevent those excesses, not to mention transgressions against the libel laws.

But that's true of anything important in a newspaper. Is the airing of criticism and challenge important, and therefore worth finding the resources for it? To me, The Times's Op-Ed page is at its best when it publishes pieces at odds with the paper's own editorial positions—when it shows it's strong enough to take the blows of differing views and thereby deepen the public debate. Likewise with informed, civilized criticism of journalistic practices: the strong can withstand it, and show their strength by absorbing it. I'm going to invoke one of Al Siegal's standard dicta, which I've known him to deploy when recalcitrant editors are reluctant to agree to a correction, to seal my point: "Because we own the printing press, we're not entitled to the benefit of any real doubt."

. . .

I don't think a physically limitless online letters site would work, for some of the reasons cited in the column but chiefly because letters require so much editorial attention: the identity of the sender must be verified; the asserted facts must by checked; many, laden with accusation, must undergo legal review. There's no way it could be done without substantial investment in additional staff.

But of all the budget-busting suggestions I've so blithely made, this might be the one that most justifies the additional expense. The 15 letters published daily on the editorial page, plus those scattered around the Sunday sections, may fairly represent the readership's views on the issues of the day. But they do not begin to reflect the reasonable complaints of those who take issue with the paper's coverage. It's heartening that The Times has appeared to commit itself to making the public editor position permanent, thereby giving the aggrieved an independent avenue of appeal. But it would be a truly worthwhile investment to add another person or two to the public editor's office just to prepare a daily online letters column, its presence advertised by a notice on the editorial page, its space made available to staff for rebuttal and amplification.

As for the letters not about personal grievance, but about how The Times covers the contentious issues of the day: To his credit, letters editor Tom Feyer has recently let his page relax a bit, allowing readers to state their cases more forcefully and more directly than before. But as Feyer remains a civilized man trying to maintain a civil conversation in an uncivil time, he's been doing this with understandable caution.

The War of the Words: A Dispatch From the Front Lines

. . .

March 6, 2005

NOTHING provokes as much rage as what many perceive to be The Times's policy on the use of "terrorist," "terrorism" and "terror." There is no policy, actually, but except in the context of Al Qaeda, or in direct quotations, these words, as explosive as what they describe, show up very rarely.

Among pro-Israeli readers (and nonreaders urged to write to me by media watchdog organizations), the controversy over variants of the T-word has become the stand-in for the Israel-Palestine conflict itself. When Israel's targeted assassinations of suspected sponsors of terrorism provoke retaliation, some pro-Palestinian readers argue that any armed response against civilians by such groups as Hamas is morally equivalent. Critics on the other side say The Times's general avoidance of the word "terrorism" is a political decision, and exactly what Hamas wants.

Here's what I want: A path out of this thicket, which is snarled with far more than "terror" and its derivative tendrils. I packed the preceding paragraph with enough verbal knots to secure the QE2, so I'll untangle them one by one.

"Pro-Israeli" and "pro-Palestinian": Adem Carroll of the Islamic Circle of North America has pointed out to me that both epithets represent value judgments. Are Ariel Sharon's policies pro-Israel? Not in the minds of his critics on the Israeli left. Is Mahmoud Abbas's negotiation policy pro-Palestinian? I doubt that supporters of Islamic jihad believe it is.

"Israel-Palestine conflict": I've heard from ardent Zionists who deplore this usage because, they say, "There is no Palestine."

"Targeted assassinations": The Israel Defense Forces use this term; Palestinians believe it implicitly exonerates Israel for the deaths of nearby innocents. The Times tries to avoid it, but an editor's attempt at a substitute on Jan. 27 — "pinpoint killings" — was even more accepting of the Israeli line.

"Settlers": Are they merely settlers when they carry out armed actions against Palestinians?

"Groups such as Hamas": According to the European Union and the United States government, which are both cited regularly by an army of readers, Hamas is a terrorist organization.

According to Times deputy foreign editor Ethan Bronner: "We use 'terrorist' sparingly because it is a loaded word. Describing the goals or acts of a group often serves readers better than repeating the term 'terrorist.' We make clear that Hamas seeks the destruction of Israel through violence but that it is also a significant political and social force among Palestinians, fielding candidates and running clinics and day care centers." According to many Times critics, that just won't do.

There was one more bugbear in that overloaded paragraph up top: "Media watchdog organizations." That's what you call the noble guardians on your side; the other guy's dishonest advocates are "pressure groups." Both are accurate characterizations, but trying to squeeze them into the same sentence can get awfully clumsy. It's also clumsy to befog clear prose by worrying over words so obsessively that strong sentences get ground into grits. But closing one's ears to the complaints of partisans would also entail closing one's mind to the substance of their arguments.

The armed conflict in the area between Lebanon and Egypt may yield the most linguistically volatile issues confronting Times editors, but I've encountered a ferocious tug-of-war between advocates of each of the following as well: Genital mutilation vs. genital cutting ("would you call ritual male circumcision 'genital mutilation'?"). Liberal vs. moderate ("you're simply trying to make liberalism look reasonable and inoffensive" as in calling Michael Bloomberg a "moderate Republican"). Abuse vs. torture ("if the Abu Ghraib victims had been American soldiers," The Times "would have described it as torture"). Partial birth vs. intact dilation and extraction (the use of the former demonstrates that The Times "has embraced the terminology of anti-abortion forces"). "Iraqi forces" vs. "American-backed forces" ("aren't the Sunni insurgents Iraqis?"). Don't get me started on "insurgents," much less homeless vs. vagrant, affirmative action vs. racial preferences or loophole vs. tax incentive.

Now a rugby scrum has gathered around the Bush Social Security plan. Republicans tout "personal accounts"; Democrats trash "private accounts." In this atmosphere, I don't think reporters have much choice other than to use "private" and "personal" interchangeably, and to interchange them often. Once one side of an ideological conflict has seized control of a word, it no longer has a meaning of its own; opting for one or the other would be a declaration that doesn't belong in the news reports.

Hijacking the language proves especially pernicious when government officials deodorize their programs with near-Orwellian euphemism. (If Orwell were writing "Politics and the English Language" today, he'd need a telephone book to contain his "catalog of swindles and perversions.") The Bush administration has been especially good at this; just count the number of times self-anointing phrases like "Patriot Act," "Clear Skies Act" or "No Child Left Behind Act" appear in The Times, at each appearance sounding as wholesome as a hymn. Even the most committed Republicans must recognize that such phrases could apply to measures guaranteeing the opposite of what they claim to accomplish.

When the next Democratic administration rolls around, Republicans will likely discover how it feels to be on the losing side of a propaganda war. (The Clinton White House wasn't very good at this: somehow, the Personal Responsibility and

Work Opportunity Reconciliation Act of 1996, which remade federal welfare policy, never hit the top of the charts.)

The Times shouldn't play along. If the sports section calls the Orange Bowl the Orange Bowl, even if its formal name is the Federal Express Orange Bowl, why can't the news pages refer to the Public Education Act of 2002, or the Industrial Emissions Act of 2005? Similarly, editors could ban the use of "reform" as a description of legislative action. It's even worse than "moderate," something so benign in tone and banal in substance that it can be used to camouflage any depredations its sponsors propose. Who could oppose health care reform, Social Security reform or welfare reform, and who could tell me what any of them means? You could call the rule barring (or at least radically limiting) the use of these shameless beards the Save the Language Act.

Of course, reform of the use of "reform," or a consistent assault on any of the linguistic cosmetics used by politicians and interest groups to disfigure public debate, could bring on charges of bias (a word which itself has almost come to mean "something I disagree with").

But I think in some instances The Times's earnest effort to avoid bias can desiccate language and dilute meaning. In a January memo to the foreign desk, former Jerusalem bureau chief James Bennet addressed the paper's gingerly use of the word "terrorism."

"The calculated bombing of students in a university cafeteria, or of families gathered in an ice cream parlor, cries out to be called what it is," he wrote. "I wanted to avoid the political meaning that comes with 'terrorism,' but I couldn't pretend that the word had no usage at all in plain English." Bennet came to believe that "not to use the term began to seem like a political act in itself."

I agree. While some Israelis and their supporters assert that any Palestinian holding a gun is a terrorist, there can be neither factual nor moral certainty that he is. But if the same man fires into a crowd of civilians, he has committed an act of terror, and he is a terrorist. My own definition is simple: an act of political violence committed against purely civilian targets is terrorism; attacks on military targets are not. The deadly October 2000 assault on the American destroyer Cole or the devastating suicide bomb that killed 18 American soldiers and 4 Iraqis in Mosul last December may have been heinous, but these were acts of war, not terrorism. Beheading construction workers in Iraq and bombing a market in Jerusalem are terrorism pure and simple.

Given the word's history as a virtual battle flag over the past several years, it would be tendentious for The Times to require constant use of it, as some of the paper's critics are insisting. But there's something uncomfortably fearful, and inevitably self-defeating, about struggling so hard to avoid it.

． ． ．

Beginning in May 2005, then picking up speed later in the year, I noticed that Hamas had acquired a new label in The Times: "a faction that calls for Israel's destruction." In some articles, identification was achieved through extended description: "Hamas has carried out many of the suicide bombings against Israelis in recent years." During one week in January 2006, Hamas was both those things, as well as "the radical group Hamas"; a group "dedicated to a continuing armed struggle against Israeli occupation"; and "a Palestinian group that the United States has designated a terrorist organization."

This is good. Each of these descriptives says much more than the naked "militants" or "terrorists"; each conveys factual exactitude rather than freighted judgment. But it's worth noting that Hamas appeared in the paper in 18 separate articles that same week, and it's reasonable to think that readers who care about Hamas and its activities no longer require a descriptive of any kind, at least not always.

By the way, James Bennet's consideration of "terrorism" was not extracted from a dispute he was having with the foreign desk, but from an analysis the desk had asked him to make.

On another linguistic front: In October 2005, after I had left The Times, I took part in a Columbia Journalism School panel addressing the subject of "loaded language" in journalism. I made my usual case against "pro-life" and "pro-choice" as terms of argument, not description, and endorsed the use of "abortion rights" and "anti-abortion." James Taranto, of The Wall Street Journal's online extension of it editorial page, Opinion Journal, replied that "anti-abortion" activists might find that term itself argumentative, and that the fair opposite of "abortion rights" would be "fetal rights." Alternatively, the opposite of "anti-abortion rights" would have to be "anti-fetal rights."

I'm still thinking about it.

A Few Points Along the Line Between News and Opinion

. . .

March 27, 2005

ONE of the more persistent criticisms of The Times comes from those who believe the news pages are the designated disseminator of views passed down from the Olympus that is the editorial page. If there's anyone among the 1,200 newsroom employees of The Times who believes this to be true, I've failed as a reporter: in 16 months, I haven't found a soul here who has ever experienced any pressure, or even endured a suggestion, to conform to the opinions expressed on the editorial page.

Hold your hoots. There may be perfectly sensible reasons why some readers believe that the news pages take direction from the editorial page, some of which I've discussed before, particularly the apparently normative, basically liberal world-view of much of the news staff on various social issues and the generally oppositional position toward those in power that typifies modern journalists. There's also the sheer forcefulness of the editorial page's voice, which in recent years has been so assertively left, and which some people unfamiliar with The Times's operations want to believe is the source of the news staff's daily marching orders.

For the record, it just isn't so — not at The Times, not at The Wall Street Journal, not at The Washington Post or at any other American paper that takes its mission seriously. Executive editor Bill Keller and editorial page editor Gail Collins run operations entirely separate from each other. They consciously, even self-consciously, avoid discussing politics or public issues. "We never ever talk about news or the editorials, under any circumstances," Collins told me in an e-mail message. Their weekly meeting with publisher Arthur O. Sulzberger Jr. and Times president Scott H. Heekin-Canedy is devoted strictly to company issues. If you don't want to believe this, feel free to be wrong. Or check out the different ways the two departments have treated Condoleezza Rice, or Alan Greenspan or Judge Charles W. Pickering Sr. (If the Pickering nomination had taken place during my tenure as public editor, I could have flogged the diverging coverage for months.)

But there is, in fact, a permeable membrane not quite separating fact from opinion at The Times, and it resides wholly within Keller's domain. It's the ragged line that careens like a wind-up toy through the news sections, zigging past the work of columnists, zagging by the views of critics and doing triple axels around several hybrid forms bearing names like Washington Memo, On Education, Personal Health, Sports of The Times, NYC, Public Lives, Reporter's Notebook and Frank Rich.

These hybrid forms are licenses: in some cases to explain, in some cases to render a reporter's subtle impressions, in some cases to analyze and opine. They all look different from news stories, yes, but also from one another. Presentation varies widely from section to section. Some columnists (Clyde Haberman, Peter Steinfels) have their names up in the equivalent of lights, large and shiny at the very top of a piece; others (Jane E. Brody, Edward Rothstein) get bylines typographically identical to those on straitjacketed news pieces. Typefaces used for "overlines"—identifying words like Personal Health or Public Lives—seem wildly inconsistent. If each style is meant to denote a specific definition—opinion piece, analysis piece, cute-but-unimportant piece—it's escaped me.

Most writers who have at least some freedom to mouth off are distinguished by the typesetting convention of what's called ragged-right formatting (you're looking at it right now), as if this were the international symbol for point-of-view. ("Hey, honey, ragged-right! Let's see what his opinion is!") But the ragged-right brigade also includes the weekly White House Letter, which is not meant to be opinion but, as correspondent Elisabeth Bumiller describes it, "a reported column that attempts to bring to life the people and behind-the-scenes events at the White House"; the election-season Political Points, which was largely meant to be amusing; and the basically-but-not-entirely news pieces like the one tagged West Orange Journal that popped up on B4 two days ago.

In the culture department, where readers are prepared to encounter the strong opinions of critics, most of the identifying overlines couldn't be clearer: Theater Review, Movie Review and the like. Critic's Notebook is only a slightly more opaque way of saying "opinion located here," but for many readers clouds descend in the vicinity of The TV Watch, and I suspect that visibility drops near zero around Connections. Starting tomorrow, an italic line attached to Rothstein's biweekly sort-of-column will declare that it's "a critic's perspective on arts and ideas": in other words, a place for judgment. It's a welcome elaboration, but only the tiniest of starts.

Many readers who object to the incomprehensibility of the labeling also object to this much opinion (or commentary, or untethered illumination, or whatever you wish to call it) rico-cheting around pages that years ago presented the news in the sonorous and noncommittal drone of a public address system. Judging by their frequent invocation of the number of years they've been reading The Times, most of these people are even older than I am.

I sympathize with them; the tone and tenor of a newspaper you've been reading all your life can grow to be as familiar, and as comforting, as your mother's voice. But all this columnizing represents an inevitable, perhaps monumental, transformation in American newspapering.

Max Frankel, who was executive editor of The Times from 1986 to 1994, once convinced me that journalistic innovation usually begins on the sports pages, and I think we're now in the middle of one of those moments when innovation is about to morph into standard practice. More and more often, the lead article in the sports section is a Sports of The Times column; just last Wednesday, Selena Roberts's take on Barry Bonds ("We Won't Have That Surly Superstar to Kick Around Anymore") dominated the section's front page.

The key word in that sentence is "take." What won Roberts's piece its prominent position, sports editor Tom Jolly told me, was the wish to provide "distinctive coverage of a widely covered event." Most readers would already have learned about Bonds's explosive meeting with the press from broadcast or Internet news sources, or even from the guy in the next seat on the subway. What Roberts could bring to the issue were her intelligence and her knowledge of the issues, the milieu and the characters; she could explain the event not just usefully but distinctively. NBC and ESPN, Sportsline.com and WFAN, The Post and The Daily News all had the details of Bonds's Tuesday pronouncements, but only The Times had Selena Roberts.

This reliance on columnists to report and explain (as the best columnists do) has spread elsewhere in the paper, but rules vary. Business editor Lawrence Ingrassia tells me that when his columnists (notably Gretchen Morgenson and Floyd Norris) write the occasional news story, special care is taken by both the writers and their editors "to make sure that the reporter's opinions aren't injected into the story." Jolly's version of special care is more confining: "We've drawn a strong line between our Sports of The Times and On Baseball columnists and our reporters. Our columnists only write columns. Our reporters only report the news."

I think Jolly's tougher policy is wise, especially in the transitional period before the newspaper of the future finally arrives; I'd like to see Morgenson and Norris continue to report these stories, but to present what they discover in the clear voices they've already established in their columns. The sports and business sections are both riding a wave toward that future, where writers' authority of voice and distinctiveness of thought will distinguish great newspapers from the rat-a-tat of more conventionally iterative (and instant) forms of journalism. On the way to that very different day, The Times needs to be careful to label opinion and its many variants. The simple addition of a slug of type reading "commentary" (not unlike "news analysis," a Times staple for nearly half a century) would be a productive step, when appropriate; so would the introduction of consistent design signals across the various sections.

After that, it's easy. You just have to make certain that your writers, and the editors who manage their work, are every bit as intellectually diverse as the readership you hope to attract.

Speaking of labels, analysis and opinion: starting April 10, this column, to date congenially accommodated by what is supposed to be the analysis-rich but opinion-free Week in Review section, will be following Frank Rich to the more appropriate turf of the Sunday Op-Ed pages. There, the public editor will be entitled to be wrongheaded on a biweekly basis.

· · ·

In early 2006, a working group appointed by Bill Keller and led by assistant managing editor Tom Bodkin (the paper's chief designer) presented a proposal outlining ways to "bring a more consistent and distinctive look to news-side columns throughout the paper." This sort of thing takes months to implement; consequently, as I write, I've no way of knowing whether the plans would, as Bodkin told me, "bring more clarity to our use of other forms such as news analysis, memos, journals, etc." Take a look for yourself.

I was properly called out by critics who noted that Keller and Collins may never discuss substantive issues, but to a degree they don't need to: both were appointed by publisher Sulzberger, and presumably he picked them because he knew what he was getting. Still, that's very different from coordinating news coverage to further editorial page causes.

This was, in fact, driven home to me by some of the internal reaction to this column: as indicated by the different rules for columnists promulgated by sports editor Jolly and business editor Ingrassia, even within the newsroom The Times operates under a doctrine much more akin to the Articles of Confederation than to the U.S. Constitution. Cross-newsroom policies exist, of course, but to a surprising degree different departments and sections operate with striking independence.

EXTRA! EXTRA! Read Not Quite Everything About It!

. . .

April 10, 2005

LAST Wednesday, a lengthy Editors' Note on Page A2 scooped a scoop I had planned on the toxicity of scoops. The note addressed irregularities in a March 31 front-page article by Karen W. Arenson, "Columbia Panel Clears Professors of Anti-

Semitism." The Times, the note explained, had been given a one-day jump on other media in exchange for its agreement not to "seek reaction from other interested parties." While acknowledging that this was in violation of Times policy, the note said "editors and the writer did not recall the policy and agreed to delay additional reporting until the document had become public." It concluded, "Without a response from the complainants"—the students who had brought the anti-Semitism charges—"the article was incomplete; it should not have appeared in that form."

Samuel Glasser, a reader in Port Washington, N.Y., who identifies himself as a former reporter and editor with three major newspaper chains, spoke for many: "The idea that editors and reporters would even have to be told not to do such a thing in the first place, let alone that they would 'forget' the policy, defies belief."

But I believe it all too readily. Unless they're enforced by a hanging judge, a mountain of policies (The Times has an Everest's worth; you can find most at www.nytco.com/press.html) will not deter editors and reporters from the heart-pounding, palm-sweating, eye-goggling pursuit of scoops. (Managing editor Jill Abramson told me that the Editors' Note "speaks for itself.") Wanting to be first, to beat the competition, to compel other media to say "as reported yesterday in The New York Times" puts the paper in a position where it can build staff spirit, expand its reputation and win prestigious journalism prizes. And be manipulated like Silly Putty, too.

I'll leave it to Columbia's faculty, students and alumni to pass judgment on their school's press strategy. From a journalist's perspective, a university trying to manage its public image at a moment of crisis is about as surprising as a tuition increase.

The recruitment handouts don't say, "Come to Columbia, where off-campus housing is extremely expensive and not very appealing." The press handouts don't say, "The report on anti-Semitism was immediately condemned by students who had brought the charges."

Columbia wanted to control how the news of the report broke. That's my version; Susan Brown, the director of Columbia's Office of Public Affairs, told me "we wanted the report to speak for itself, to stand on its own." Same thing. Eventually it exploded in Columbia's face and in The Times's, after The New York Sun, some aggrieved students, and (he said immodestly) some rude inquiries from the public editor messed things up. But until then, Columbia landed its version of events on the front page. Its controversial report was insulated from its controversy, presented to a large degree unchallenged. (Arenson did insist on interviewing the one professor the report cited for misbehavior.) The Times was able to tout its possession of an important document "obtained by The New York Times and scheduled for release today." And the readers got an incomplete story that wasn't made whole until Arenson's article about student reaction appeared the next day—but not on A1, of course.

The first Columbia story would probably have made Page 1 in any case, but the fact that it was an exclusive guaranteed it. Beating the competition is so much more rewarding when you can shout it through an amplifier.

In March of 2004, when the top half of the front page was given over to the carnage wrought by terrorists' bombs that killed 191 people in Madrid, many readers were offended by the presence, at the bottom of the same page, of an article headlined, "In Science's Name, Lucrative Trade in Body Parts." The Madrid story demanded to be there that day; the story about what happens to cadavers in the United States, and the stomach-churning juxtaposition this brought to readers' breakfast tables, did not. When I asked why it hadn't been held a day or two, a masthead editor told me, "We heard The Los Angeles Times was on to the same story and would be running it in the next few days."

Last June, when I tut-tutted the Page 1 placement of Michiko Kakutani's review of Bill Clinton's "My Life," I think I missed the point: a front page position for an opinion piece may have been odd, but publishing a review of a 957-page book barely 24 hours after it arrived in Kakutani's hands was even odder, unless you buy the premise that speed equals virtue. The Pulitzer judges who awarded Kakutani her prize in 1998 cited "her passionate, intelligent writing on books and contemporary literature," not her speed-reading capabilities.

The timing of both the cadaver story and the Clinton review, and their consequent claim on front-page real estate, are symptoms of a persistent genetic disposition. Some newspaper people seem to regard beating the competition as the opposable thumb of journalism, an essential characteristic that distinguishes winners from losers. I think it's more like the tailbone, a vestigial remnant from the era when reporters were still swinging from the trees—that distant time when New York had eight daily papers, and newsboys in knickers prowled the streets shouting "Extra!" whenever their papers had something the other guys didn't.

Darwinian selection might have weeded out the weaker specimens, but the traits that kept them alive for years haven't disappeared. Today, breaking news belongs to those who deliver electronically, so reportorial wiles become the chief weapons in this meaningless war.

A reporter doesn't even need to make a deal to protect a scoop, gratify a source and stiff the readers. This is especially easy in Washington, where puppet masters on both sides of the aisle use hypercompetitive reporters as their willing playthings. A pol gives a hot piece of news about, say, an impending appointment—late afternoon is an especially propitious time for this dodge—to a reporter. The reporter knows that if he seeks comment from someone likely to be opposed to the appointment, that person has plenty of incentive to bust the balloon by calling the reporter's competitors, grabbing some television face-time and otherwise making it a very bad day for the scoopster. But if the reporter doesn't make that call, the leaker gets the story the leaker wants, unmolested by thorough reporting.

When I ask why being first inspires high fives from colleagues and love notes from bosses, some editors look at me dumbly, as if I'd asked why words have vowels. Some, though, have convinced me that the footrace can benefit readers, who are well served by the competitive instincts that impel journalists to do better than the other guy. And some make the very good point that the scoops that truly matter aren't those that arise from someone's slipping a document (or, in the Robert Novak-Valerie Plame case, a name) to a reporter, but those resulting from a reporter's sustained diligence.

Not every good story requires more than 500 interviews, conducted over 15 months, like reporter Walt Bogdanich's unimpeachable series on safety at railroad crossings that won a Pulitzer last week. But a component of all good reporting is an unrelenting thoroughness even under time constraints, and an element of all good management is a willingness to wait another day when time can't be stretched.

I wish I could say the Columbia story was an aberration. I

wish as well I could prove it was not. Reporters who make secret quid pro quo agreements with sources don't pick up the phone to tell me they've just concluded a deal. I've stumbled across several pieces in the last few months that emit a slightly fishy aroma, but it would be unfair to cite specifics when reporters deny they've made deals and I can't prove otherwise.

But there are some telltale signs that could lead readers to draw their own conclusions. The first tip-off, of course, is a string of words like "to be announced tomorrow," "obtained by The Times and scheduled for release today," or any other per-mutation that suggests this is in The Times, just The Times, and you won't see it anywhere else for at least a day. Then, if the only people quoted in the article are those who benefit from spreading its substance, be wary. And be angry, too. You deserve better journalism than that.

Many people at The Times know this, and they take it seri-ously. Among them I would include Steven A. Holmes, one of the editors who handled the Columbia story. "I do think jour-nalists can be too scoop crazy," he told me last week. But, he added with palpable rue, "That's a lot easier to say when it's somebody else's scoop."

. . .

This one grabbed a nerve and pinched it: nearly everyone I spoke with at the paper thought the Columbia deal was improper and shouldn't have been made. (A few thought I wasn't harsh enough, noting that the deal was discussed in that day's 4:30 Page 1 meeting, yet still it wasn't scuttled.) Where I got far less unanimous agreement was on my general assault on scoops. It may be that my roots in magazine journalism cause my disdain—as an editor of Time once said, "A newsmagazine with a scoop is like a whore with a baby"—but I still believe that the desperate wish to be one day—or sometimes, one minute—ahead of the competition is profoundly silly. (I also believe that the winners of the Stupidest Reason to Knock The Times Prize were surely those commentators who blasted the paper for being scooped by the Philadelphia Inquirer's Web site—it beat The Times by a matter of hours—on Judith Miller's release from jail.)

Bill Keller understands the scoops problem; in a talk to the news staff in 2005, he said "There is a large lesson . . . about our sometimes heedless passion for incremental scoops—the little stories that leapfrog us ahead in the footrace with our rivals but do not add anything fundamental to the fund of public knowledge, those exclusives that probably nobody cares about except us." There's no way of measuring whether acute scoopitis has abated at The Times, but it's pleasing to think that meaningless scoops are not considered cause for praise.

The Hottest Button:
How The Times Covers Israel and Palestine

. . .

April 24, 2005

LET ME offer two statements about this paper's coverage of the conflict in the Middle East. First: I find the correspondents at The Times to be honest and committed journalists. Second: The Times today is the gold standard as far as setting out in precise language the perspectives of the parties, the contents of resolutions, the terms of international conventions.

Neither of these comments is my own. The first is a direct quotation from Michael F. Brown, executive director of Partners for Peace, an organization that seeks, it says, "to end the occupation of the Palestinian territories." The second comes from Andrea Levin, president and executive director of the Committee for Accurate Middle East Reporting in America, the muscular pro-Zionist media monitor. With partisans on each side offering respectful appraisal in place of vituperation and threat, you would think that we had reached a milestone moment in The Times's coverage of the Israel-Palestine conflict.

You would be wrong. Less temperate groups on each side find The Times guilty of felonies ranging from outright dishonesty to complicity in the deaths of civilians. A group called the Orthodox Caucus has led boycotts of The Times for "simply not telling the truth." I have met with representatives of If Americans Knew, an organization that says The Times conscientiously reports on the deaths of Israeli children but ignores the deaths of Palestinian children—children, they say, usually "shot in the head or chest" by the Israeli soldiers.

On the edges, rage and accusation prevail; nearer the middle, more reasoned critics still find much to criticize. Michael Brown and Andrea Levin can cite chapter, verse, sentence and punctuation mark. They watch this paper with a truly awesome vigilance.

It's this simple: An article about the Israeli-Palestinian conflict cannot appear in The Times without eliciting instant and intense response. A photograph of a grieving mother is considered a provocation, an interview with a radical on either side is deemed willful propaganda. Detailed studies of column inches devoted to one or another subject arrive weekly. One reader, Leo Rennert of Bethesda, Md., has written to me 164 times (as of Friday) over the past 17 months to comment on the Middle East coverage. His messages are seldom love letters.

On this issue, love letters are as common as compromise, and The Times's exoneration from charges of bias is as likely as an imminent peace.

After reading thousands of criticisms (as well as insults, accusations and threats) of The Times's Middle East coverage, I'm still waiting for one reader to say the paper has ever been unfair in a way that was damaging to both sides. Given the frequency of articles on the subject, it would be hard to imagine that such a piece has not been published. In fact, I've seen a few myself. But to see them, I have had to suppress my own feelings about what is happening in Israel and Palestine.

I can't say I'm very good at it. How could I be — how could anyone be — when considering a conflict so deep, so unabating, so riddled with pain? Who can be dispassionate about an endless tragedy?

This doesn't exonerate The Times, nor does the fact that criticism comes from each side suggest that the paper's doing something right. But no one who tries to walk down the middle of a road during a firefight could possibly emerge unscathed.

Critics will say The Times attempts nothing of the sort, that it has thrown in its lot with one side in the conflict. But let's keep motive out of this discussion. Neither you nor I know what the motives of the editors might be. Nor should their motives even matter. We can judge them only on what they do.

Some things The Times does and does not do (apart from having extremely opinionated opinion pages, which color the way the rest of the paper is read but are not the issue under discussion today):

It does not provide history lessons. A report on an assassina-

tion attempt on a Hamas leader in Gaza that kills nearby innocents will most likely mention the immediate provocation—
perhaps a Palestinian attack on an Israeli settlement. But, says
the angered reader, what about the murderous assault that provoked the settlement attack? And, says his aggrieved counterpart
on the other side, what about the ambush that preceded the
assault? And so on back to the first intifada, and then to 1973 and
1967 and 1956 and 1948—an endless chain of regression and
recrimination and pain that cannot be represented in a year,
much less in a single dispatch in a single day.

It eschews passion. If your cause needs good publicity—as
both the Palestinians and the Israelis definitely do—conventional news story tropes can only be infuriating: bland recita-
tions of presumed facts followed by challenges to those facts,
assertions by spokesmen instantly countered by opposing
spokesmen. The paper's seeming reluctance, for instance, to
report evidence of incitement to racial or religious hatred
derives in part, I believe, from a subconscious effort to stick to
the noninflammatory middle and to keep things civil, even
when civility leaked out of the conflict long ago.

But partisans desire heat. Detachment itself becomes suspect. If you are not with us, you are therefore against us.

It makes selections. For people on either side who see the
conflict as a life-and-death issue—as it certainly is—the Middle
East is the only story that matters. Each day's reports in The
Times are tiny fragments of a tragic epic. Yes, there were
demonstrations against settler relocation this morning, but how
can you ignore the afternoon's additional construction on the
West Bank barrier? Or, I know you gave my version of events
yesterday, but why are you presenting only the other side's version today?

This dilemma is aggravated by the way certain events force themselves into the newspaper. Violence trumps virtually everything else. If you are covering a debate and a terror bomb detonates two blocks away, you race to the bombing site. Terrorists have a horrifying way of influencing news coverage, but it works.

It does not cede definitive authority to other organizations and sources. Last Tuesday, "Israel, on Its Own, Is Shaping the Borders of the West Bank," by Steven Erlanger, angered Michael Brown for its unelaborated statement that Palestinians "argue that all Israeli settlements beyond the green line are illegal." The Times, Brown believes, is obligated to note that "it's not just the Palestinians who say it's illegal, but U.N. Security Council resolutions."

Ethan Bronner, the paper's deputy foreign editor, counters: "We view ourselves as neutral and unbound by such judgments. We cite them, but we do not live by them." He adds, "In 1975, when the U.N. General Assembly labeled Zionism as racism, would it have been logical for The Times to repeat that description as fact from then on? Obviously not. We take note of official views, but we don't adopt them as our own."

Nor does the paper accept as authoritative the reporting of others. A common criticism I receive is built around "proof" of something The Times has not itself reported. Frequently such evidence is drawn from openly partisan sources, and when I cite to critics contrary evidence provided by Times reporters, that evidence is in turn dismissed as partisan. The representatives of If Americans Knew earnestly believe that the information they presented to me about the killing of Palestinian children to be "simple objective criteria." But I don't think any of us can be objective about our own claimed objectivity.

It is limited by geography. The Times, like virtually every American news organization, maintains its bureau in West Jerusalem. Its reporters and their families shop in the same markets, walk the same streets and sit in the same cafes that have long been at risk of terrorist attack. Some advocates of the Palestinian cause call this "structural geographic bias."

If the reporters lived in Gaza or Ramallah, this argument goes, they would feel exposed to the daily struggles and dangers of life behind Palestinian lines and would presumably become more empathetic toward the Palestinians.

I don't know about empathy, but I do know that the angle of vision determines what you see. A reporter based in secular, Europeanized Tel Aviv would experience an Israel vastly different from one living in Jerusalem; a reporter with a home in Ramallah would most likely find an entirely different world. The Times ought to give it a try.

It's only a newspaper. It eventually comes to this: Journalism itself is inadequate to tell this story. Like recorded music, which is only a facsimile of music, journalism is a substitute, a stand-in. It's what we call on when we can't know something firsthand. It's not reality, but a version of reality, and both daily deadlines and limited space make even the best journalism a reductionist version of reality.

In preparing to write this article, my conversations with Michael Brown and Andrea Levin, with various other parties of interest and with The Times's editors consumed hours. My e-mail encounters with readers have consumed months. To all who would assert that squeezing what I've drawn from this research into these few paragraphs has stripped the many arguments of their nuance or robbed them of their power, I have no rebuttal. The more important and complicated an issue, or the closer it is to the edge of life and death and the future of nations, the less likely its essences can be distilled by that wholly inadequate but absolutely necessary servant, daily journalism.

A postscript:

During my research, representatives of If Americans Knew expressed the belief that unless the paper assigned equal numbers of Muslim and Jewish reporters to cover the conflict, Jewish reporters should be kept off the beat.

I find this profoundly offensive, but not nearly as repellent as a calumny that has popped up in my e-mail with lamentable frequency—the charge that The Times is anti-Semitic. Even if you stipulate that The Times's reporters and editors favor the Palestinian cause (something I am not remotely prepared to do), this is an astonishing debasement. If reporting that is sympathetic to Palestinians, or antipathetic to Israelis, is anti-Semitism, what is real anti-Semitism? What word do you have left for conscious discrimination, or open hatred, or acts of intentional, ethnically motivated violence?

The Times may be—is—imperfect. It is not anti-Semitic. Calling it that defames the accuser far more than it does the accused.

. . .

The leaders of CAMERA, who had long seemed to think I was doing a fair and honest job as public editor, and had particularly liked my earlier take on the use of "terrorist" and "terrorism," now found my logic peccable, my arguments egregious. A message from the group's executive director, Andrea Levin, quoted this comment from a CAMERA supporter: "Very calm, very reasoned, very articulate. Very inadequate. He obviously doesn't get it at all—you can't ignore the fact that one side wants to live in peace and the other wants to make war." Levin also objected to my citing Partners for Peace's specific complaints while not citing CAMERA's—and, she added, I got her organization's name wrong: It's Committee for Accuracy in Middle East Reporting in America, not ". . . Accurate Middle East Reporting. . . "

Alison Weir of If Americans Knew posted on the Web a denial and denunciation that soon appeared in many online venues; among other things, Weir maintained that it was I who had suggested that Jewish reporters should be kept off the beat. She and I have different recollections of our meeting.

Michael Brown of Partners for Peace thought my piece was reasonably fair.

The one reaction to the column that took me by surprise came from a well-known journalist, very experienced in the Middle East, who asked that I not use his name. He said that an American reporter operating out of a bureau in the occupied territories or Gaza would be putting his or her life at risk.

Briefers and Leakers
and the Newspapers Who Enable Them

· · ·

May 8, 2005

SOMETIME in the next few days The Times's staff will be presented a statement titled "Preserving Our Readers' Trust." Prepared by a committee of reporters and editors led by assistant managing editor Allan M. Siegal, the document will offer recommendations addressing such subjects as sourcing, bias, the division between news and opinion, and communication with readers. Staff members will be invited to comment, and then executive editor Bill Keller will determine which recommendations to adopt, adapt or dismiss.

I haven't seen the recommendations, but I suspect that those having to do with anonymous sources will be the most controversial among the reporting staff. Reporters who work the corridors of criminal justice, the foreign policy world and the intelligence community cannot do their jobs without unidentified sources. Many who cover those twin cesspools of duplicity, self-regard and back-stabbing—Hollywood and politics—are addicted to the practice. And implicit in much of the criticism aimed at any journalist who uses a blind quote is the unpleasant suggestion of dishonorable behavior.

Since I've been in this job, use of anonymous sources has been the substantive issue raised most often by readers. They challenge the authenticity of quotations. They question the accuracy of the information in the quotations. They believe reporters who invoke unidentified sources are lazy or, far worse, dishonest. As Leonard Wortzel of Atlanta wrote, "Whenever I come across a phrase like 'according to a high-ranking official,' I translate it to mean, 'I, the reporter, will now state my opinion and disguise it as news.'"

Reporters bristle when they hear this sort of thing, just as you would if your integrity were challenged. But I don't think it matters if it's fair or not. If readers perceive deception or dishonesty, The Times has a problem.

The paper knows it; that's why the Siegal group, generally referred to as "the credibility committee," was convened. That's why Philip Taubman, the Washington bureau chief, informed his staff last week that The Times had joined a group of news organizations in a broad effort to reverse the flood of "background briefings" in Washington, where officials hand out their version of events and policies and are allowed to remain unseen by the paper's readers.

Credibility is also why many reporters will now acknowledge that the profession's worst habits must be broken—the vague descriptions of phantom sources, the readiness to disregard their motivations, the willingness to let them say what they wish without public accountability. White House correspondent David E. Sanger, much of whose recent work has been in the extremely sensitive area of nuclear proliferation, told me, "In the post-Iraq world"—the world in which artful leakers convinced reporters and their readers that Saddam Hussein possessed weapons of mass destruction—"using identifiers like 'intelligence officials' or 'officials with access to intelligence' just doesn't hack it."

But getting to the point where journalists incorporate this awareness into their work isn't easy. The psychic rewards a newsroom can bestow still go to the reporter who publishes something the competition doesn't have. Valuable sources, insisting on anonymity, continue to dangle tantalizing details as if they were biscuits offered to hungry dogs. Even background briefings have their appeal, when the alternative is a two-dimensional view of policy. Assistant secretary of state Richard A. Boucher told me that he and other officials are compelled to go on background "when describing views of other governments that are important to understand but for which we are not authorized to speak. Other governments might take exception when their views are characterized by our official spokesmen, but they can't object as easily when we're anonymous."

David Leavy, who was National Security Council spokesman during the second Clinton term, agrees: "It's the law of political physics. You'll be a lot more forthcoming and rely on a lot less diplomatese if your name isn't attached to what you're saying." And, presumably, reporters (and readers) will learn much more. But policy makers want to get their story out, and even without the anonymity of a backgrounder, I bet they'll find a way.

Of course, there's another reason why some print reporters are partial to background briefings: as soon as briefers go on the record, the television lights start gleaming, the cameras start rolling, and the broadcast reporters start performing. That tends to make the print guys very grumpy.

All of this helps explain why some well-intended plans have gone unfulfilled. In March 2004, management issued a revised policy on anonymous sources that included this stricture: "When we use such sources, we accept an obligation not only to convince a reader of their reliability but also to convey what we can learn of their motivation."

A couple of months later, I reported on a study of sourcing practices conducted by Jason B. Williams, then a graduate student at New York University. Examining every A-section article published in the first full week of April 2004, one month after the new policy was announced, Williams found that barely 2 percent of stories citing anonymous sources revealed why anonymity was granted, and only 8 percent of unidentified sources were described in a meaningful fashion. (Meaningless fashion: "a Congressional official." Meaningful fashion: "a Congressional official opposed to Mr. Bolton's nomination.")

Several weeks ago, I asked Williams to look at the first full week of April once again, a year later. The policy has now been around long enough for editors to get used to it, and for reporters to get used to editors' nagging them about it. The results are . . . well, at best they're O.K. The number of anonymous sources in the paper was down 24 percent. But the percentage of stories citing unnamed sources barely slipped, from 51 percent to 47 percent. Meaningful description and reason for granting anonymity were up—from very rarely to pretty rarely. A full 46 percent of anonymous sources were identified only as "officials" or "aides," and those terms were commonly preceded by such unhelpful qualifiers as "Congressional," "administration" or—my special favorite—"several."

It wasn't until Washington news editor Greg Brock pointed it out that I noticed how frequently responsibility was put on the source, not on the paper: "The officials requested anonymity because" carries one implication; "The Times granted anonymity because" suggests a very different one. "If we are indeed committed to giving readers as much information as possible," Brock suggests, "we should start by acknowledging that we made the decision."

I'm fairly certain that if the syntax cops who preside over the paper's language insisted on this inversion, Jason Williams's numbers would plummet. It's one thing to let someone take advantage of you; it's another to proclaim that you encouraged it.

There are good reasons to use information provided by unidentified sources. The best is that it can lead you to someone who will confirm it on the record, so readers can learn something valuable. But the burden of proof is enormous when no one will

stand publicly behind a bold assertion. So should be the barrier to publication.

There is also value to unattributed material that comes from
what Pentagon reporter Thom Shanker calls "not a leak but a
puncture." Shanker explains: "What may look like a coherent
story based on information from a single source actually represents days of work stringing together separate facts from lots of
people. The sources are extensive; the motivations vary. Some
were not 'motivated' at all; they did not even know they were
contributing an important fact, which was only important when
placed alongside other observations gathered during the course
of many conversations with many other people."

This isn't overreliance on anonymous sourcing; this is what's
called "reporting." It's what separates journalists from stenogra-
phers, and I'm all for it.

But I'm also for a newsroom culture that could be symbolized by a new piece of wall decor. Imagine a little box with a
glass door; behind the glass, a certificate with the words
"Permission to use anonymous source." A small hammer hangs
from the box, and a notice reads, "Break glass in case of emergency"—an emergency not for the editors or reporters, but for
The Times's readers.

"We need to get our policies hard-wired into the brains of our
reporters and editors that we are obliged to tell readers how we
know what we know," Bill Keller told me the other day. "There
are cases when we can't, for excellent reasons—but they have to
be exceptional, and they have to be explained to the reader."

He also said, when I asked why the last policy iteration
didn't take, "We're still a little new at this." Fair enough—but
the credibility issue is growing old.

. . .

By the end of 2005, Keller—who cared deeply about this issue—could fairly claim that the hard-wired reporters and editors had had new circuit boards installed. By my very rough count, the frequency of anonymous sourcing hadn't decreased much, but readers almost always had the reason for anonymity explained to them (even if too many of these explanations said, in effect, that "the source insisted on anonymity because revealing his name would mean someone who could make life hard for him would know who he was.") Descriptive identifications were clearer, and unattributed quotations seemed to show up much less frequently in soft news pieces. There's been real progress, and it's meaningful.

Still, I'm convinced that reliance on the anonymice would decrease yet further if the paper really stuck to Greg Brock's recommendation. Can you imagine, for instance, a piece of copy containing a sentence like this one: "The source was granted anonymity because no one on the president's staff would speak on the record, and fairness required that Democrats' criticism be balanced by White House comment." My guess is that this would lead an editor to ask, why is it unfair if we've solicited an on-the-record comment and they've chosen not to give us one?

Or this: "The source was granted anonymity because The Times believed he had already spoken to one of its competitors." Having to publish something like that might make an editor think the comment isn't worth including at all.

13 Things I Meant to Write About but Never Did

. . .

May 22, 2005

AND so all good (and tense and terrible and exciting) things must come to an end. When I began in this job in December 2003, I had a list of about 20 topics I knew I wanted to address. In the ensuing months, I got to about half of those, and devoted the rest of my time and space to issues that exploded out of the pages of the paper and my e-mail in-box. The 10 I never got to are now hanging in a closet with about 50 others. What follows, you will soon see, is an all but random selection.

1. In my very first column I identified myself as "an absolutist" on the First Amendment. Apart from having come to realize that absolutism in the pursuit of self-definition can be a bit reckless, my thoughts on journalism and the First Amendment have changed considerably. I still cherish the First; I still think it's the cornerstone of democracy. But I would love to see journalists justify their work not by wrapping themselves in the cloak of the law, but by invoking more persuasive defenses: accuracy, for instance, and fairness.

As a corollary, in some arenas the First Amendment may not even be the most effective legal defense. The idea that Times reporter Judith Miller and Time magazine's Matthew Cooper may soon be imprisoned for not naming a source is nausea-inducing—especially since the source remains free. (No one is suggesting that Miller and Cooper may have broken the law; the source may well have.) Reporters Glenn Kessler and Walter Pincus, both of The Washington Post, were represented by criminal lawyers in the same case and are today going on with their lives, while those who have depended on a First Amendment defense may soon be packing for jail.

2. Op-Ed columnist Paul Krugman has the disturbing habit of shaping, slicing and selectively citing numbers in a fashion that pleases his acolytes but leaves him open to substantive assaults. Maureen Dowd was still writing that Alberto R. Gonzales "called the Geneva Conventions 'quaint'" nearly two months after a correction in the news pages noted that Gonzales had specifically applied the term to Geneva provisions about commissary privileges, athletic uniforms and scientific instruments. Before his retirement in January, William Safire vexed me with his chronic assertion of clear links between Al Qaeda and Saddam Hussein, based on evidence only he seemed to possess.

No one deserves the personal vituperation that regularly comes Dowd's way, and some of Krugman's enemies are every bit as ideological (and consequently unfair) as he is. But that doesn't mean that their boss, publisher Arthur O. Sulzberger Jr., shouldn't hold his columnists to higher standards.

I didn't give Krugman, Dowd or Safire the chance to respond before writing the last two paragraphs. I decided to impersonate an opinion columnist.

3. Question: What do these characterizations have in common?:

"At the first sound of her peremptory voice and clickety stiletto heels, people dart behind doors and douse the lights." —

Television critic Alessandra Stanley on Katie Couric, April 25.
"A semicelebrated hustler Ms. Lakshmi may be."—Fashion
writer Guy Trebay on Padma Lakshmi, Feb. 8.

"Le mot juste here is 'jackass.'"—Book reviewer Joe
Queenan on writer A.J. Jacobs, Oct. 3.

Answer: Each is gratuitously nasty, and inappropriate in a
newspaper that many of us look to as a guardian of civil discussion. I'll put the chart that appeared in the Feb. 20 edition of
The Times's T: Women's Fashion magazine, touting Oxy-
Contin as a status symbol, in the same repellent category.

4. Last July, when I slapped the headline "Is The New York
Times a Liberal Newspaper?" atop my column and opened the
piece with the catchy one-liner "Of course it is," I wasn't doing
anyone—the paper, its serious critics, myself—any favors. I'd
reduced a complex issue to a sound bite. The column itself, I'll
stand by; I still believe the paper is the inevitable product of its
staff's experience and worldview, and that its news coverage
reflects a generalized acceptance of liberal positions on most
social issues.

For The Times's ideologically fueled detractors on the right,
though, there was no reason to invoke this somewhat more
complex analysis when they could paint my more incendiary
words on a billboard: "According to The Times's own Daniel
Okrent. . . ." I may wish they'd live by one of the same standards
they ask The Times to adhere to—the fair representation of
controversial opinions. But I handed them a machine gun
when a pistol would have sufficed.

5. Reader Steven L. Carter of Bala Cynwyd, Pa., asks, If
"Tucker Carlson is identified as a conservative" in The Times,
then why is "Bill Moyers just, well, plain old Bill Moyers"?
Good question.

6. There are few traits more valuable to a great cultural critic than a consistent aesthetic viewpoint. But a consistent aesthetic viewpoint inevitably fosters blind spots in the field of vision. If a critic just doesn't like the work of a particular playwright (or painter or singer or novelist), both the playwright and the readers lose out. He never gets a fair chance; we never get a fresh take. How about term limits—say, 10 years—for critics?

7. If you've been noticing more and more unfamiliar bylines in the paper, it's no accident. Additional sections, the demands of The Times's Web site and its television operation, and generalized economic pressures have spread finite staff resources across the requirements of a much wider mission, and have increased the paper's dependence on freelance writers.

Now, I've got nothing against freelance writers; I've been one myself, and tomorrow morning I'll become one again. It's a respectable way to make a living (even if a fiscally preposterous one). Though Times freelancers agree to abide by the paper's ethical rules and professional standards, there's no way someone who's working for The Times today, some other publication tomorrow and yet another on Tuesday can possibly absorb and live by The Times's complex code as fully as staff members. Unrevealed conflicts, violations of Times-specific reporting rules and a variety of other problems have repeatedly found their way to my office over the past 18 months.

The economic pressures on all newspapers are real, of course, and no modern newspaper can thrive unless it commits resources to new forms of distribution. I'm sure The Times devotes a larger share of its revenue to reporting than any other paper in the nation. But the price of stretching a staff too thin, and of patching the weak spots with day labor, could be much, much more expensive.

8. In the Travel section, the Escapes section and the occasional travel editions of the Sunday magazine now called T: Travel magazine, why are the restaurants almost always delightful, the hotels hospitable, the views glorious, the experiences rewarding? This is a weird form of crypto-journalism; if the theater critics were so chronically uncritical, they'd be hooted off the stage.

9. It's a story, say, about the New York City public schools. In the first paragraph a parent, apparently picked at random, testifies that they haven't improved. Readers are clearly expected to draw conclusions from this.

But it isn't clear why the individual was picked; it isn't possible to determine whether she's representative; and there's no way of knowing whether she knows what she's talking about. Calling on the individual man or woman on the street to make conclusive judgments is beneath journalistic dignity. If polls involving hundreds of people carry a cautionary note indicating a margin of error of plus-or-minus five points, what kind of consumer warning should be glued to a reporter's ad hoc poll of three or four respondents?

10. Six months ago, I applied the adjectives "arrogant" and "condescending" to the culture editors who had so badly botched their radical revision/evisceration of the Sunday arts listings. Therefore, on the heels of last month's reintroduction of the vastly improved listings in the Weekend section, and the total remake of a coming-events page in Arts & Leisure, I owe them new adjectives—like "responsive" and "deft." They did a wonderful job.

11. Thank yous: I've mentioned my associate Arthur Bovino several times in my column, but at no point have I said that without him there wouldn't even be a public editor's office; the

roof would have caved in months ago. Copy editors Steve Coates and John Wilson have at many points prevented me from making a fool of myself (when they failed, it wasn't for lack of trying). My old friend Corby Kummer, moonlighting from his job at The Atlantic Monthly, read and commented on all my columns before they went into the paper. Susan Kirby edited the periodic letters columns. Several score members of the staff of The Times were helpful, tolerant and pleasant, yet always true to the institution.

Mostly, of course, I have to thank the paper's readers. I especially cherish those whose periodic unhappiness with The Times, even at its most intense, is the byproduct of their loyalty to the paper, and their appreciation of its importance to their lives.

This attitude was best symbolized by a lengthy message I received my first week on the job, from the economist and former Wall Street Journal editorialist Jude Wanniski. His letter coursed through page after page of criticism of The Times's coverage of topics as diverse as its unquestioning acceptance of the assertion that Saddam Hussein gassed thousands of Kurds during the Iraq-Iran war (Wanniski maintains the Iranians were responsible for the atrocity) and the paper's abiding disregard for supply-side economics. At the end of this acidulous letter, Wanniski appended a P.S. "Having said that," he wrote, "it remains one of my life's great daily pleasures."

12. I wish I hadn't made so much noise, in print and in various interviews, about how hard this job was. Dexter Filkins, in Baghdad, has a hard job; Steven Erlanger, in Jerusalem, has a hard job. By any reasonable standard, public editor is a walk in the park.

13. During a tense encounter with a group of writers 17

months ago, economics reporter Louis Uchitelle asked what I hoped my legacy would be. I really had no answer, but like any good reporter, Uchitelle persisted; like any unprepared news subject, I dodged.

But a response came to me on the subway that evening, and I sent it to Uchitelle the next morning. "The true contribution that I can make to The Times," I wrote, "will be the product of 18 months of policies restated, staff members angered, readers disgruntled, procedures revised, and all the other missteps and false starts that must arise from an effort as new, as untested, and as inchoate as this one. When I move on, my successor will know how to do the job, and the people at The Times will know how to deal with it."

Ladies and gentlemen, please welcome Barney Calame.

. . .

Last thoughts:

1. As it turned out, The Times's legal maneuvers ended in ruins. My own supposition is that when Miller was first subpoenaed, somebody on the 14th floor of the Times Building—either Sulzberger, then-CEO Russ Lewis, or both of them—grabbed a flag from the nearest stanchion and said, "To the barricades." Or, if need be, the Supreme Court.

Apparently, no one said, "Let's think this over long and hard and see if we can resolve it without compromising a meaningful principle." The assumption was that there was no compromise possible—never a good way to begin a battle.

2. Wow. I brought on my own headache with this one. My one sentence on Paul Krugman—which didn't say that he lied, or that he made numbers up, or even that he was inaccurate—produced more hostile comment than anything else I had written in

18 months. On my way out the door, Krugman and I went at each other in an e-mail exchange followed by a few postings on the public editor Web site[@], in a contretemps that gawker.com appropriately labeled "The Battle of the Bureau of Labor Statistics."

I'm willing to grant that Krugman (and the legions of supporters arrayed behind him) may have gotten the best of me on a few specifics; I was never better than a B student in economics. But I'm pretty good at reading newspapers, and I feel that columnists serve a worthwhile function when they support their arguments with reporting, and when the reporting does not neglect, or withhold from the readers, evidence that might support the opposing point-of-view. Otherwise, they're just entertainment for the fans in the balcony.

Krugman haters who asked why, if I was so down on the guy, I didn't go after him before this, missed the point: columnists are entitled to shape, slice and dice in the service of gratifying their supporters. I just don't happen to like it.

Maureen Dowd was really, really angry in her first e-mail to me; pissed but polite in her second one; and perfectly cordial the next time we encountered one another. I never heard from Safire.

3. Of this trio, the only one who got in touch with me was a very displeased Alessandra Stanley. I hadn't encountered it at the time, but I later came across "some hardwon guidelines for responsible reviewing," by the critic John Leonard, a former editor of the Times Book Review. Among them: "First, as in Hippocrates, do no harm. Second, never stoop to score a point or bite an ankle. Third, always understand that in this symbiosis, you are the parasite." Words to live by.

8. Now, *this* I really regret. I had long intended to write about

the various travel-related sections, never got around to it, never interviewed the editors to get a better understanding of what they do, and instead tossed off an insult as I was walking out the door. It was bad journalism, bad columnizing and I apologize for it.

9. David Herszenhorn, the author of the piece about the school system, begged—shouted—to differ. We had a vigorous back-and-forth, in which he made the case for choosing one individual to represent the many people he had interviewed, and why such a lead was preferable to a dry recitation of polling data or expert testimony. I don't really think dry recitation was the only alternative.

13. The question comes up often: what was your proudest accomplishment at The Times? Easy: The Times chose to continue the public editor experiment by appointing another one. Byron S. Calame, formerly of the Wall Street Journal, stepped right into the job as I was leaving. In many ways—upbringing, professional background, tone of voice — we couldn't be more different. But both Barney and I demanded independence; Keller and Sulzberger granted it; and I would like to believe that the paper's readers have come to expect the presence of an uncensored critic in the paper's pages.

It's one of the nice things about newspapers: generally speaking, readers will get what they ask for.

ACKNOWLEDGMENTS

Besides those whom I thanked in my final column, I owe my gratitude to a number of other people without whom this would be a much poorer book—for without their generous counsel I would have been a far poorer public editor. Notable among these are Taylor Branch, John Carroll, Chris Chinlund, Liz Darhansoff, Max Frankel, Jim Gaines, Mike Getler, Lisa Grunwald, Marian Heiskell, John Huey, Dave Jones, Chuck Lewis, Craig Pyes, Jack Rosenthal, Jack Shafer, and Glen Waggoner. Alex Jones supported me both early and late: as I was beginning in the job, with sage advice; as I was writing the new material in this book, with a fellowship at the Joan Shorenstein Center on the Press, Politics, and Public Policy at Harvard's John F. Kennedy School of Government. The encouragement offered by Neal Shine, my very first boss in the journalism business, was precious to me. I couldn't have found publishers more helpful (and more patient) than Peter Osnos, David Patterson, and Melissa Raymond of PublicAffairs. Thanks are also due Ernie Imhoff, who provided me with the book's epigraph, and to the membership of the Organization of News Ombudsmen— a rare collection of dedicated journalists whose advice and support I appreciated daily.

At The Times, there were scores of people who were helpful, and I'm grateful to all of them. But Bill Borders, Andy Rosenthal and Paul Winfield deserve specific thanks for tolerating my incessant badgering with special patience (and satisfying it with large helpings of wisdom). Managing editors Jill Abramson and John Geddes, and editorial page editor Gail Collins, were notably tolerant, even when I was being critical.

It should be needless to say that Bill Keller and Arthur Sulzberger made this book possible, but to say only this would diminish their contribution. From their decision to create the public editorship to their steadfast determination to honor their commitment to the position's absolute independence, they never failed to honor their end of the deal—not only by allowing me the freedom to do my work without impediment, but by publishing America's finest newspaper.

Still, of all those at The Times, I have to single out Al Siegal. His belief in great journalism, his dedication to ethical journalism, and his deep and generously shared knowledge of The Times, its practices, and its history were, for me, treasures beyond price. My immense gratitude to Al is matched only by my admiration for him.

Finally: John, Lydia and Becky. My kids read my columns, and told me they were proud of me—the most valued of compliments. My wife talked me into taking the job at The Times when I was wavering, and supported me cheerfully and steadfastly throughout my tenure. Of course, Becky's been doing that for nearly thirty years, so I guess I shouldn't have been surprised. What I should be, and am, is immeasurably grateful that I am able to share my life and my love with the most wonderful person I will ever know.

INDEX

PublicAffairs is a publishing house founded in 1997. It is a tribute to the standards, values, and flair of three persons who have served as mentors to countless reporters, writers, editors, and book people of all kinds, including me.

I.F. Stone, proprietor of *I. F. Stone's Weekly,* combined a commitment to the First Amendment with entrepreneurial zeal and reporting skill and became one of the great independent journalists in American history. At the age of eighty, Izzy published *The Trial of Socrates,* which was a national bestseller. He wrote the book after he taught himself ancient Greek.

Benjamin C. Bradlee was for nearly thirty years the charismatic editorial leader of *The Washington Post.* It was Ben who gave the *Post* the range and courage to pursue such historic issues as Watergate. He supported his reporters with a tenacity that made them fearless and it is no accident that so many became authors of influential, best-selling books.

Robert L. Bernstein, the chief executive of Random House for more than a quarter century, guided one of the nation's premier publishing houses. Bob was personally responsible for many books of political dissent and argument that challenged tyranny around the globe. He is also the founder and longtime chair of Human Rights Watch, one of the most respected human rights organizations in the world.

· · ·

For fifty years, the banner of Public Affairs Press was carried by its owner Morris B. Schnapper, who published Gandhi, Nasser, Toynbee, Truman, and about 1,500 other authors. In 1983, Schnapper was described by *The Washington Post* as "a redoubtable gadfly." His legacy will endure in the books to come.

Peter Osnos, Founder and Editor-at-Large